Stonehenge City

Books by Leon Stover

Anthropology and History

China: An Anthropological Perspective
(with Takeko K. Stover)
The Cultural Ecology of Chinese Civilization
Imperial China and the State Cult of Confucius (McFarland)
Stonehenge and the Origins of Western Culture

Fiction

Stonehenge (with Harry Harrison)
Stonehenge: Where Atlantis Died
(the above revised and expanded)
The Shaving of Karl Marx

Criticism

La Science Fiction Américaine
Robert A. Heinlein
Harry Harrison
*The Prophetic Soul: A Reading of
H.G. Wells's "Things to Come"* (McFarland)
Science Fiction from Wells to Heinlein (McFarland)

The Annotated H.G. Wells (McFarland)

Volume 1. *The Time Machine*
Volume 2. *The Island of Doctor Moreau*
Volume 3. *The Invisible Man*
Volume 4. *The War of the Worlds*
Volume 5. *When the Sleeper Wakes*
Volume 6. *The First Men in the Moon*
Volume 7. *The Sea Lady*
Volume 8. *Man Who Could Work Miracles*
Volume 9. *Things to Come*

Anthologies

Apeman, Spaceman (with Harry Harrison)
Above the Human Landscape (with Willis McNelly)

Stonehenge City

A Reconstruction

Leon Stover

McFarland & Company, Inc., Publishers
Jefferson, North Carolina, and London

The present work is a reprint of the illustrated case bound edition of Stonehenge City: A Reconstruction, *first published in 2003 by McFarland.*

Facing the title page:
Leon Stover sitting atop one of the trilithons,
a helper standing to the left.

LIBRARY OF CONGRESS CATALOGUING-IN-PUBLICATION DATA

Stover, Leon
Stonehenge city : a reconstruction / Leon Stover.
p.   cm.
Includes bibliographical references and index.

ISBN 978-0-7864-4512-7
softcover : 50# alkaline paper ∞

1. Stonehenge (England)   2. Extinct cities — England — Wiltshire.
3. Megalithic monuments — England — Wiltshire.
4. Wiltshire (England) — Antiquities.   I. Title.
DA142.S875   2009   936.2'31— dc21   2003004259

British Library cataloguing data are available

©2003 Leon Stover. All rights reserved

*No part of this book may be reproduced or transmitted in any form
or by any means, electronic or mechanical, including photocopying
or recording, or by any information storage and retrieval system,
without permission in writing from the publisher.*

Front cover images ©2009 Art Today;
back cover photograph by H.W. Stone

Manufactured in the United States of America

*McFarland & Company, Inc., Publishers
Box 611, Jefferson, North Carolina 28640
www.mcfarlandpub.com*

To the memory of
Walter Charleton, M.D.
1619–1707

Among the living I dedicate this book
to my astronomer friend
and former student,
William Drish

Nor is Thy STONE-HENG a less Wonder grown,
Though once a *Temple* thought, now prov'd a *Throne*.
 — Robert Howard,
 "To my Worthy Friend, Dr. Charleton" (1663)

Table of Contents

Table of Figures — xi
Table of Plates — xvii
Preface — 1

Introduction — 3
1. The Polymathic Dr. Charleton — 7
2. The Monument — 21

Between pages 62 and 63 are 8 color plates containing 17 illustrations

3. The Builders — 63
4. The Reconstruction — 89
Epilogue: Looking Back from the Iron Age — 117

Appendix I "To my Honour'd Friend, Dr. Charleton," by John Dryden (1663) — 121
Appendix II Excerpts from *Stone-heng* by Walter Charleton (1663) — 125
Appendix III A Novelization of Charleton's Theory, by Leon Stover — 155
Appendix IV Excerpt from *Stonehenge* by William Stukeley (1740) — 163
Bibliography — 173
Index — 181

Table of Figures

Fig. 1	Stonehenge seen from the northwest. Photograph by Hans Schaal, a former student.	4
Fig. 2	Matchbox cover from The Stonegallows, a pub near Stonehenge listed in Dunklin and Wright 1987.	8
Fig. 3	Walter Charleton's realistic drawing of the ruins of Stonehenge. Despite heavy weathering, any reconstruction should look nearly as rough-hewn.	9
Fig. 4	Reconstruction by Inigo Jones, fantastically interpreted as a Roman temple built along lines of the Tuscan Order.	10
Fig. 5	Bas-relief medallion honoring Olaus Wormius (1588–1654).	11
Fig. 6	Late nineteenth-century painting of round barrows in the Stonehenge cemetery; from Barclay 1895.	13
Fig. 7	Aerial photograph of Stonehenge, with a nearby round barrow at top right. From an official guidebook published by Her Majesty's Stationery Office (HMSO).	13
Fig. 8	Photograph of a display of stone ax-heads in the Salisbury and South Wiltshire Museum.	14
Fig. 9	One of the grey-wether boulders uprighted at Avebury among others forming its various stone circles (Hans Schaal).	15
Fig. 10	Other emplaced stones in outer ring at Avebury. In background is the huge earthwork encircling all the stone rings within (Hans Schaal).	15
Fig. 11	Two bluestones in foreground at right, another to the left. View toward the southwest, with trilithon uprights in back of bluestones, a fallen one extreme left. In background is a surviving pillar of the sarsen ring (Hans Schaal).	16

Table of Figures

Fig. 12	Famous engraving of a Druid by Aylett Sammes from his *Britannia Antiqua Illustrata* (1676).	18
Fig. 13	Mock Druids, themselves a tourist attraction, gather at Stonehenge for their annual sunrise ceremony (HMSO).	19
Fig. 14	Earliest photograph of Stonehenge. From archival sources discovered by Hans Schaal, a former student and photography major; heretofore unpublished.	22
Fig. 15	Ground plan of Stonehenge from the official guidebook (HMSO).	23
Fig. 16	Aerial view of Stonehenge, illustrating ground plan in fig. 15.	24
Fig. 17	Portion of the broken sarsen ring (Hans Schaal).	25
Fig. 18	One of the photogenic trilithons (Hans Schaal).	25
Fig. 19	Fallen Slaughter Stone in Avenue, with intact entrance to the monument in background (Hans Schaal).	26
Fig. 20	Drawing of Slaughter Stone (no. 95), with Heel Stone (no. 96) further down the Avenue; from Barkelay 1902.	27
Fig. 21	Ground plans of Stonehenge's three main building phases. From Atkinson 1980 (HMSO).	28
Fig. 22	Statue menhir from southwest France; Warwick and Trump 1972.	30
Fig. 23	Top of a pillar in the sarsen ring, showing its two tenons for holding lintels in place (HMSO).	32
Fig. 24	Tongue-in-groove connections between lintels in the sarsen ring; from Stone 1924.	33
Fig. 25	Section of the broken sarsen ring seen close up (Hans Schaal).	33
Fig. 26	View of main trilithon's remaining pillar, top left, its fallen lintel at foot of complete trilithon top center (Hans Schaal). Pillar uprighted from a tilt in 1901.	34
Fig. 27	Display of greenstone mauls in the Salisbury and South Wiltshire Museum.	35
Fig. 28	Dagger carving (left) next to ax-head carving on stone 53; from a 1953 newspaper report.	37
Fig. 29	Use of a wooden A-frame to raise sarsen upright; from Atkinson 1956.	37
Fig. 30	The Atkinson method of raising sarsen pillars, illustrated in one of the official guidebooks (HMSO).	38
Fig. 31	The Atkinson method of raising and seating lintels, as illustrated in one of the official guidebooks (HMSO).	40
Fig. 32	Map of the Stonehenge region, showing pattern of round barrows grouped around scattered long barrows. Types of round barrows given in the legend are controversial and may be ignored. From Grinsell 1978.	41
Fig. 33	Official ground plan of interior structure within the chambered tomb on the Stoney Littleton farm (HMSO).	42

Table of Figures

Fig. 34	Long shot of Stoney Littleton, front end (photograph by the author).	43
Fig. 35	Close-up of Stoney Littleton entrance (photograph by the author).	43
Fig. 36	Passageway inside Stoney Littleton, with corbelled arching above (photograph by the author).	45
Fig. 37	Plan of a Danubian long house in Czechoslovakia; in Ashbee 1970, from a Czech language report.	47
Fig. 38	Boulder-bounded long barrows in northern Germany; in Ashbee 1970, from a German language report.	48
Fig. 39	Aerial view of the West Kennet chambered tomb in Wiltshire: The stone burial chambers are beneath the mound at its widest end, bottom left (HMSO).	48
Fig. 40	Ground plan of West Kennet: General view left, details of mortuary house right (HMSO).	49
Fig. 41	View looking into West Kennet from the entrance (photograph by the author, with the help of a friendly curator from Devizes Museum).	50
Fig. 42	Isometric drawing of West Kennet's burial chambers, outer facade and forecourt (HMSO).	50
Fig. 43	Plan of Bryn Celli Dhu (HMSO).	52
Fig. 44	Bryn Celli Dhu, looking at the entrance (photograph by the author).	53
Fig. 45	Bryn Celli Dhu, showing peristoliths encircling the mound (photograph by the author).	54
Fig. 46	Stonehenge compared to the ground plans of a variety of chambered tombs; from Newall 1929.	55
Fig. 47	Plan of Stonehenge with arrows indicating the directions to which the Station Stones point (HMSO).	61
Fig. 48	The five directions at Stonehenge (drawing by the author).	61
Fig. 49	Archaic grave goods on display in the Devizes Museum. Note pair of boar's tusks at top in this best preserved example of this burial type (HMSO).	66
Fig. 50	Head of vice-regal sceptor from Clandon Barrow, in Dorchester Museum (HMSO).	68
Fig. 51	Major Indo-European language families (boldface) with some representatives, an asterisk indicating a dead language; from Stover 1978.	73
Fig. 52	Basic types of Beaker pottery: bell, long-necked, and short-necked; from Bray and Trump 1970.	79
Fig. 53	Corded-ware beaker from Saxo-Thuringa in Germany; from Bray and Trump 1970.	80
Fig. 54	Collared Wessex vessel and so-called "grape-cup" from the Stonehenge III cemetery; from Crittall 1973.	81

Fig. 55	Bronze worker's kit at Kalinovka in the Caucasus region, not far north of the Kuro-Araxes site where bronze casting began; from Mongait 1961.	83
Fig. 56	Flat ax from northern Scotland (left) and corresponding open mold from Ireland (right); from *Inventaria Archaeologica GB* 26.	84
Fig. 57	Flanged bronze ax-head (left) and stone ax-head from Stonehenge; from Crittall 1973.	85
Fig. 58	Possible ways of hafting flat axes (drawings by the author).	85
Fig. 59	Mycenaean dagger carving next to native ax-head carving (drawing by the author).	86
Fig. 60	Flat ax (4³⁄₁₀ inches long) and hilt (4¼ inches) of Mycenaean short sword from same barrow in Cornwall; in Truro Museum.	86
Fig. 61	Mycenaean cup of corrugated gold (height 3¼ inches) from a barrow near Rillaton in East Cornwall; electrotype in Devizes Museum, original in British Museum.	87
Fig. 62	Tin ingot cast by Mycenaean smiths in Cornwall; length 2 feet 10 inches, weight 158 pounds; in Truro Museum, photograph courtesy Cornwall County Museum.	87
Fig. 63	The five main features of the Stonehenge landscape; adapted from Atkinson 1956.	90
Fig. 64	Five similar features at Tara; adapted from Raftery 1994.	90
Fig. 65	Bronze Age rock carving in Scandinavia (drawing by the author after Gelling and Davidson 1969).	92
Fig. 66	Line drawing of large gold plate, 8½ inches across, from Bush Barrow.	93
Fig. 67	Map of the five regions comprising the five Stonehenge kingdoms; simplified in Stover 1978 from Grinsell 1958, map II.	94
Fig. 68	"Wicker Image" from Aylett Sammes, *Britannia Antiqua Illustrata* (1676).	95
Fig. 69	Vlad the Impaler and his grisly work, from a German woodcut of 1499.	96
Fig. 70	Plan of Woodhenge; from Cunnington 1929.	98
Fig. 71	Official reconstruction of Woodhenge as a temple (HMSO).	99
Fig. 72	Architectural drawing of the restored palace shown in elevation, scale in feet; student drawing.	100
Fig. 73	Architecture of the yurt as built by steppe peoples (from a source provided by the student who did fig. 72).	101
Fig. 74	Reconstruction of Iron Age fort in northern Scotland; from Hamilton 1968, HMSO.	103
Fig. 75	Cross-section of two-storey housing depicted from the outside in fig. 74.	103

Table of Figures

Fig. 76	Excavated portion of Durrington Walls; from Wainright and Longworth, 1968.	104
Fig. 77	Layout of the Tara hall from the Yellow Book of Lecan; after Petrie 1839.	107
Fig. 78	Seating arrangements in the Tara hall diagrammed by MacAlister (1931): C = cauldron, H = hearth.	108
Fig. 79	Burial mound at Kivik; from a Swedish engraving published in the 1780s.	111
Fig. 80	Drawings of carvings on slabs lining stone cist at Kivik; from Gelling and Davidson 1969.	112
Fig. 81	The Cursus, looking east; from Stukeley 1740.	113
Fig. 82	Old print of Stonehenge in Camden's encyclopedia reproduced by Charleton.	127
Fig. 83	Imaginary ground plan of Stonehenge by Inigo Jones.	129
Fig. 84	Dagger carving on stone 53, with bronze ax-head carving at bottom left and part of another at top right.	156
Fig. 85	World map of the war between Mycenae and Atlantis; from Stover 1983.	158
Fig. 86	Map featuring details of the Island of the Yerni; from Stover 1983.	159
Fig. 87	Stukeley's drawing of a British Druid standing at the doorway into the Stonehenge sanctuary, another within.	165
Fig. 88	Stukeley's field drawing of the ruins of Stonehenge, the Altar Stone at AA under seated figure.	166

Table of Plates

I:1 *top*	Ax-head and dagger carvings on stone 53.
I:2 *bottom*	Casting ax-head in flat mold.
II:1 *top left*	Bush Barrow grave furniture.
II:2	Flat axe left, flanged axe right.
II:3 *bottom*	View inside royal grave, Bush Barrow.
III:1 *top*	Cutaway view of Tara Hall.
III:2 *bottom*	Cutaway view of Stonehenge Hall.
IV:1 *top*	Cross section of Bush Barrow.
IV:2 *bottom*	Cutaway of Stonehenge palace.
V:1 *top*	Footrace at the Cursus.
V:2 *bottom*	Stonehenge election court.
VI:1 *top*	Sacrificial arrow-shooting at election court.
VI:2 *bottom*	Sacrificial impaling in election court.
VII:1 *top*	Burning of Wicker man, election time.
VII:2 *bottom*	Detailed view of Stonehenge electors.
VIII:1 *top*	Raising a trilithon upright.
VIII:2 *bottom*	Election stone at Tara.

Preface

By the beginning of the twentieth century, Stonehenge had accumulated a bibliography of nearly a thousand items (Harrison 1901). Since then the bibliography has exploded to include a remarkably new variety of works, ranging from goofy mystery mongering to matter-of-fact archaeological reporting.

My title, *Stonehenge City*, may seem a bit eccentric, but it bases on good archaeology and ventures a reasonable theory.

As the world's foremost prehistoric monument and busy tourist attraction, the great stones of Stonehenge naturally dominate all else long vanished and now unseen, save for the hundreds of weathered-down and unpicturesque burial mounds extending miles in every direction.

This little book offers a reconstruction of the principal buildings belonging to a well-attested Bronze Age city in southern England. It centers on a series of reconstructive paintings I commissioned from the artist David Alexovitch, a former student who knew exactly what I wanted.

The frontispiece is a photograph of the author sitting atop one of the still standing trilithons at Stonehenge. Its wardens allowed me that wonderful privilege because they favored my political theory (Stover 1978) over the reigning astronomical one (Hawkins 1965). Before, I had considered only the conspicuous megalithic structure, but now the whole invisible urban complex.

Leon Stover, Ph.D., Litt.D.
Professor emeritus of anthropology
Illinois Institute of Technology

Introduction

My point of departure is a seventeenth century book by the learned physician to Charles II to whose memory the present work is dedicated. Chapter 1 explains why Dr. Charleton's book is unusually insightful for its day.

Chapter 2 describes the monument itself, built over a period of a thousand years, from the Neolithic to the Bronze Age. The visible ruins tourists come to see (fig. 1) belong to the latter stage, as defined locally.

Next is a chapter on the builders of the Bronze Age monument that gives the Stonehenge site its name. I relate them to the warrior society of Mycenaean Greece remembered in Homer's *Iliad*.

The foregoing leads up to the book's purpose for being: a display of color plates showing my reconstruction of Stonehenge City. Chapter 4 discusses that series of imaginative paintings.

The Epilogue concludes with a retrospective on the British Bronze Age from the view platform of the Celtic Iron Age in Ireland, documented in literary history. I argue that this record gives a voice to the builders of Stonehenge. The Bronze Age, after all, is continuous with the following Iron Age; and if the novelties of the latter are subtracted, the former condition is exposed.

Finally I attach four appendices. The first is a poetic dedication to Charleton's book by the great poet and dramatist John Dryden. It illustrates how much science and literature once were one culture.

Appendix II offers generous excerpts from Charleton's book, by way of showing the reasonable grounds for his useful conclusion. Appendix III explains how I came to write the present work by researching it for a successful novelization of Charleton's theory. Appendix IV is a selected chapter from *Stonehenge* (1740) by William Stukeley, a later author who introduced Druids into British folklore.

Fig. 1. *Stonehenge seen from the northwest. Photograph by Hans Schaal, a former student.*

Although one of the most learned men in Europe, Dr. Charleton could not possibly know anything about the concepts and methods of modern archaeology. For that reason today's professionals too easily dismiss his work as that of a hopelessly amateurish antiquarian.

Archaeologists, ever scornful of their antiquarian predecessors, trace their modernity to one Christian Thomsen, curator of the National Museum of Denmark from 1816 until his death in 1865. His decisive contribution to the study of prehistory was to classify the museum's antiquities in three successive parts, from Stone Age to Bronze Age to Iron Age.

Thomsen's Three Age system established a persistent idea. Later it was refined, with Stone Age divided into Old and New, Paleolithic and Neolithic. Soon enough it became evident these were developmental stages, not chronological stages with fixed dates everywhere. More, the stone, bronze and iron tools displayed in the Danish National Museum came to be associated not merely with technological change but with wider socioeconomic and political changes.

Prehistory by definition means before history, before writing began. Most of the world existed in a state of prehistory, everywhere except in ancient Sumer (Tigris-Euphrates valley) where, in about 3500 B.C., the first Bronze Age civilization emerged. This event is known as the urban revolution (civilization = city life), which in turn rests on the so-called Neolithic revolution in the Middle East: a change from mobile hunting and gathering to settled food production with domesticated plants and animals.

Introduction 5

In time these revolutionary elements diffused to the Stonehenge region. Its impressive ruins are the most famous prehistoric monument in the world.

For prehistoric it is. Although Bronze Age metallurgy and urbanism came to Stonehenge, writing did not. For historical records bearing on its builders I turn to Iron Age sources, justified in the Epilogue.

1

The Polymathic Dr. Charleton

Walter Charleton's book on Stonehenge is titled *Chorea Gigantum*, Latin for "giant's dance," as if the great stones were giants dancing about, frozen in motion, petrified. The phrase, in English, is from local folklore, centuries old (Grinsell 1975). Charleton, however, chose to use the more dignified Latin phrase, derived from a twelfth-century book partially given to the subject, *Historia Regum Britanniae* by Galfridas Monemutensis (Geoffrey of Monmouth). The Anglo-Saxon "stone-heng" Charleton deemed a vulgar usage.

Geoffrey's book, translated as *The History of the Kings of Britain* (Geoffrey 1966), is more fable than documented fact, including the legend of King Arthur. But as a work of myth-making power, active for five centuries, it decisively shaped the idea of a British kingdom (Hanning 1966). As the first to account for Stonehenge, Geoffrey says it is a memorial raised by Merlin the magician, at the behest of Ambrosius (Arthur's predecessor), to honor the hundreds of British nobles under King Vortigern murdered by invading teutonic Saxons.

The word stonehenge itself means "hanging stones." The usual interpretation is that they refer to the structure's impressive lintels hanging high on their pillars. The proper emphasis, however, should be on *hanging* stones, not hanging *stones*. Taylor (1876) quite rightly thinks the word must derive from something Germanic like *steinhengē* (hanging stones).

Sure enough, the gibbet in Anglo-Saxons times was formed of two uprights and a crosspiece, unlike the later and more familiar upside-down "L" with corner brace. In a nearby town I found a pub named The Stonegallows (fig. 2*). Here may be preserved a folk memory older than Geoffrey's *chorea gigantum*.

---

*This book contains 17 color plates on an 8-page insert; in addition, 88 figures (photographs and illustrations) appear throughout the text.

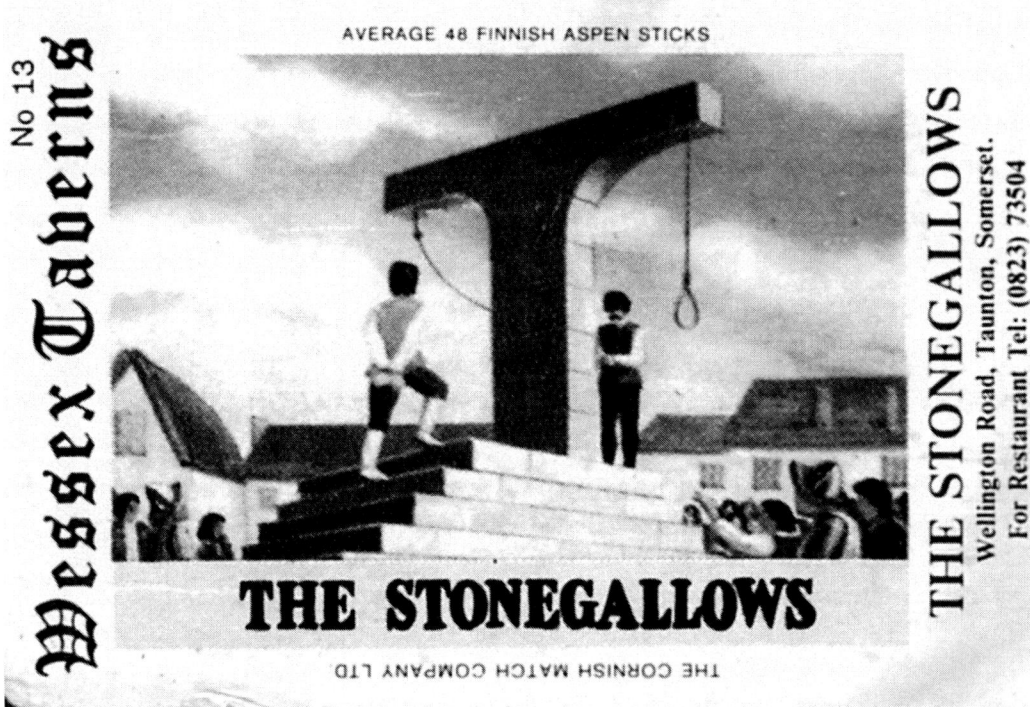

Fig. 2. *Matchbox cover from The Stonegallows, a pub near Stonehenge listed in Dunklin and Wright 1987.*

Dr. Charleton's book was commissioned by Charles II, whom he served as royal physician. He took pains to demolish, in every detail, a previous book commissioned by James I, *The Most Notable Antiquity of Great Britain*, done by Inigo Jones (1655), the king's royal architect.

Inigo Jones is famous, after a tour of Italy, for bringing antique Roman architecture to Britain. His book on Stonehenge reimagines it in his own classical style as a Roman temple.

Dr. Charleton made a realistic sketch of the craggy Stonehenge ruins (fig. 3), which completely rebuts the smooth Inigo Jones restoration, altogether marble-like. Worse, and even more creative, Jones pictured *six* trilithons in symmetrical hexagonal array, beyond the actual five in horseshoe-shaped array.

That is the point of Robert Howard's dedicatory poem (see epigraph). Stonehenge is not a temple but a throne, not Roman but Danish, built by Viking invaders in the time of King Alfred. The book's florid dedication to the monarch who commissioned it clearly celebrates the Restoration: the reassuming of the throne by Charles II following the execution of his father, Charles I, by Oliver Cromwell, winner of the English Civil War. For his highly partisan royalist sympathies alone, today's archaeologists dismiss Charleton's thesis out of hand. For them his Viking idea is no less absurd than Inigo Jones's Roman.

1. The Polymathic Dr. Charleton

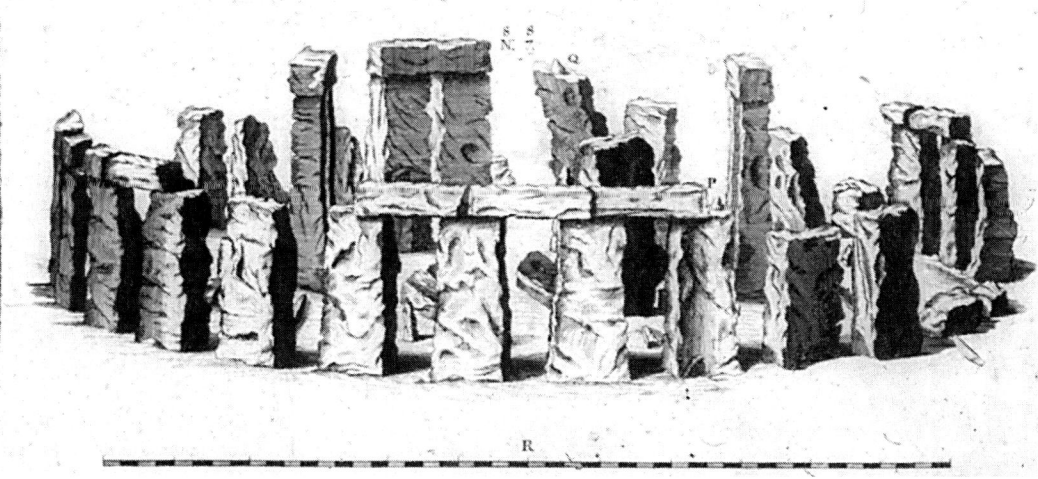

Fig. 3. *Walter Charleton's realistic drawing of the ruins of Stonehenge. Despite heavy weathering, any reconstruction should look nearly as rough-hewn.*

But the good doctor did his homework. First he reviewed all the existing literature, then consulted with Europe's foremost antiquarian, the great Olaus Wormius. Never mind Charleton's completely mistaken and anachronistic identification of the monument's builders. His perceptive thinking about its political function remains incisive.

For a seventeenth-century intellectual, Charleton's wide-ranging interests are remarkably modern in temper. John Dryden's poem (see Appendix I) celebrates a powerful intellect we too should respect. His book on Stonehenge, for all its historical nonsense, deserves the serious attention I give its theoretical premise.

The polymathic Dr. Charleton not only served as president of the College of Physicians, he was a charter member of the Royal Society of London for Improving Natural Knowledge. International in membership, it begins the scientific enterprise now well established in both its branches: pure research and applied research for useful application.

In the medical field he anticipated Harvey's discovery of blood circulation between arteries and veins, among his books on physiology. Other books make original contributions to mathematics and physics, not to mention a practical manual on wine making from a chemical standpoint. He also wrote novels.

On top of all that Charleton did the definitive biography of his king. From it we learn why he commissioned the Stonehenge book. Following the defeat by Cromwell of the royal army under Charles I, and then his regicidal beheading, the son fled south to France. On the way he hid among the stones of Stonehenge, and when restored as Charles II he asked his learned physician to explain them.

More superficial was the curiosity shown by James I in the monument when he assigned his own renowned architect Inigo Jones "to produce out of his own practice in architecture, and experience in antiquities abroad, what he could dis-

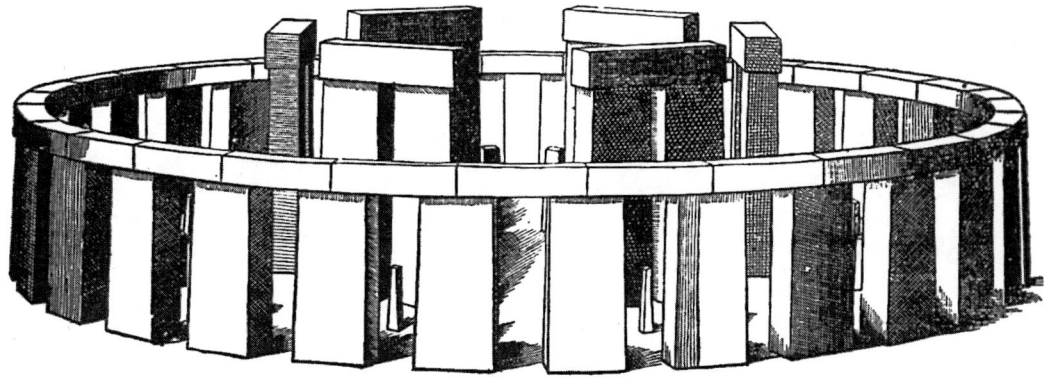

Fig. 4. *Reconstruction by Inigo Jones, fantastically interpreted as a Roman temple built along lines of the Tuscan Order.*

cover concerning this of Stonehenge." While staying as a guest of the Earl of Pembroke at Wiltshire House, King James visited nearby Stonehenge. As it happens his architect in 1633 had designed a magnificent new front for Wiltshire House, itself now a national landmark. Inigo Jones indulged the king by projecting his own Roman-derived architectural style onto the monument (fig. 4).

Very different is Dr. Charleton's response to a royal request, one seriously interested in solving the problem. His most important move was to correspond, in Latin, the language of international scholarship, with Olaus Wormius (Ole Worm), physician to the king of Denmark and a fellow member of the Royal Society. Dr. Wormius made his reputation with a seminal museum of natural history, embracing archaeological relics (antiquities). I often thought about Dr. Wormius's model when working for the preeminent American Museum of Natural History in New York.

He of course had not yet arrived at the current taxonomy of stone and metal age artifacts introduced by Christian Thomsen, first curator of the National Museum of Denmark (which inherited some relics from Worm's private museum). Dr. Wormius *did*, however, do pioneering field surveys of prehistoric monuments, stone circles and the like (many of which have since perished), richly and precisely illustrated in *Danicorum monumentorum* (Copenhagen, 1643). Happily I have a portrait of the man, worth inserting here (fig. 5).

A fellow physician attending royalty, like Dr. Charleton, he also did original anatomical research, for whom the "Wormian bones" in the skull are named. Polymathic men like these (including Sir Isaac Newton) glorified the Royal Society of London. Their like is no longer seen today, now the scientific enterprise they established is divided into specialties. The wonderful day of the omnicompetent generalist is over.

Dr. Charleton wisely turned to Dr. Wormius for advice. From his classification of Danish monuments he offered five possibilities:

Sepulchra (tombs)
Fora (places of judicature)
Duelorum strata (places of camp-fights)
Trophea (battle monuments)
Comitalia loca (election places)

Taking this last as his clue, Charleton concluded that Stonehenge was built by invading Danes as a "Court Royal, or Place Royal for the Election and Inauguration of their kings." Not a bad idea, perceptive and wrong at the same time. For one thing the Danes (= Vikings) never got that far inland for King Alfred to have driven them out, although he did fight them on the eastern coast.

Charleton also missed the essential connection between the monument and *sepulchra*. Stonehenge centers in the midst of an immense cemetery in which are buried the builders of Stonehenge. It was not until the late nineteenth century that the monument was correctly judged to be prehistoric, and that the cemetery was part of it (Long 1876).

Fig. 5. *Bas-relief medallion honoring Olaus Wormius (1588–1654).*

The oddest thing about Charleton's book is his mention of a metal tablet, inscribed with writing, dug up at the time of Henry VIII, in whose collection of antiquities (now vanished) he does not say. See pages 138–139 in Appendix II. He reports that two linguistic experts of the time attempted to decipher it but would not. They could have if it had been inscribed in letters of the runic alphabet, the Norseman's form of writing. Charleton candidly admits this does not help his theory, and so leaves it that Stonehenge is an unlettered Danish monument.

The tablet no doubt once existed, and only now can be explained. Most certainly it was deposited at Stonehenge in Iron Age times, perhaps during the Roman occupation, when the site may still have been active as a magic place of Druidic resistance.

Today it is known that the Druids in Britain, like their Celtic brethren in post-conquest Gaul, cursed their enemies by depositing thin ragged sheets of lead at native votive sites, the curse inscribed thereon (Green 1997:99). The script, now deciphered, is a strange mix of Etruscan, Roman and Greek letters, however derived. The brief texts of the cursing magic spells are the only examples of the Gaulish language written down. So, the Stonehenge tablet reported by Dr. Charleton must have been of that sort.

Nor is his Viking connection altogether ludicrous. The prehistoric monuments of Denmark examined by Dr. Wormius are today taken as evidence of Viking beginnings, a long-term cultural continuity now well established (Brøstedt 1965). Let us remember that Denmark was not only Worm's homeland but also the seat of Thomsen's National Museum, from which sprang everything modern archaeologists adduce from man's unwritten record, the longest record of all.

In popular imagination, Viking voyaging and conquests are among the most spectacular events in Western history. Rightly so. They have much to tell, in their origins, about prehistoric Europe — and the builders of Stonehenge. In the archaeologist's view of prehistory, both cultural change and cultural continuity are seen over long horizons of time and space. Stonehenge is a place where local developments and influences from afar meet in a well-studied setting of dramatic change and less visible but equally dramatic signs of amazingly persistent patterns of continuity ranging over the entire Indo-European cultural domain, from India to Ireland.

That is why I titled my earlier book *Stonehenge: The Indo-European Heritage* (Stover 1978). Here it is improved by further study, and a new appreciation of Dr. Charleton's work. At last I have been led to the urban concept of Stonehenge City, reconstructed in a series of paintings done for this book: its purpose being to display and explain them.

At Stonehenge the big change, evident in its surrounding cemetery, is from long barrows to round barrows, from Neolithic to Bronze Age, from collective tombs to individual burials. The interesting continuity I have in mind rests with the hundreds of round barrows dominating the cemetery (figs. 6 and 7). Inside each barrow are the skeletal remains of a Bronze Age warrior, often buried with a stone battle ax (fig. 8), sometimes with a bronze-headed ax (most of these looted by gold-seeking tomb robbers).

Now for the Viking connection. The warriors buried at Stonehenge are quaintly dubbed the Battle-ax Folk (Vlahos 1968), whose like trace all across Europe and into India: the Indo-European invaders of archaeological record (more in chapter 3). They transformed Old Europe (= Neolithic Europe), making for a new cultural order. Out of that same movement, later, arose the Iron Age Vikings, whose invasions and conquests are continuous with those of the Battle-ax Folk. Instead of moving overland, they moved by boat over water and fought with iron axes: a change of little difference.

I do not say that Dr. Charleton understood anything of this, but his brilliant insight into the political function of Stonehenge, however wrongly attributed to Vikings, is the basis for the present book. He did, after all, have the historical sensibility to see that kings once were not dynastic, like his royal Charles II, but were indeed elevated in election courts: his idea of Stonehenge exactly.

More, Dr. Charleton rightly observed that Stonehenge looks the way it does because of the local building materials from which it was constructed. For some unaccountable reason, today's archaeologists believe that the monument's great sarsen stones were laboriously hauled from Marlborough Downs about twenty miles

Fig. 6, top. *Late nineteenth-century painting of round barrows in the Stonehenge cemetery; from Barclay 1895.* Fig. 7, bottom. *Aerial photograph of Stonehenge, with a nearby round barrow at top left. From an official guidebook published by Her Majesty's Stationery Office (HMSO).*

Fig. 8. *Photograph of a display of stone ax-heads in the Salisbury and South Wiltshire Museum.*

to the north. Strewn with lumpy sarsen boulders called grey wethers, they were arranged, unshaped, to form the great stone circles of Avebury, second only to Stonehenge as a tourist attraction. Figures 9 and 10 are examples, showing how absurd it is to assume that the domino-shaped stones of Stonehenge were hewn from such rude raw material. Without steel chisels and sledgehammers?

All futile speculation on this head is demolished by Dr. Charleton's field observation. He said that the squared-off sarsens at Stonehenge were taken from tabular stones lying about locally. Today such slabs no longer occur, they having been long broken up and used for building material in nearby houses. That is why Charleton is disbelieved. But we have an eyewitness account of him clambering over the monument's unused slabs. This comes from a biographical sketch done by John Aubrey (*d.* 1697), among other famous people he happened to know (see in Dick 1949). Aubrey himself was a famous personality, a notable antiquarian, whose name will come up again.

The geologist E.H. Stone, in *The Stones of Stonehenge* (1924), agrees with Charleton: the building material is local. He explains that the so-called sarsens are of highly compacted sandstone formed at oceanic depths during the Eocene period, 55 to 44 million years ago. When in the course of geological time this ancient Eocene seabed surfaced, remnants of it appeared in the countryside of southern England, as tabular slabs in the Stonehenge region, as misshapen boulders in the Avebury region.

The term sarsen, coined about 1635, refers to a hardness of composition said

Fig. 9, top. *One of the grey-wether boulders uprighted at Avebury among others forming its various stone circles (Hans Schaal).* Fig. 10, bottom. *Other emplaced stones in outer ring at Avebury. In background is the huge earthwork encircling all the stone rings within (Hans Schaal).*

Fig. 11. *Two bluestones in foreground at right, another to the left. View toward the southwest, with trilithon uprights in back of bluestones, a fallen one extreme left. In background is a surviving pillar of the sarsen ring (Hans Schaal).*

to be harder than the tempered steel of Saracen swords used against the less adequately armed Christian knights during the medieval period of the Crusades. That rock is indeed the hardest known to geology. So how did the builders of Stonehenge shape it to their purpose? E.H. Stone says easily enough, even with a primitive technology. Sarsen stone, he says, is grained just like wood. The builders had only to split it along the grain to get the size of slab they wanted to erect: carpentry applied to stone (more in chapter 2).

Charleton of course knew nothing of geology, a new science that did not evolve until the advent of Sir George Lyell, with his *Principles of Geology* (1830–1833). For that reason Dr. Charleton had no basis for distinguishing between the minerological content of the sarsen stones at Stonehenge and its associated bluestones.

The bluestones, actually, are not very blue, their alleged coloration given off by embedded particles of mica when glinting in sunlight. Examples are pictured in fig. 11, each standing about six feet tall, much smaller than the taller sarsen stones. A good many of them were originally arranged both within and around the massive trilithons at the monument's center, encircled by the linteled sarsen ring. Like the sarsen stones, however, quite a few bluestones have been quarried for local home building.

These bluestones figure in yet more speculation about their origin: again not local but transported from a distant source, all the way from the top of a mountain in Wales. Why? The eminent British archaeologist Glyn Daniel explains in his book *Megaliths in History* (1972). He thinks, and others have followed him, that Geoffrey of Monmouth's legendary story of 1136 may have some truth behind it: his account of *chorea gigantum* lifted entire from afar by Merlin. But only the bluestones, the sarsen stones already accounted for by their transport from Marlborough Downs. The rationale for this argument is that spotted dolorite, technical term for the bluestones, is found only atop Mount Presely in Pembrokeshire, Wales. Rare enough as its occurrence is there, however, it is not the *only* place.

The rarity of spotted dolorite on Mount Presely is a chance deposit, or terminal moraine, of the Pleistocene Ice Age. The geologist G.A. Kellaway (1971), however, has ascertained that derelicts of that same deposit strayed onto Salisbury Plain. So, Charleton was right after all: *all* the stones of Stonehenge are local.

The most enduring Stonehenge idea was cultivated by the eighteenth century antiquary William Stukeley, a scholar of wide learning who also spent much time in the field mapping and sketching ruins we now know to be prehistoric. His chief work, *Stonehenge, a Temple Restor'd to the British Druids* (1740), activated a Druidic cult that lives on to this day.

Stukeley studied all the classical sources, Greek and Roman, bearing on Druids in continental Europe. These include Athenaeus the writer of miscellanies, Strabo the geographer, Diodorus Siculus the historian, and Julius Caesar in his commentaries on the Gallic War. All these sources, however, derive almost entirely from one close observer, Posidonius the Greek historian and ethnographer, whose lost work is known only by quotation and allusion (Tierney 1960).

Therefrom Stukeley concluded that Stonehenge was a temple built by the British Druids, to which he affixed the strangely specific date of 460 B.C., centuries before the Roman invasion. At all events, he drew upon the popular image of a bearded wiseman illustrating a 1676 translation of Caesar's *Battle for Gaul* (fig. 12), making his own version of it (fig. 87) even more popular. This image persists among today's mock Druids, who come to Stonehenge every year at dawn to celebrate the rising of the midsummer sun (fig. 13), as they think their forebears did.

The white-robed individuals in fig. 13, some wearing false white beards, belong to the Albion Lodge of the Ancient Order of Druids, a late Victorian invention inspired by Stukeley and modeled on Freemasonry (Piggott 1968). Today they alone are admitted to the monument, now that it is closed to damaging public traffic. Tourists by the million each year still continue to visit, even if allowed only to walk a path around the site. All the more my privilege it was to climb one of the trilithons (frontispiece).

Druids by name are from the plural forms *druidas* in Greek and *druidae* or *druides* in Latin, words used by the classical authors for a class of priests in Gaul. They are described as transmitters of oral history, keepers of the calendar and rites of sacrifice, composers of poetry, and most importantly as memorizers of the genealogies of their royal patrons. My own guess is that the word Druid can be read as dri-

Fig. 12. *Famous engraving of a Druid by Aylett Sammes from his* Britannia Antiqua Illustrata *(1676)*.

Fig. 13. *Mock Druids, themselves a tourist attraction, gathering at Stonehenge for their annual sunrise ceremony* (HMSO).

wid, or tri-wit, meaning thrice wise. This would fit with the fondness in all Indo-European languages, Gaulish included, for triple intensifiers. Elsewhere in the most ancient texts of Indo-European oral literature warrior heroes are termed thrice strong (Lincoln 1981:104).

Next to Dr. Charleton's book, none are made more fun of than Stukeley's. Archaeologists are confident that Iron Age Druids cannot be read back into Bronze Age Stonehenge. Yes they can, in my opinion (see Epilogue). It is altogether reasonable to suppose that protodruids planned the building of Stonehenge; their remains are among those found in the cemetery's round barrows. Not only warrior heroes and kings are buried there.

Although enlightened archaeologists are pleased to rise above even the most sophisticated of their antiquarian forerunners, yet many of them fall for the trendiest theory of recent times. I refer to that of the archaeo-astronomers, or astro-archaeologists, whose guiding light is the ever-popular *Stonehenge Decoded* by Gerald Hawkins (1965). My previous book (Stover 1978) went out of its way to explode Hawkins; happy to say it converted at least one shaken archaeo-astronomer (Aveni 1980).

The present work takes the matter settled, and moves on to the set-piece reconstructions of Stonehenge City. It were futile to further debate the culture-bound assumptions of space age mythology underpinning the fanciful, not to say science-fictional flights of the archaeo-astronomers: as if the ancients were interested in what the observatory at Mount Palomar does. The latest addition to this genre is John North, *Stonehenge*, whose grandiloquent subtitle is *A New Interpretation of Prehistoric Man and the Cosmos*.

However, in preparing the way for the next chapter, it is no waste of time to summarily review the basic fallacy of Hawkins's thesis. He takes the monument, which he pretends to decode, as one construct built at one time, by one people, for one purpose: as a solar and lunar observatory that also functioned as an eclipse computer. This is to ignore the manifold building phases, for different purposes, not to say the significance of the associated cemetery. Worse, later phases actually obscure earlier ones: they cannot be conflated in a single scheme.

2

The Monument

Tourism at Stonehenge began in the eighteenth century, following the popularity of Stukeley's book, complete with souvenir vendors. Some enterprising tradesmen rented sledgehammers with which to strike off chips of stone for the making of Stonehenge tea, a curative infusion suggested by Geoffrey's still resonant claim that the stones had magical medicinal qualities.

The oldest known photograph of Stonehenge (fig. 14) was taken by a nineteenth century tourist (1853?), no doubt with a heavy tripod-held camera. To the extreme left are his horse and carriage, and his manservant sitting on a recumbent stone. To the right is a flock of sheep grazing what was then open pastureland. One of them, as if owning the place, dominates another fallen stone at center foreground.

By the twentieth century, tourism had expanded to huge international proportions, American and Japanese camera toters the most numerous. From about 1970 large groups of bead-wearing drug-taking American hippies, together with their European brethren, camped out in tents and trailers around the site, taking in its "good vibes." Because they invaded private property, woods and fields, they faced local police with a virtual insurgency beyond control. Later, members of the New Age movement camped in the same way, come there to soak up ancient wisdom. New Age books on the subject now outnumber astro-archaeological ones in goofiness.

While the fad lasted, these crowds had gathered during the summer solstice to share with the mock Druids a mystical event. The latter's assembly still draws tourists, but only as a picturesque event. It may have happened before, in Bronze Age times. One distinguished British archaeologist believes the nearby Cursus was a seasonal camping ground for visitors come to witness a ceremonial spectacle at Stonehenge, whatever that might be. He found posthole impressions within the Cursus, taken as evidence for skin tents erected on poles (Wainwright 1989).

Fig. 14. *Earliest known photograph of Stonehenge. From archival sources discovered by Hans Schaal, a former student and photography major, and heretofore unpublished.*

Today Stonehenge is under the government's Department of the Environment, formerly under the Ministry of Public Works and Antiquities. The environmental concern is for the wear and tear of increased tourism that is no less destructive than the hammer-wielding makers of Stonehenge tea. Once covered with grass for grazing sheep, that, long ago wore down and was replaced with gravel. In time, millions of shuffling feet raised a cumulative amount of erosive dust that did more than millennia of strong wind-blown weathering.

For that reason the site years ago was closed to the public, except for a walk-around pathway for looking and picture-taking from the outside, not very far away. To the advantage of all, however, the Department of the Environment has issued, and continues to issue, informative guidebooks keeping up with the latest researches done by the best of archaeological authorities. These books and pamphlets cover every notable antiquity in Great Britain, including sites in the Stonehenge region not ordinarily associated with its main attraction.

No discussion of Stonehenge is possible without naming its parts. The best source for recognizing them is the ground plan provided as a large foldout in every edition of the official guidebook. See fig. 15. Curiously enough, it but reproduces a survey done by the great Egyptologist Sir Flinders Petrie, including the stone numbers (Petrie 1880).

STONEHENGE

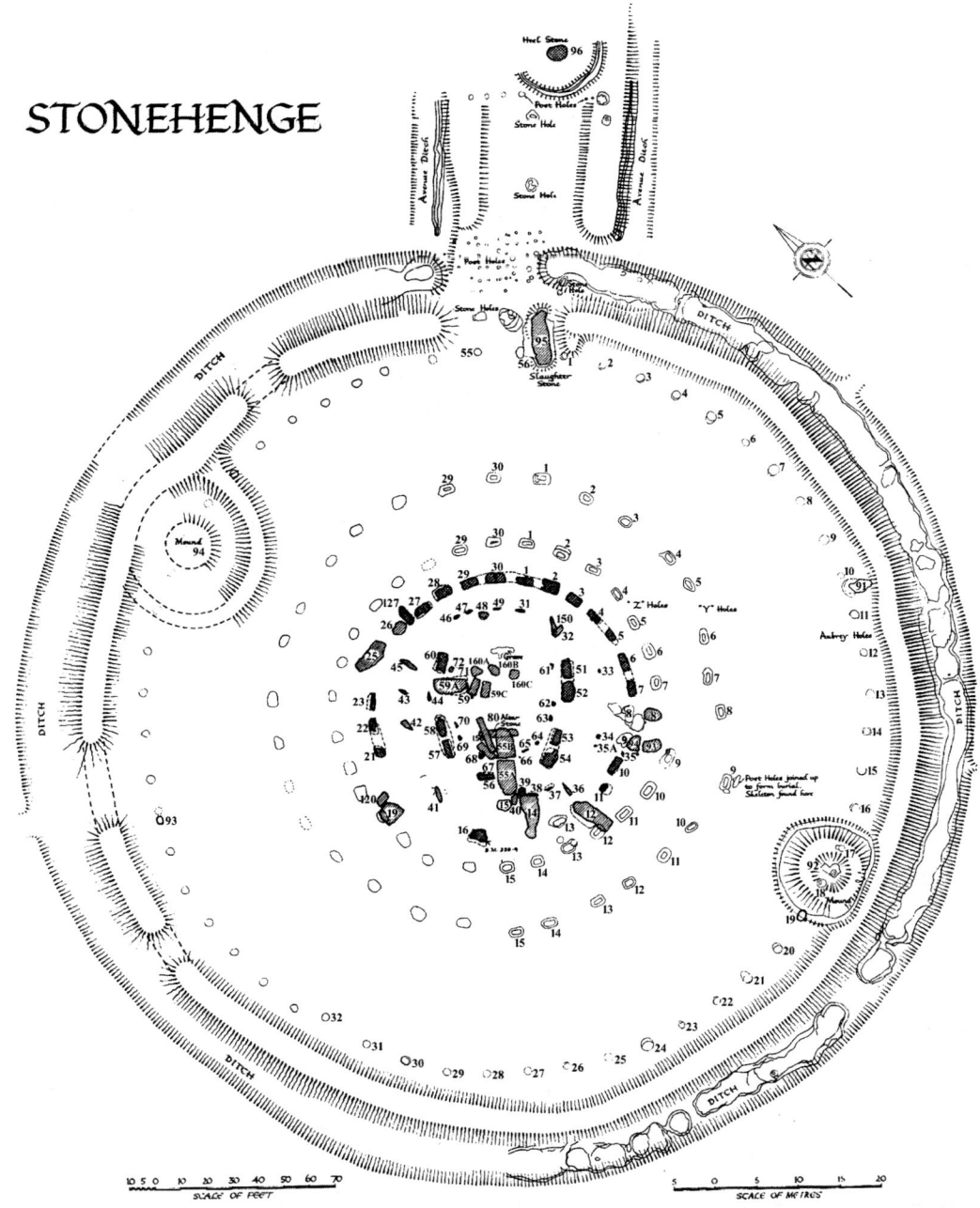

Fig. 15. *Ground plan of Stonehenge from the official guidebook (HMSO).*

The first thing to note is the earthen embankment, with excavation ditch, that defines the site. Directly inside are the Aubrey holes, named after John Aubrey who discovered them (Aubrey 1665). Further inside (black oblongs) is the so-called sarsen ring. At the center, in horseshoe-shaped array, are the five great trilithons, so named by William Stukeley (1740). To the northwest is the Avenue, with Heel Stone at top. Other details in due course.

To help visualize the layout in three dimensions, the aerial view in fig. 16 is useful. Ignore the opening at the bottom, a gravel-laid pathway for public access before the site was closed. The real entrance, when the monument was active, is at the left. Here the Avenue leads up to its front door, so to speak, where the ruined sarsen ring is most complete: four uprights and three continuous lintels. Rotating clockwise from them is a broken section of the ring shown in fig. 17. Inside the ring are the trilithons, three of the five and one pillar still standing. See fig. 18 for the most photographed example. Their arrangement is not circular but, as planned, U-shaped like a horseshoe.

Also dimly seen are the intact bluestones, already illustrated in fig. 11. Now is a good time to give basic specifications for all the monument's principal features. These are tabulated below.

- Bank and ditch. 320 feet from crest to crest, originally 6 feet high. Ditch from which this earthwork was thrown up is now less deep than when excavated, as a result of erosion and silting.
- Aubrey holes. 56 chalk pits just inside the ditch.
- Sarsen circle. 100 feet in diameter. 30 uprights uniformly 13½ feet high, each weighing about 25 tons, some of their uneven length rooted below ground. Lintels 10½ feet long, 7 tons each. Spacing between uprights, 3½ feet, except for the two framing the entranceway, one foot wider.

Fig. 16. *Aerial view of Stonehenge, illustrating ground plan in fig. 15.*

Fig. 17. *Portion of the broken sarsen ring (Hans Schaal).*

- Trilithons. Graded in three sizes. Largest one at heel of horseshoe, one pillar standing, rises 25½ feet to top of lintel and weighs 50 tons. Next in size is the neighboring pair, one of them altogether fallen, measuring 21¼ feet high. The next pair, one of their uprights fallen, stands 20 feet high.
- Bluestones, not all standing or surviving. Plan called for 60 in a circle around the trilithons, 19 within matching their U-shaped curve. Each 6 feet high at 10 tons.

Also visible in the aerial view is a large undressed sarsen stone (no. 95) lying recumbent just inside the Causeway, a break in the embankment leading into the interior. Fig. 19 shows it in a camera shot aimed over it to focus on the sarsen ring's entranceway. On the official ground plan it is known as the Slaughter Stone,

Fig. 18. *One of the photogenic trilithons (Hans Schaal).*

Fig. 19. *Fallen Slaughter Stone in Avenue, with intact entrance to the monument in background (Hans Schaal).*

or Sacrificial Stone, terms applied by eighteenth-century antiquarians, terms evoking the image of a Druidic victim spread-eagled on a bloody stone table for evisceration. The Slaughter Stone, however, once stood upright and had a companion next to it.

Another sarsen stone, farther down the Avenue, is the Friar's Heel, or Heel Stone, so termed from local folklore dating from the eighteenth century — Christian legend suggesting that Stonehenge is the Devil's work. A vigilant friar, hiding nearby, saw him do it. The Devil, having spotted the friar, then threw that particular stone at him, hitting him on his heel. This caused a dent in the stone, leaving a clue as to the monument's evil purpose (Grinsell 1975).

Legendary history often conceals a hidden truth. In this case the story of the Friar's Heel may tell something about the *pattern* of the monument's ruination. To be sure, the missing stones can be accounted for by local residents' quarrying them for building material, as they did the plentiful supply of sarsens that used to lie about, unincorporated into the monument. But these other stones, taken from the monument's ruins, already had been toppled over by those who thought to desecrate the place. Who were they?

The pattern of ruination certainly reveals a motive. Look again at that aerial view in fig. 16. The front part, to which the Avenue leads, is the least damaged. Tearing down Stonehenge, for whatever reason, is no easier than erecting it. So, if desecration were the motive, the main effort had to be concentrated on the monument's business end, its back end where the so-called Altar Stone lies, not its front door.

2. The Monument 27

Fig. 20. *Drawing of Slaughter Stone (lower right, no. 95) with upright Heel Stone (no. 96) farther down the Avenue; from Barkelay 1902.*

One theory has it that the Romans did it, in order to deactivate a center of Druidic resistance. Another that medieval Christians did it, to desanctify a pagan sanctuary, a conspicuous heathen relic of old, as remembered in the legend of the Friar's Heel.

Later that term was transferred from stone 95 to the now-designated Heel Stone, numbered 96 on the official ground plan, which once also had a companion upright. See figs. 15 and 20 for its place in the Avenue. Why the confusing shift in terminology is probably explained by the suggestive heel print on its frontal face. Henceforth it was dubbed Hele Stone, or Sun Stone, by rationalizing archaeologists: a stone for observing the summer solstice.

Important to note, the Heel Stone once had a twin, paired next to it in the Avenue. A socket for this other is detectable in the ground. The twin, however, is much ignored, perhaps because it is not embanked like the Heel Stone. For that reason astro-archaeologists make too much of the existing stone, taking it as a marker for sighting the rising of the midsummer sun, just like the mock Druids. Its true significance, when paired with the other, must be reserved for later discussion.

Four other stones are important to notice, the so-called Station Stones, located just inside the outer earthwork. In fig. 15 they are numbered, clockwise from upper left, 94, 91, 92, and 93. Nos. 94 and 92 are embanked, the other two not. All, however, obscure some of the Aubrey Holes beneath, a very inconvenient fact for

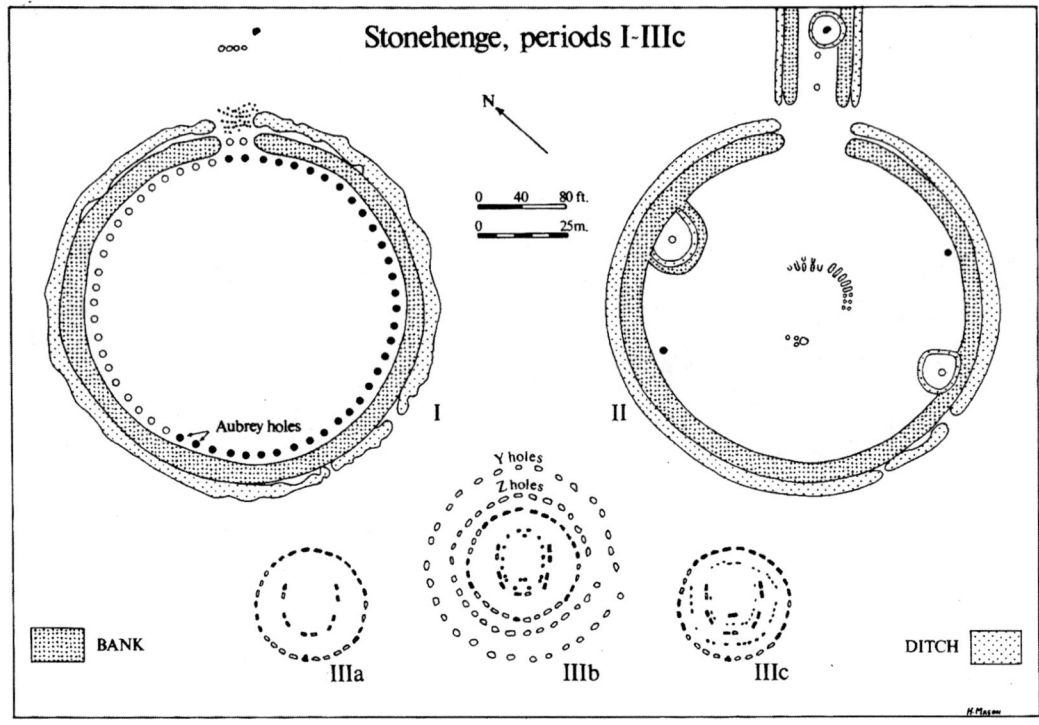

Fig. 21. *Ground plans of Stonehenge's three main building phases; from Atkinson 1980 (HMSO).*

Gerald Hawkins, who in *Stonehenge Decoded* takes them as part of a single machine for computing eclipses, among other celestial observations. The whole idea is manifestly absurd.

Now is the time to spell out the monument's three building phases. These first were determined by Britain's top Stonehenge archaeologist, R.J.C. Atkinson (1956), with many other excavated sites to his credit. He was then professor of archaeology at the University of Cardiff in Wales, himself a charming Welshman. He took the lead in attacking the seductive nonsense promoted by Hawkins in *Stonehenge Decoded* with a sarcastic review article titled "Moonshine on Stonehenge" (Atkinson 1966), so my easy dismissal of it keeps good company.

When Atkinson (1980) revised the details of his periodization, he was kind enough to autograph it for me. Even more generously, he endorsed my reconstruction of the enigmatic Woodhenge site, picturing it as a palace for the king of Stonehenge. What he would think of my other reconstructions in chapter 4 I cannot pretend to guess. At least *part* of my overview of Stonehenge City is not wildly out of place.

Fig. 21 displays Professor Atkinson's latest and last estimate of the monument's three main phases, carried out over a thousand years, from about 3000 B.C. to 2000 B.C. His dating relies on the radiocarbon method, which of course cannot date the stones but only organic material associated with them. Under them are found antler picks and cattle scapulae used as shovels, also found in the ditch from which the circumambient bank was excavated: all datable tools left behind by workmen at each period.

To simplify, Stonehenge I is Neolithic, locally known as the Wessex Neolithic, a division of similar farming cultures in Old Europe before the Indo-European invasions. Stonehenge II is early Bronze Age, known locally as the Wessex Culture. Stonehenge III a–c ranges from early to middle Bronze Age, or Wessex Culture II. (The regional name Wessex is a traditional usage that memorializes the geographical reach of King Alfred's West Saxon — Wessex — kingdom, the nucleus of a unified England. The area centers on present-day Wiltshire.) In all that follows the focus is on Stonehenge IIIb, passing over the less significant variations marked a and c.

The main building phases, then, sequence the following features:

- Stonehenge I. Ditch and bank, Aubrey holes, Heel Stone. Associated with long barrows in the cemetery.
- Stonehenge II. Uncompleted double ring of bluestones. Avenue, Heel Stone embankment within it. Station Stones, two of them embanked. Associated with round barrows in cemetery.
- Stonehenge III. Trilithons. Bluestones rearranged amidst them. Alter Stone. Y and Z holes. Associated with more round barrows.

As to be expected, not all authorities agree with Professor Atkinson's scheme. Some believe that the Y and Z holes, in which no stones were ever set, date to the early Iron Age. They reason that the holes, whatever their purpose, have not the precision of placement characterizing the rest of the monument; therefore Stonehenge was coming to the tired end of its active Bronze Age life. I incline to that notion.

On another point, the good professor omits marking the socket hole for the Heel Stone's twin. I asked him about that and he answered, yes, it exists but he could not date it to any one of his periods. Logically it must belong to Stonehenge III, and I so take it.

Also controversial is the so-called Altar Stone. Atkinson has it lying flat in front of the principal trilithon (IIIb). Actually it lies awry, broken in half. Other authorities, perhaps wary of its lurid repute in popular imagination as a Druidic Slaughter Stone — a table for human sacrifice — think it once stood upright behind the trilithon, for which there is in fact a socket for it. I favor this logic for a reason more complicated than disbelief in its use for human sacrifice at Stonehenge.

For one thing, the Altar Stone is a rare mica-flecked variant of the bluestones, carefully worked, by grinding and pounding, to resemble the squared off shape of the naturally occurring domino-shaped sarsen stones, from which the main trilithon was erected.

First of all, the bluestones and the Altar Stone as well belong to a class of megalithic pillars or slabs called statue menhirs. They are quite common in south and west France, where they typically feature carvings, very schematically, of the

Fig. 22. *Statue menhir from southwest France; Warwick and Trump 1972.*

attributes of a human figure, at times including details of clothing or weapons. See fig. 22. But they may also be featureless (Bray and Trump 1972:218), as are those at Stonehenge.

In fig. 22, the statue menhir bears a shaft-hole battle ax, whether of stone or of bronze is not apparent. Whatever, it definitely belongs to the so-called battle-ax culture, a vernacular term tagging early Indo-European peoples moving into central and western Europe. Sometimes their stone battle axes are, technically speaking, skeuomorphs; they copy in stone the shape of bronze originals, right down to the casting seams. While those buried in the round barrows of the Stonehenge cemetery (fig. 8) have not this feature, they do show no sign of use: they are strictly ceremonial, perhaps family heirlooms passed down in a distinguished line of warrior heroes. In iron, the same was the favored weapon of the Vikings, in practical use into medieval times.

The bluestones of Stonehenge II, if statue menhirs, may very well commemorate notable Indo-European warriors who helped to subjugate the Wessex farmers of southern England, as they did the Neolithic communities everywhere in Old Europe. One must imagine that the builders of Stonehenge II, with its incomplete array of bluestones, were familiar with the name of each warrior represented there, oral tradition always being perseverant in a preliterate culture. Significantly, the round barrows of these conquering heroes are placed next to the Neolithic long barrows in the same cemetery associated with Stonehenge I: invaders assimilating to local custom.

Now then for the Altar Stone, yet another statue menhir. My guess is that this special one represents the royal lineage of the kings of Stonehenge III, whose election place was none other than the monument's hugest trilithon. The other four I take to be electoral platforms for his underkings, drawn from neighboring regions. My reconstruction of the monument as a royal election court, following Dr. Charleton's brilliant insight, is further explained at the end of this chapter. Here I introduce the complicated argument that the architecture of Stonehenge is sepulchral, closely connected to the cemetery in which it is set.

How the monument was built is not as perplexing as the professional mystery mongers make out. The most foolish of these has to be Erich von Däniken, a Swiss-German popularizer of space age mythology, a new cult of unreason. His books have sold in untold millions, exploiting a gullible public susceptible to the occult and even to the more reasonable-seeming astro-archaeological theorists. From his very first book, *Erinnerungen an die Zuklunft* (1968), translated into English as *Chariots of the Gods?*, von Däniken advanced the lunatic theory that ancient astronauts, *Gods from Outer Space* (1970), constructed every tourist-drawing stone monument anywhere, from the great pyramids of Egypt to the giant statues on Easter Island to Stonehenge in southern England. The latter is said to be a landing beacon for flying saucers (the god-like "chariots"), still buzzing about as UFOs flown by space-faring aliens. It was they who built Stonehenge, far beyond the moronic capacity of prehistoric man. Oppositely, the ancient astronomers posited by Hawkins and his like were Einsteinian geniuses anticipating modern science, a reverse twist on space age mythology.

There is, however, no mystery to the mechanical construction of Stonehenge. Any one of my freshman engineering students could easily have figured out how to do it. Half a century ago, Professor Atkinson's own students did experiments showing how simple it is to raise the heavy stones, first the pillars then the lintels. The results are pictured in various official guidebooks (see below). They hauled and raised cast concrete slabs the size and weight of sarsen stones, one upright and one lintel. The hauling part was done by sledge, after use of log rollers, as commonly supposed, proved quite impractical (the rollers broke when passing over uneven ground). Although Atkinson is one of those archaeologists who assume all the stones were brought from afar, he is quite correct to understand the need for transport, even from a nearby quarry, the only possible source according to the geologists upon which I rely.

Before raising the stones, however, they must be worked, prepared, shaped. The methods of erection demonstrated experimentally by Professor Atkinson and his students come into play only after that. These methods apply the most elementary principles of mechanical engineering, allowing for the manhandling of the heaviest sarsen stones with surprisingly little manpower. No mystery to it at all. Even more simple is preparation of the stones. To be sure, this process entailed intensive labor, but on the part of only a few skilled stone masons.

This section deals with their labors. The unusual point to be made here is that the stones of Stonehenge have been worked with techniques not unrelated to carpentry, the working of wood. Nothing could be more simple or easily explained.

Although in local terms the Stonehenge monument belongs to the early Bronze Age, its technical basis is altogether Neolithic, not alone in its method of working stone but in its wood-working implications. Carpentry is also a Neolithic art which must be assumed, even though wooden structures are so perishable no direct evidence remains. The same with clothing and basketry. Stone and metal tools are all that survive for archaeologists to classify within their Three Age system: Stone Age (Old and New), Bronze Age and Iron Age. For the present we may pass over certain refinements later added to this preliminary nineteenth-century system.

The term Neolithic (= New Stone Age, or age of polished stone) was coined to contrast with the preceding Paleolithic (= Old Stone Age, or age of flaked stone). The one did not automatically replace the other, even though the two worked radically different raw material. Paleolithic artifacts are chipped from flint or quartzite, Neolithic from compact stone, abraded to shape. Both types are found at Stonehenge, which is not surprising, given that the flint industry continued to flourish in eighteenth-century Europe and America for use in strike-a-light tinder boxes (before the advent of phosphorous matches) and for the firing of gunpowder in muskets (flintlocks).

Now then, the dressing of the Stonehenge sarsens (a very compact form of sandstone) is a strictly Neolithic technique: pounding, abrading, grinding. At the same time sarsen uprights are joined to their lintels by techniques derived from carpentry. Take the sarsen ring for example. Their pillars are locked onto their lintels by means of mortise-and-tenon joints. Atop each upright are two tenons (see fig. 23) that fit into a mortise at each end of adjoining lintels. More, the lintels themselves are linked horizontally by means of tongue-in-groove joints (fig. 24), another wood-working method. Only in this case the tenons are formed by the Neolithic

Fig. 23. *Top of a pillar in the sarsen ring, showing its two tenons for holding lintels in place (HMSO).*

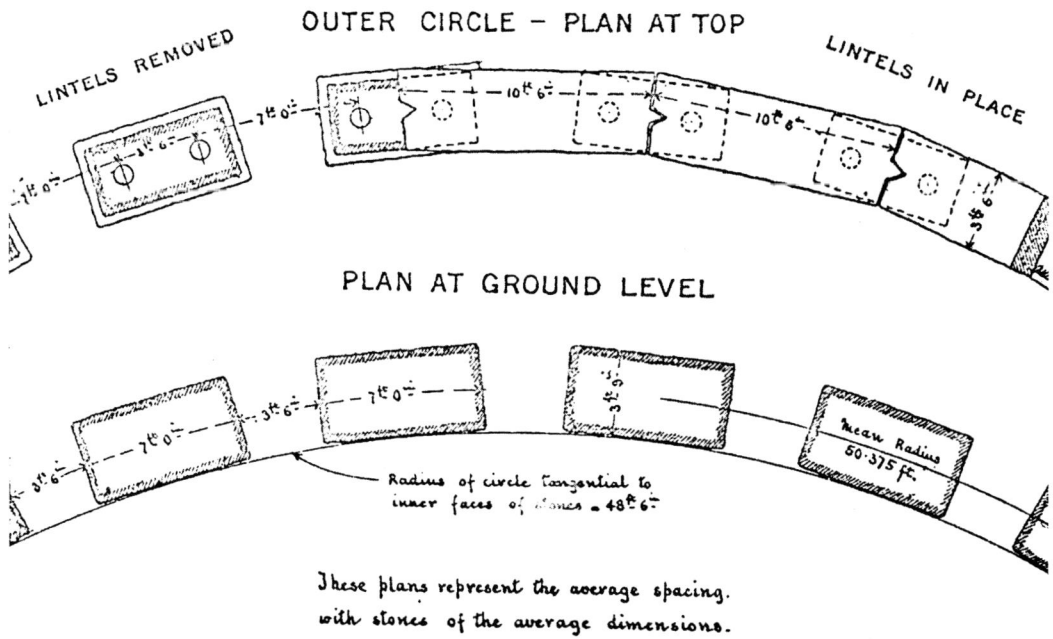

Fig. 24. *Tongue-in-groove connections between lintels in the sarsen ring; from Stone 1924.*

technique of pounding and grinding away the stone around them. Digging out the mortise holes, absent iron chisels, would have been much more difficult, suggesting a very patient devotion to a model set by the art of wood joinery. By comparison the tongue-in-groove joints would have been easier to form in stone. Note also the abrasion required to give the lintels their slightly curved shape when viewed in plan (as in fig. 24).

With the aid of fig. 25, a close view of a section of the ruined sarsen ring, the reader may imagine how it was assembled. The right-hand pillar has one of its two tenons sticking up into the mortise hole beneath the lintel, whose neighbor is missing. Exposed at the lintel's right end is the groove into which fitted the tongue of the fallen lintel next to it. This groove, much weathered, is just barely visible in the photograph, seen as a nick silhouetted against the skyline.

Fig. 25. *Section of the broken sarsen ring seen close up (Hans Schaal).*

Fig. 26. *View of main trilithon's remaining pillar, top left, its fallen lintel at foot of complete trilithon top center (Hans Schaal). Pillar uprighted from a tilt in 1901.*

The trilithons were assembled the same way, except their five lintels are separate, one per five paired uprights. In fig. 26 the one standing pillar of the hugest trilithon at the heel of the horseshoe-shaped array rises high to the left. Its massive tenon is starkly visible at top. At its foot is the fallen lintel, its cavitied mortise hole exposed to the right of it, seen against the foot of the complete trilithon. This is the one I sat upon in the frontispiece. Note that its lintel is wider at the top than at bottom, so that when one is looking up from below the optical illusion of its narrowing upward is countered: a sophisticated architectural trick known as entasis.

The designers of Stonehenge III certainly were not professional architects, not job specialists in the modern sense. They rather were religious specialists. In chapter 3 I shall be calling them proto–Druids, and for good reason, nothing startling nor mystifying. A revelation of my reasoning must wait upon that later chapter. I cannot say everything at once.

Meanwhile, further discussion of how the sarsen stones were dressed is in order. As already mentioned, the stones were available locally for building material, huge tabular formations of compact sandstone naturally occurring. However, these did not occur in the exact width useful to the monument's designers. Therefore the raw material required trimming to their specifications, quite a simple process actually.

Like wood, sarsen stone is grained, and can be split like wood. How this was

2. The Monument

Fig. 27. *Display of greenstone mauls in the Salisbury and South Wiltshire Museum.*

done is suggested by the recovery at Stonehenge of a number of stone mauls, large and small. In fig. 27 the smallest one is the size of an orange. A maul of about that size would have been gripped in one hand by stonemasons to pound down and abrade away the tops of sarsen pillars, leaving their tenons revealed. The biggest maul, however, is about the size of a basketball (top left), not a one-handed pounding tool. Mauls of that mass must have been used in quite a different way, in a two-handed hurling of them, in unison, onto a sarsen slab by a team of masons in order to split it along the grain.

The method of cleaving the stones of Stonehenge was deduced by the geologist Edward H. Stone from his experience as an engineer with the government of India during the British raj. Stone concluded that a technique once used by the subjects of the Nizam in Hyderabad for the quarrying of stratified granite would have worked on the stratified sandstone of Salisbury Plain.

> In the neighborhood of the city of Hyderabad there occurs in several places a formation of stratified granite (or "gneiss") which can be separated into layers of varying thickness.
>
> To obtain stone for building purposes a layer of this granite is split up by native quarrymen, in a very simple manner, by the use of spherical masses or "mauls" of granite. These mauls are precisely similar to the largest mauls found in the excavations at Stonehenge.

> A number of men stand in line across the layer in the direction in which the slab is to be split. Each man has a maul which he holds between his two hands above his head. At a signal from the foreman each man dashes down his maul simultaneously on the granite layer, which is thereby split across with a fairly even fracture.
>
> The pieces thus obtained are long blocks similar in size and shape to the sarsen stones of the outer circle at Stonehenge. These blocks are afterwards broken into pieces of suitable size for building purposes [Stone 1924:77*f*].

Stone, author of *The Stones of Stonehenge*, is a wonderfully apt name for the one geologist most obsessed with the subject. His opinion as to how the sarsens were cut carries indefeasible authority. The only point in doubt is his last sentence in the above quotation. He says that gneiss can be split across the grain as well as with it for width and thickness. Were sarsen pillars and lintels cut to length the same way? That is not possible to know. Remnants of unworked sarsen slabs no longer are extant, those John Aubrey saw Dr. Charleton clamber over. One thing, however, is known: all the sarsen uprights are of different lengths, whatever height above ground was planned. The difference in each excavated case is buried below ground where the bottoms are rounded, as if to rock the pillar back and forth in its hole until properly vertical: calculated with remarkable precision.

Dressing of the stones is one thing, raising them is another, a question of mechanical engineering. In the event it turns out to be simplicity itself, as demonstrated by field experiments conducted by Professor Atkinson and his students. What they did in practice merely tested a likely method suggested by E.H. Stone. Not only did his method prove workable, he was right again when he argued that it was possible to local builders without the aid of a more sophisticated architect from outside.

The idea of a foreign agent gained currency when in December 1953 Atkinson discovered a suggestive dagger carving on the face of one of the trilithons (stone no. 54). This was a front page story in the *New York Times*, and what a sensational story it was, picked up by other papers as well. Those were the days when important archaeological discoveries were big news.

The dagger carving soon attracted tourists who fingered it with their greasy hands. That is why it shows up black in plate II:1. To the right of it is the blackened outline of a bronze ax-head of the sort found inscribed all over the place. The dagger carving is unique. See fig. 28 for a side by side comparison. To the right is the common ax-head carving, to the left the out-of-place dagger carving.

As for raising the sarsens, first the pillars must be uprighted in their sockets, then the lintels elevated and seated. Atkinson toyed with both problems experimentally, solving them to such complete satisfaction that his results are now a commonplace in the professional literature. This includes official guidebooks, always written by a variety of the most distinguished authorities.

Fig. 29 illustrates his experimental raising of a concrete slab the size and weight of one of the uprights in the sarsen ring. To the right, the slab, with properly

Fig. 28, top. *Dagger carving (left) next to ax-head carving on stone 53; from a 1953 newspaper report.* Fig. 29, bottom. *Use of wooden A-frame to raise sarsen upright; from Atkinson 1956.*

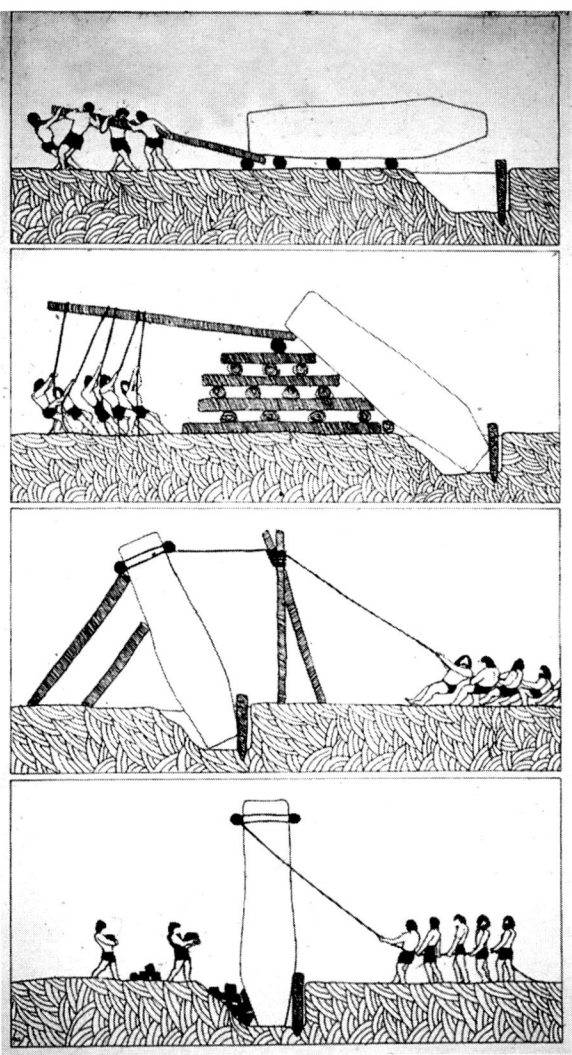

Fig. 30. *The Atkinson method of raising sarsen pillars, illustrated in one of the official guidebooks (HMSO).*

rounded bottom, is placed on log rollers in front of a prepared pit (*not* rollers used for transport of the slab to its erection site: a sledge was used for that). After the slab was pushed toward the hole, it fell foot first into it, then was raised fully upright by means of a simple A-frame, seen at left. Further steps shown in fig. 30. The A-frame, simple as it is, allows for a tremendous mechanical advantage. Only a few men are needed to pull a weighty stone into place. See plate VIII:1 for an imaginative pulling into place of one of the great trilithon uprights.

Going back to fig. 29, note how the socket is prepared in Atkinson's experiment. A ramp of 45° incline in front of the slab about to be lowered makes possible, by force of gravity, the falling into place of the slab at the same degree of incline, then to be raised up to full height by means of a wooden A-frame. Wooden stakes at the back end of the hole keep it from crumbling when the toe of the slab drops in. Evidence for this has been learned from excavation of empty socket holes once holding now fallen or missing sarsen uprights.

Interviewed by the science journalist at the *Times*, Atkinson explained that he could date that dagger carving to 1500 B.C. In outline it matched the shape of real daggers buried in the royal shaft graves at Mycenae. These burial pits also contained trade pottery of a distinctive type from Egypt, datable exactly in accord with the accurate Egyptian solar calendar. Therefore, Stonehenge III was designed in 1500 B.C. by a Mycenaean architect. Later, with the radiocarbon date of 2000 B.C. in hand, Atkinson gave up on Mediterranean influence. Bronze Age Mycenae did not arise until 500 years *after* Stonehenge, so its construction was a strictly native project. All the same, a Mycenaean presence at that time was real enough, the significance of which is discussed in chapter 3 on the builders of Stonehenge.

Lintel-raising calls for another technique altogether, but still simple in concept. Although it calls for a plentiful supply of wooden planking for the building of timber cribs around the uprights, dense woodlands near Stonehenge once were common, and carpenters in the Neolithic tradition surely knew how to split trees into planks. Fig. 31 shows the method, extrapolated from preliminary steps conducted by Atkinson. The lintel is first levered up onto the lowest level platform of the timber crib, and then upward to the top level, where the lintel is levered over above its pillars. When lowered its mortises lock firmly with the tenons below. There is no other way to rationally explain, or demonstrate, the construction process.

Much more difficult to explain is the symbolic meaning of the monument's architecture. All becomes clear, however, once its megalithic details are related to structural features found inside the many long barrows distributed throughout the vast cemetery in which the monument situates. To build up a case for what I call sepulchral architecture, it is necessary to review the history of burial practices at Stonehenge. These mortuary details change over time no less than the central monument itself during its three main building phases.

To begin with Stonehenge I. Within the earthen embankment lie the 56 Aubrey Holes, as already mentioned, the significance of their number unknowable. What is evident, however, is their intended purpose, to serve as cinerary pits. Dug out of chalk and then refilled, these holes are about 3 feet 3½ inches wide and as deep, with sheer walls. Excavated ones reveal cremated remains. In one case the bottom rim of a fired clay pot, a container for the deceased's ashes, was found; other finds include bone hair pins, flaked stone implements and one elegant shaft-holed macehead of polished stone.

There is no accounting for cremation evidenced in the Aubrey Holes (now covered with white concrete discs), when all the burial mounds of whatever phase in the surrounding cemetery contain inhumed remains, no cremations. The only difference (apart from shape) between the long barrows of Stonehenge I and the round barrows of Stonehenge II and III is that the former house collective burials, the latter individual burials.

A close look at the long barrows is now in order, because the structure of their buried mortuary houses has remarkable significance for the sepulchral architecture of Stonehenge III. But, although I have repeatedly stressed the immensity of the Stonehenge cemetery, nobody knows how many burials once filled it. Uncountable numbers of them have been ploughed under in recent centuries. Although aerial photography has detected the outlines of a dozen or so, the total number comes to only about 460, many more lost to reckoning. One thing is sure, however: Bronze Age round barrows outnumber Neolithic long barrows and the former are arranged in distinct groups around the latter. See fig. 32.

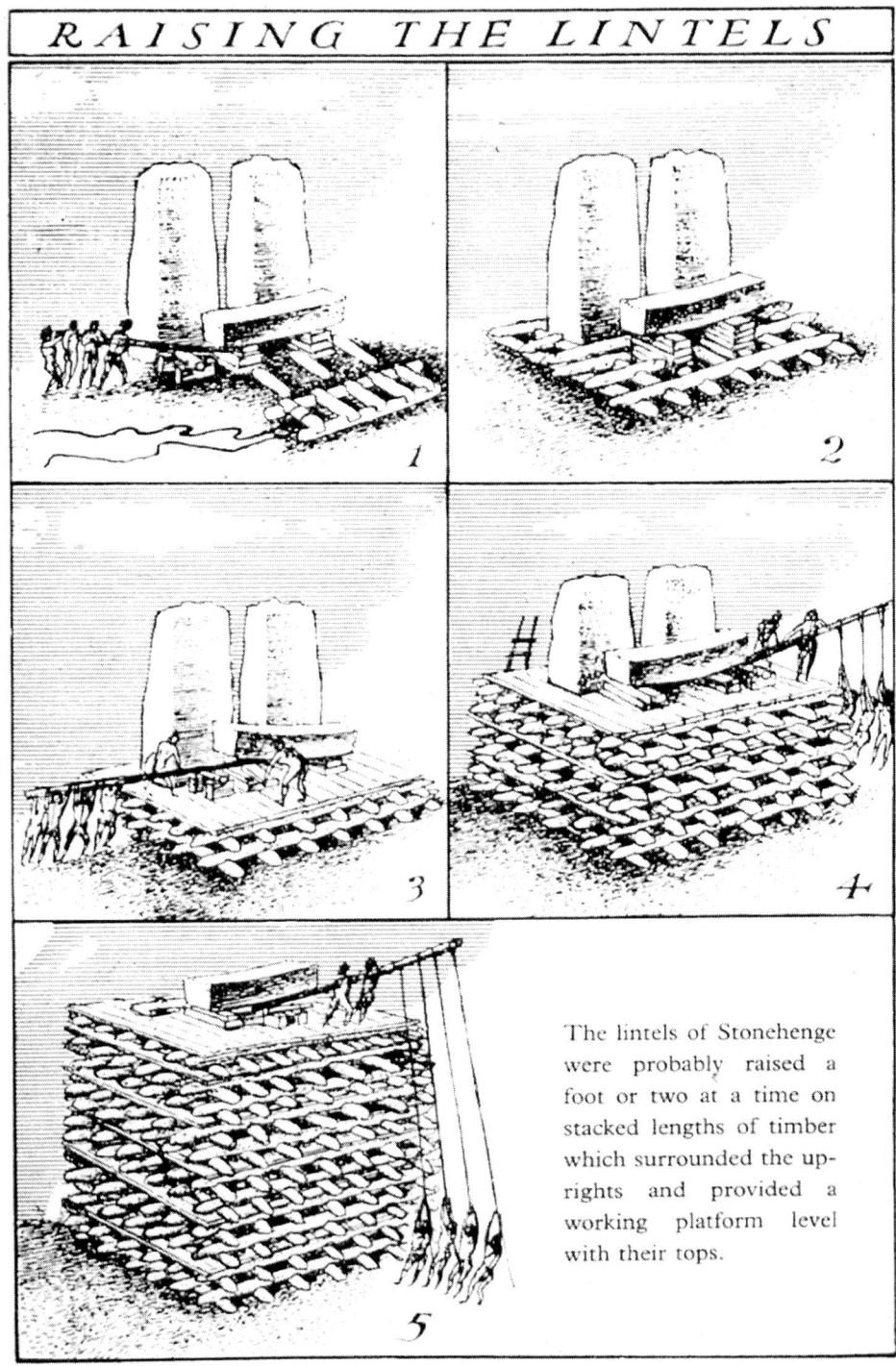

Fig. 31. *The Atkinson method of raising and seating lintels, as illustrated in one of the official guidebooks (HMSO).*

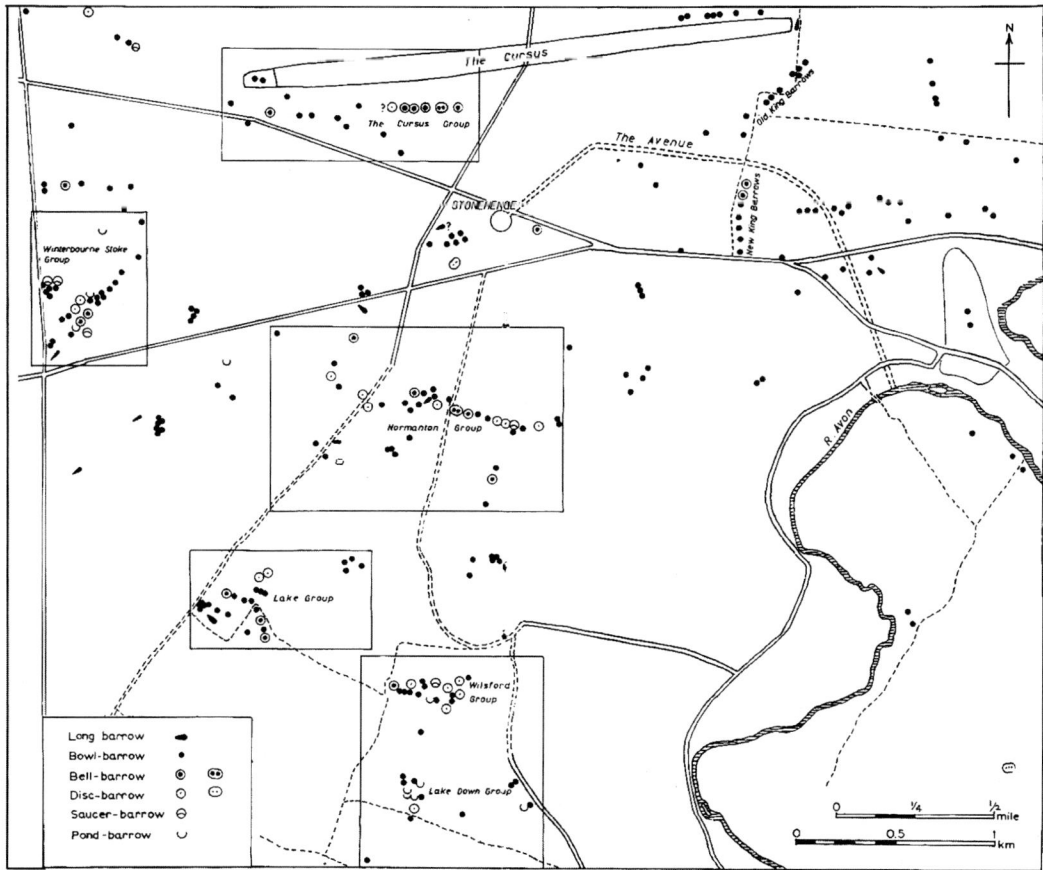

Fig. 32. *Map of the Stonehenge region, showing pattern of round barrows grouped around scattered long barrows. Types of round barrows given in the legend are controversial and may be ignored. From Grinsell 1978.*

The long barrows of Stonehenge I are a product of the Wessex Neolithic, although many others throughout southern and eastern Britain still survive. These are long, wedge-shaped earthen or chalk mounds anywhere from 100 to 300 feet in length and 30 to 100 feet wide which, at the widest end, covered wooden or turf mortuary houses. Where the mortuary house is made of stone they are known as chambered tombs. All have continental origins (Ashbee 1970).

A perfectly restored example of the chambered tomb is located in the Cotswold Hills of southwestern England, known for the region's fine Cotswold wool. Under protection of the Department of Environment, the site is named after the Stoney Littleton farm on whose property the hilltop site resides. When visiting it I paid the owner a small fee to borrow his government key to unlock the iron gate to a fence built to keep cattle out.

After walking about half a mile of pastureland and up the hill, I beheld from on high a scenic view of the Cotswolds, and tried to imagine the landscape at the

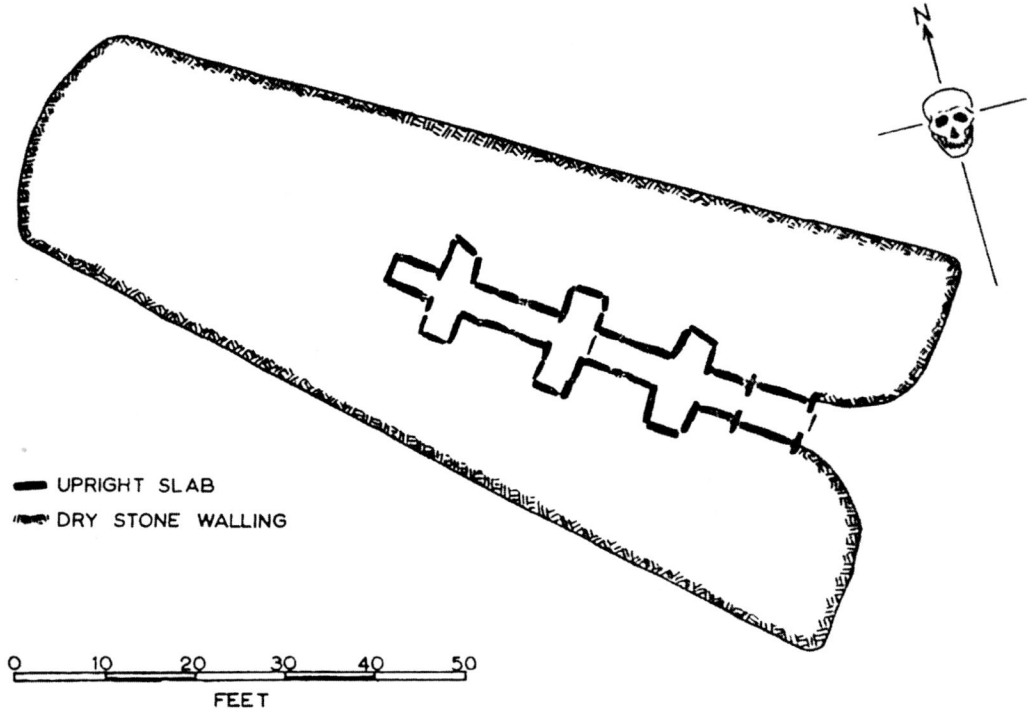

Fig. 33. *Official ground plan of interior structure within the chambered tomb on the Stoney Littleton farm (HMSO).*

time of burial. Most certainly it would show fewer tilled fields, more pastureland for cattle and less for sheep, and much more forest cover. Some sheep because the British woolen industry most likely has Neolithic beginnings.

The official pamphlet on Stoney Littleton provides a ground plan of its burial chambers, but not of the earthen mound covering them. This is 107 feet long and 54 feet wide at the entrance. Typical of all Neolithic long barrows, with or without stone-built mortuary houses, the mound tapers front to back, its tail the longest part.

My photograph of the front end's entranceway in fig. 34 is a distant view, showing the rolling Cotswold hills beyond, where many other Neolithic tombs of the same type are common, although none are preserved as well as Stoney Littleton. Although far from the largest chambered tomb of its type, the earthwork still is impressive. A considerable amount of organized effort went into building it. My wife standing diminutive on top suggests the monumental scale.

Fig. 35 is a close-up of the doorway. It is framed by two horns of revetted dry-stone walling that curve inwards to a low entrance constructed of stone slabs, as diagrammed in fig. 33. The left-hand jamb has a fine fossil ammonite impression worthy of any museum of paleontology, here purely decorative, evincing aesthetic taste in the selection of stone. Crawling inside (it was not a walk-in place

2. The Monument

Fig. 34, top. *Long shot of Stoney Littleton, front end (photograph by the author).* Fig. 35, bottom. *Closeup of Stoney Littleton entrance (photograph by the author).*

like some other tombs), I took the picture in fig. 36. Off to the sides of a narrow passageway were three paired burial chambers and one at the end: there are seven altogether.

Chambered tombs are nothing if not collective tombs, gathering the remains of related family lineages over long periods of time. Typically a chambered tomb remained open until closed many generations later. The often-taken implication of collective tombs is that Neolithic society was a kind of folk society, communal, egalitarian, and non-hierarchical. This may not be the case, as evidenced by the organized labor required to raise long barrows and by the mace of authority found in one of the Aubrey Holes belonging to Stonehenge I and its Wessex Neolithic constructors.

Just to the north of Stonehenge is the looming presence of Silbury Hill. The largest earthen mound in all of Europe, Silbury Hill is a truncated cone standing 130 feet high on a base covering 5¼ acres, one of the greatest enigmas of British archaeology. Once thought to be the gigantic tomb (like unto the Egyptian pyramids) of some Bronze Age king, during a digging program between 1968 and 1970, Professor Atkinson determined that it was Neolithic and contained no burial. His most interesting discovery was that Silbury Hill is no mere piling up of dirt but a complex structure engineered to hold its mixed building material in place. Otherwise the whole thing long ago would have slid into a shapeless mass.

The top of Silbury Hill is leveled to form a sizeable platform. Standing on it, after a steep climb, I got to thinking about its possible use. The mountainous hill itself, in this line of thought, would but serve to elevate a high place from which something conspicuous could be seen for miles around. What came to mind was the ancient Irish fire festival Beltaine held on 1 May. Beltaine means "bright fire" or "goodly fire," from which meaning the term *bonfire* derives. To this day in the British Isles, Mayday is marked by the lighting of bonfires, at times called Beltaine fires. In ancient Ireland, the Celtic Iron Age there, Beltaine fires were often set on mountain tops by the king of each region, thereby asserting his command over traditional usages.

Reflecting on these matters while standing atop Silbury Hill, I was led also to think about long-term cultural continuities. It may very well be that Silbury Hill (Neolithic) anticipates a significant event on the Celtic calendar, just as I believe the symbolic meaning of Stonehenge III (Bronze Age) anticipates the political geography of Ancient Ireland (Iron Age). More on the logic of that in chapter 5. But for now attention must be directed at the monument's architecture as it relates to the sepulchral design of long barrows belonging to the Wessex Neolithic of Stonehenge I.

If my reading of Silbury Hill is correct, the Wessex Neolithic was no egalitarian folk culture, nor was it a stratified society. Yet it was structured enough to organize labor for big work projects like Silbury Hill and the complex long bar-

Fig. 36. *Passageway inside Stoney Littleton, with corbelled arching above (photograph by the author).*

rows. It was not until the Indo-European invaders of Old Europe transformed its Neolithic order and made for real stratification, a new stratified order, or layered society, with priests and warriors holding sovereignty over once autonomous Neolithic producers. This is exactly the cultural revolution behind the builders of Stonehenge III, identified in the archaeological literature as the Wessex Culture.

The megalithic monument created by that culture is not unconnected with tomb-building features of the long barrows arrayed in the Stonehenge I cemetery. It is a mistake, however, to conclude that the collective burials within represent a communal society: the Neolithic idealized.

But of course the Neolithic is not the same thing everywhere at any one time, given the process of cultural diffusion and local adaptation. The temptation to overgeneralize must be resisted. The Wessex Neolithic is a distinctive extension of the continental Danubian culture, which in turn derives from the original Neolithic in the Near East, where it paid for the rise of urbanism in the original Bronze Age civilization. Diffusing from that center the Neolithic, but not yet urban culture, spread throughout Europe (henceforth Old Europe) with many local variations.

The first penetration of farming into Europe is known as the Danubian culture. It is best excavated in central European places like Germany, Poland, and the Czech and Slovak republics. Indicated in those sites is a style of slash-and-burn agriculture conducted within a heavily forested environment. It seems these homesteaders would cut down trees, burn them for fertilizing ash, clear their fields, and then move on when the soil leeched out after a few years. Moving from one stead to another, they eventually returned to another home base in a repeated cycle. These rotating homes, meant for reoccupation over many generations, were solidly built of heavy timber, plastered walls, and gabled roofs, measuring from 30 to 120 feet long by about 20 feet wide. In ground plan these homes were trapezoidal long houses. See fig. 37. The concept of a long house is widely known from the Iroquois example in North America. Their rectangular long houses, up to 130 feet long, were communal dwellings, housing extended families or related clan members. The same is reasonable to assume for Danubian long houses.

Why they take the queer trapezoidal shape they do is unanswerable. At bottom all cultural conventions are ultimately arbitrary, beyond explanation. One thing is clear, however. Danubian long houses influenced the design of Danubian long barrows, collective tombs reflecting the communal dwellings of the living. See fig. 38. These in turn have influenced the wedge-shaped design of long barrows and chambered tombs associated with the Wessex Neolithic in southern Britain, although no long houses are evidenced there.

The next piece of evidence in my case for sepulchral Stonehenge is the truly monumental chambered tomb, 380 feet long, the so-called West Kennet Long Barrow. See the aerial view in fig. 39. Located a few miles west of Silbury Hill, it was excavated by the highly honored professor of prehistoric archaeology at the University of Edinburgh, Stuart Piggott, assisted by the promising young R.J.C. Atkinson, in their digging campaigns of 1955–1956 (Piggott 1962). Thereafter it was restored by the Ministry of Works to become the tourist site it now is under the Department of the Environment.

As can be seen in fig. 40, the stone-built mortuary house occupies a very small space within the business end of the massive earthen mound. Even so it is a tremendously large cathedral-like place when walked into standing up as I did to snap the picture in fig. 41. In view is the passageway running between burial chambers on either side and one at the end. At Stoney Littleton I had to crawl inside the tomb, but the scene is the same, only on a different scale.

At last it is time to relate the tomb architecture of West Kennet to the sepulchral features of Stonehenge III. For the moment I pass over the actual burial practices revealed by excavation of the tomb, details reserved for the next section. More urgent now is the need to hasten my argument for the funerary aspects of Stonehenge's design, basic to everything else.

Look at fig. 42 (page 50), the isometric drawing of the burial chambers within West Kennet. These chambers were accessed by a central passageway before the blocking stones (bottom right) were put in place. Archaeologists name such chambers *transepts*, a term borrowed from ecclesiastical architecture. Transepts are any major transverse part of a church, running at right angles to either

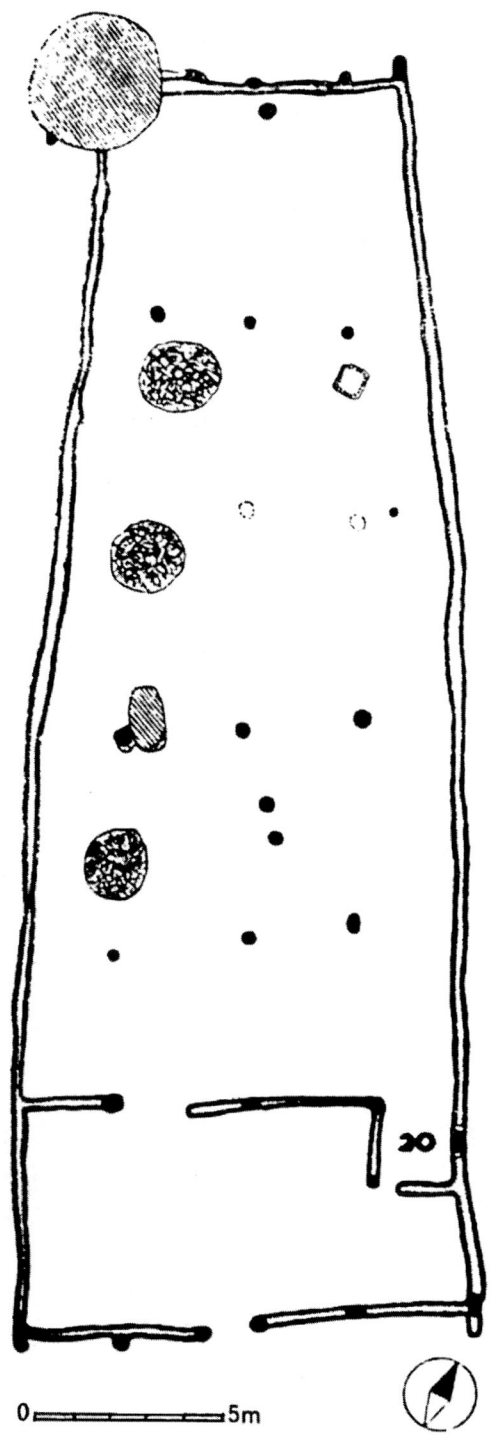

Fig. 37. *Plan of a Danubian long house in Czechoslovakia; in Ashebee 1970, from a Czech language report.*

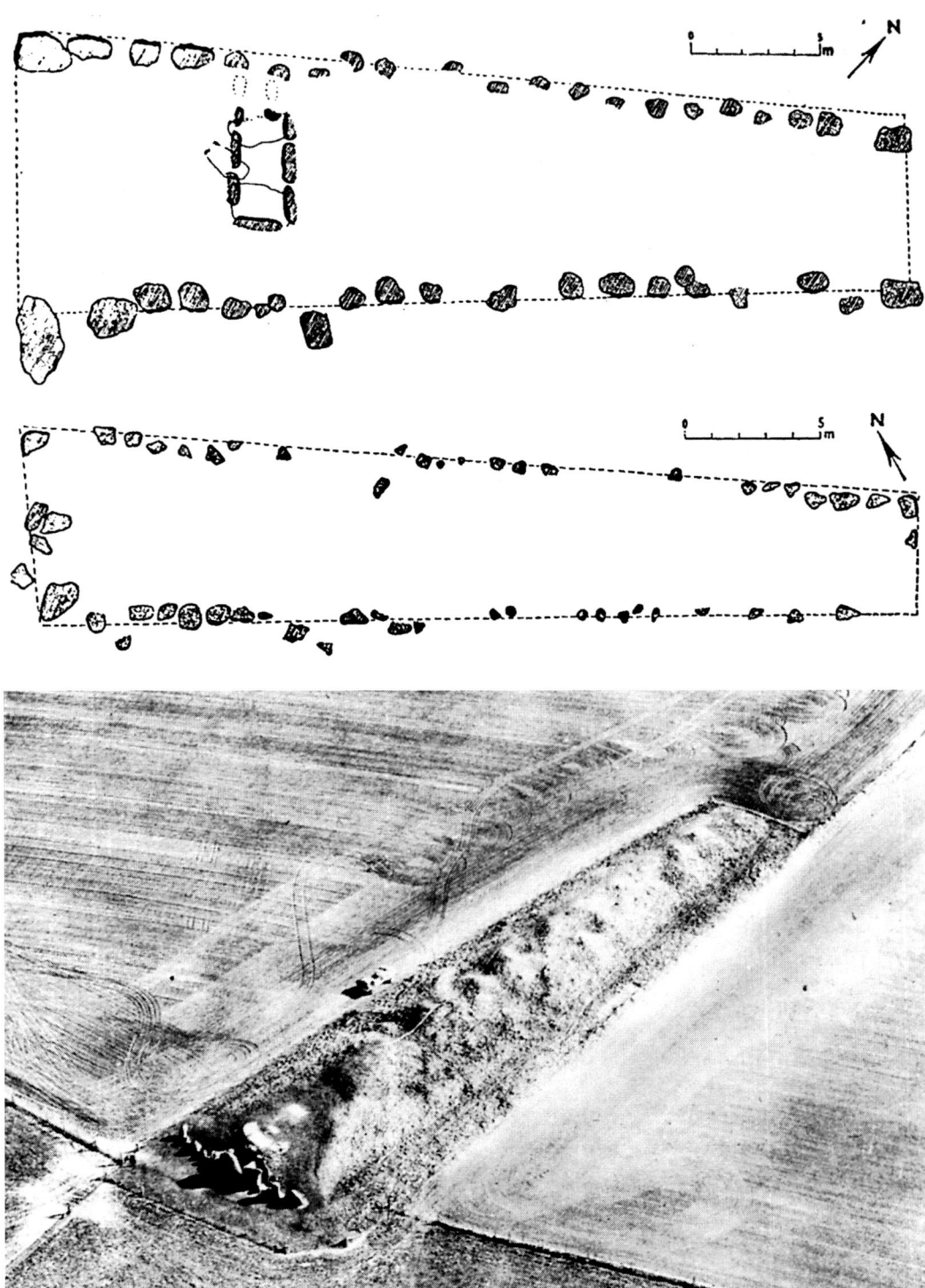

Fig. 38, top. *Boulder-bounded long barrows in northern Germany; in Ashbee 1970, from a German language report.* Fig. 39, bottom. *Aerial view of the West Kennet chambered tomb in Wiltshire: The stone burial chambers are beneath the mound at its widest end, bottom left (HMSO).*

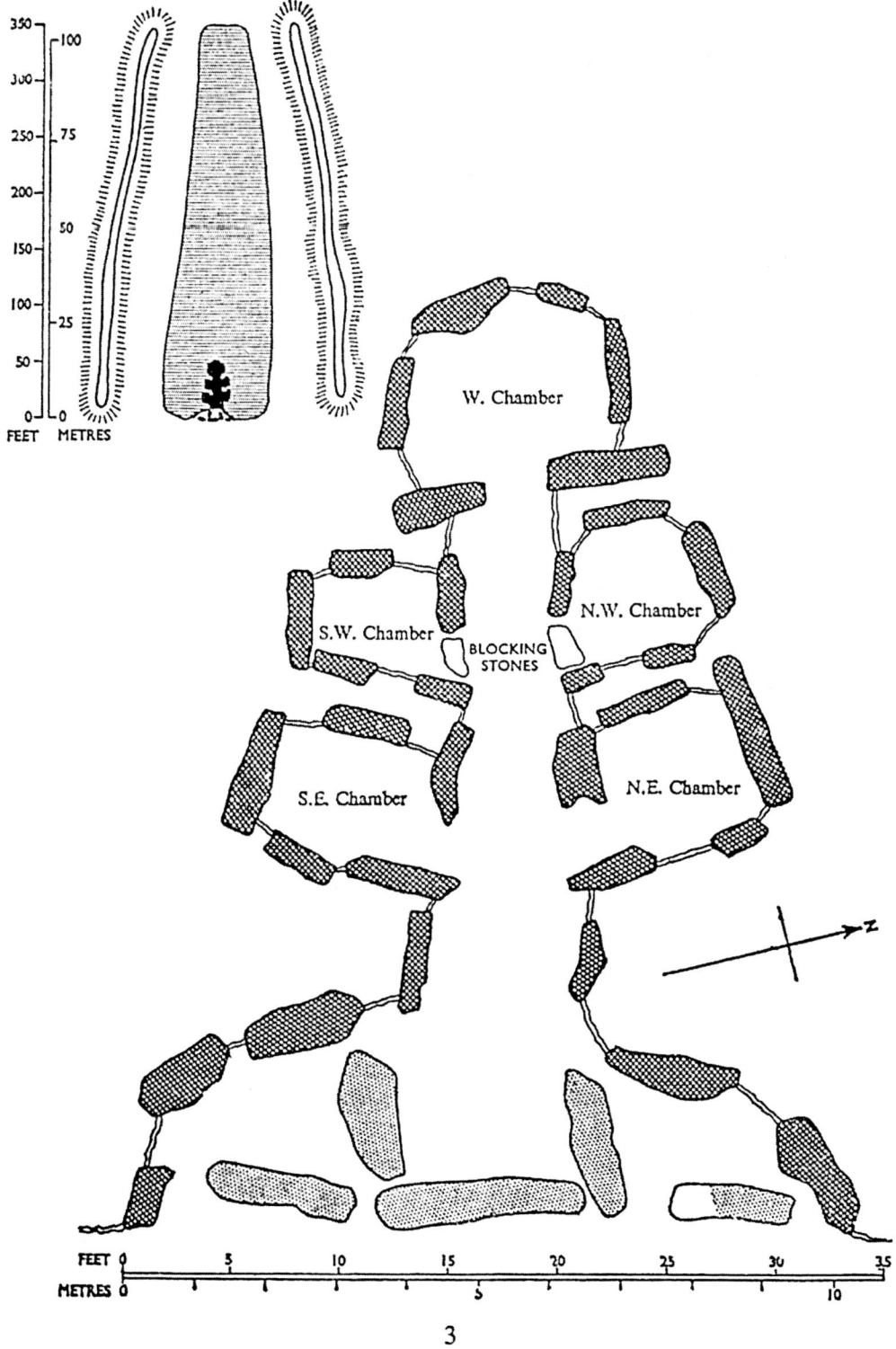

Fig. 40. *Ground plan of West Kennet: General view left, details of mortuary house right (HMSO).*

Fig. 41, top. *View looking into West Kennet from entrance (photograph by the author, with the help of a friendly curator from Devizes Museum).* Fig. 42, bottom. *Isometric drawing of West Kennet's burial chambers, outer facade and forecourt (HMSO).*

side of its aisle. It is so with the five chambers inside West Kennet, except that the west chamber (top left) is terminal, not off to the side of the aisle.

Important to note, illustrated for the north chambers, all transepts are roofed over with a massive slab of sarsen stone. Indeed, all stones are tabular sarsens from the Stonehenge region. The builders of Stonehenge III most likely were aware of West Kennet, which remained open for about a thousand years, from just after Stonehenge I (Neolithic) to Stonehenge II (early Bronze Age).

Although I am not by any means the first to associate burial practices with Stonehenge, my two books (Stover 1978 and the present one) are the only works since 1899 and 1929 to develop these early suggestions. The very first hint of this idea was thrown out almost casually by Sir Arthur Evans, who devoted his life and immense wealth to the excavation and partial restoration of the spectacular palace complex at Knossos on the island of Crete, home of the Minoan civilization (his term) contemporary with the Mycenaean on the Greek mainland. Thirty years later R.S. Newall, a distinguished Stonehenge archaeologist, followed through with another brief article elaborating a little on the same idea. But as author of the 1959 edition of the Department of Environment's guidebook he says no more about it. It simply vanished into the oblivion of theories too quirky to credit.

Sir Arthur argued that Stonehenge was far from unique among megalithic monuments, that it shared some structural features with even more ancient megalithic tombs on Malta and in Iberia. He shrewdly says,

> As I have elsewhere endeavored to point out, this original sepulchral connection of Megalithic Circles is of primary importance in its bearing on their origin. It enables us in fact to trace the smaller and simpler circles that actually mark the limits of the primitive grave-mound. The three component parts of the most characteristic of the Megalithic Circle, the circle itself, the stone avenue opening from it, and the cist or dolmen contained by it, are all of them mere amplifications of the simplest sepulchral forms. The Circle is an enlarged version of the ring of stones placed round the grave mound; the Dolmen represents the cist within it; the avenue is merely the continuation of the underground gallery. The only difference lies in the greater size of the stones in the Megalithic Circles, and that in this case they are no longer covered by or in juxtaposition with the earth mound, but have become freestanding....
>
> And in Stonehenge itself we have to deal with a monument which, though of a more complicated arrangement and displaying greater technical skill, must still be regarded as belonging to the same general class as the simpler forms already alluded to.... The triliths are indeed a new feature in connection with the stone circle, but ... are themselves only the perpetuation of a part of the sepulchral structure, the actual gateway of the subterranean chamber, which remains a ritual survival when ... the galleried chamber to which it led has itself been modified away [Evans 1899:313*f*].

Picking up on this exotic notion, R.S. Newall (1929) carried through with a systematic comparative study, published in *Antiquity*, Britain's most prestigious archaeological journal. It made nary a ripple in professional circles, and I came across it by accident: a stunning discovery. His comparative diagrams are reproduced in

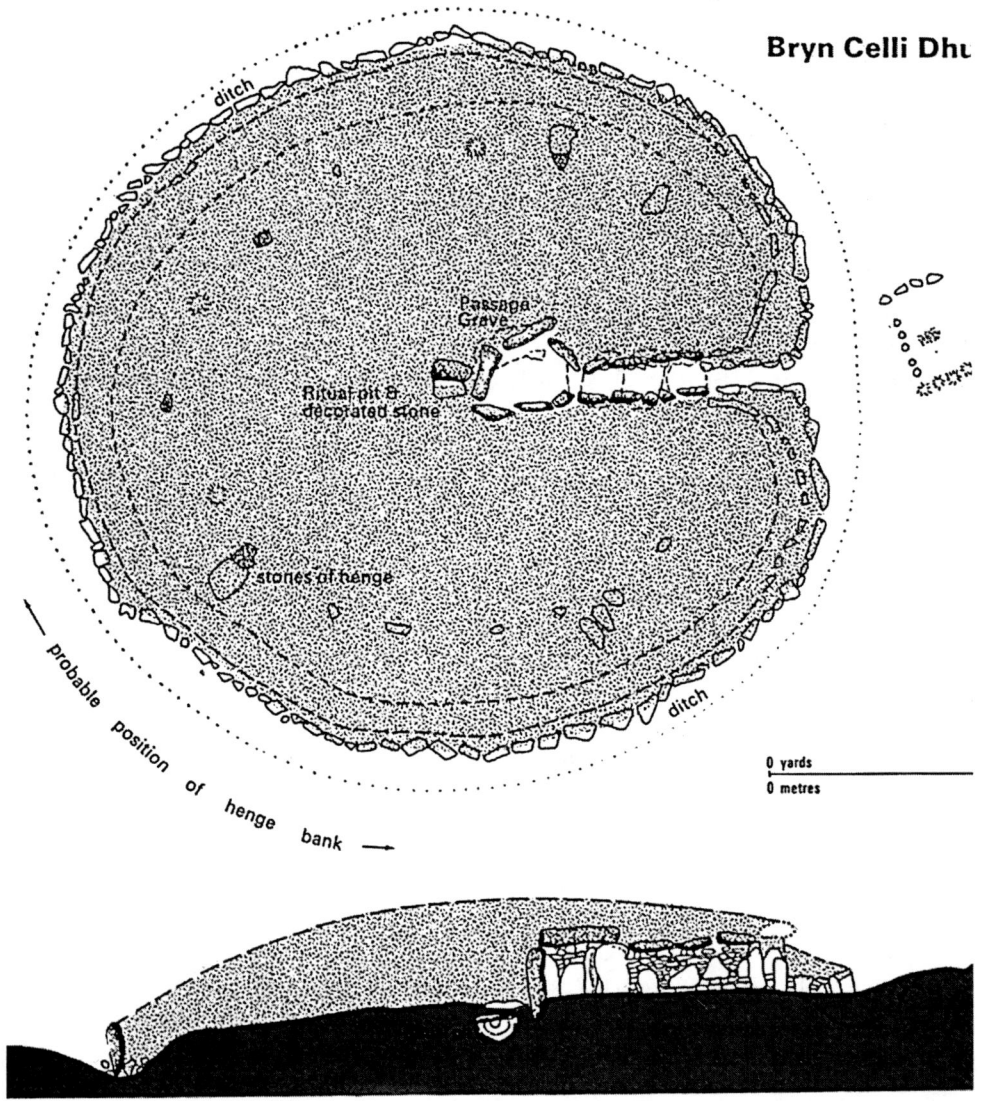

Fig. 43. *Plan of Bryn Celli Dhu (HMSO)*.

fig. 46 and are the basis for discourse in this crucial section. Allow me, however, to add one other example: a site in Angelsey, Wales, called Bryn Celli Dhu in Welsh.

Its ground plan here reproduced in fig. 43 is from a government pamphlet issued by the Ministry of Works (before it was trendily renamed the Department of the Environment). Technically Bryn Celli Dhu is a variant of the chambered tomb called a passage grave. The passage leads into a vaulted chamber, built on the principle of the corbelled arch, the whole covered by an earthen mound. Buried in the earth behind the chamber is a statue menhir, with three lesser ones near the perimeter, comparable to the open air bluestones at Stonehenge. The passage is entered through a linteled doorway seen in fig. 44. Ringed around the mound is a circle of stones (fig. 45) called peristoliths in French archaeology, a term used by Newall in his analysis of Stonehenge.

It is not amiss at this point to mention how political the field of archaeology can be. The English monarch's interest in publishing official guidebooks (HMSO imprint) is not unrelated to the issue of maintaining sovereignty over Wales and Scotland, parts of the United Kingdom, or Great Britain, in which British archaeologists have done their work outside England proper. All along there have been irredentist movements in Wales and Scotland. Recently the Scots won the right to an independent parliament, and patriotic Welshmen (like Professor Atkinson) aim at same. Interestingly, as I know from doing two books on the origin and development of Chinese civilization, the present government of China challenges the legitimacy of its borders with Russia and India on the basis of a wider spread of its Neolithic pottery.

Archaeology is thus often hotly topical, as, it must be said, is this book. It argues that Stonehenge is witness not only to a funeral cult, but to a political process for the elevation of kingly figures. I bring together the insights of R.S. Newall and of Dr. Charleton in my reconstruction of Stonehenge as a Royal Court of Election

Fig. 44. *Bryn Celli Dhu, looking at the entrance (photograph by the author).*

Fig. 45. *Bryn Celli Dhu, showing peristoliths encircling the mound (photograph by the author).*

(see plate V:2). I also reconcile dear Professor Atkinson's insistence (1980) that the monument is a temple with my equally strong conviction that it served a political purpose, a seeming contradiction that dissolves the instant we think of Westminster Abbey, where for centuries the kings and queens of England have been coronated.

Finally, my conflation of temple and election court is not unrelated to the siting of Stonehenge in the midst of a cemetery, when the burial of notables beneath the flooring of Westminster Abbey is evident to all visitors. The picture is completed with R.S. Newall's powerful insight that the monument's architecture derives from design features belonging to the chambered tomb, not alone in the immediate region but elsewhere.

Newall's brief article is largely occupied by a full page display of comparative ground plans (fig. 46), in which he rested his conclusion. The text is mostly given to naming, locating, and describing his British examples, all of this esoterica meant for his fellow archaeologists. Such details are passed over here for the sake of elaborating on his rather abstract conclusion, authoritative as it is. The object here is to relate it to a wider generalization regarding the functional purpose of Stonehenge as part of Stonehenge City: this book's focus.

The reader is advised to study fig. 46 long enough to learn the vocabulary of the points of comparison Newall illustrates. At bottom middle is the Stonehenge ground plan, extending outward (downward in the schematic) from the center to two pairs of stones in the Avenue distant from the center. Surrounding are those examples of chambered tombs Newall finds illuminating Stonehenge as an outdoor, uncovered version of the same architectural variety. As Sir Arthur Evans first

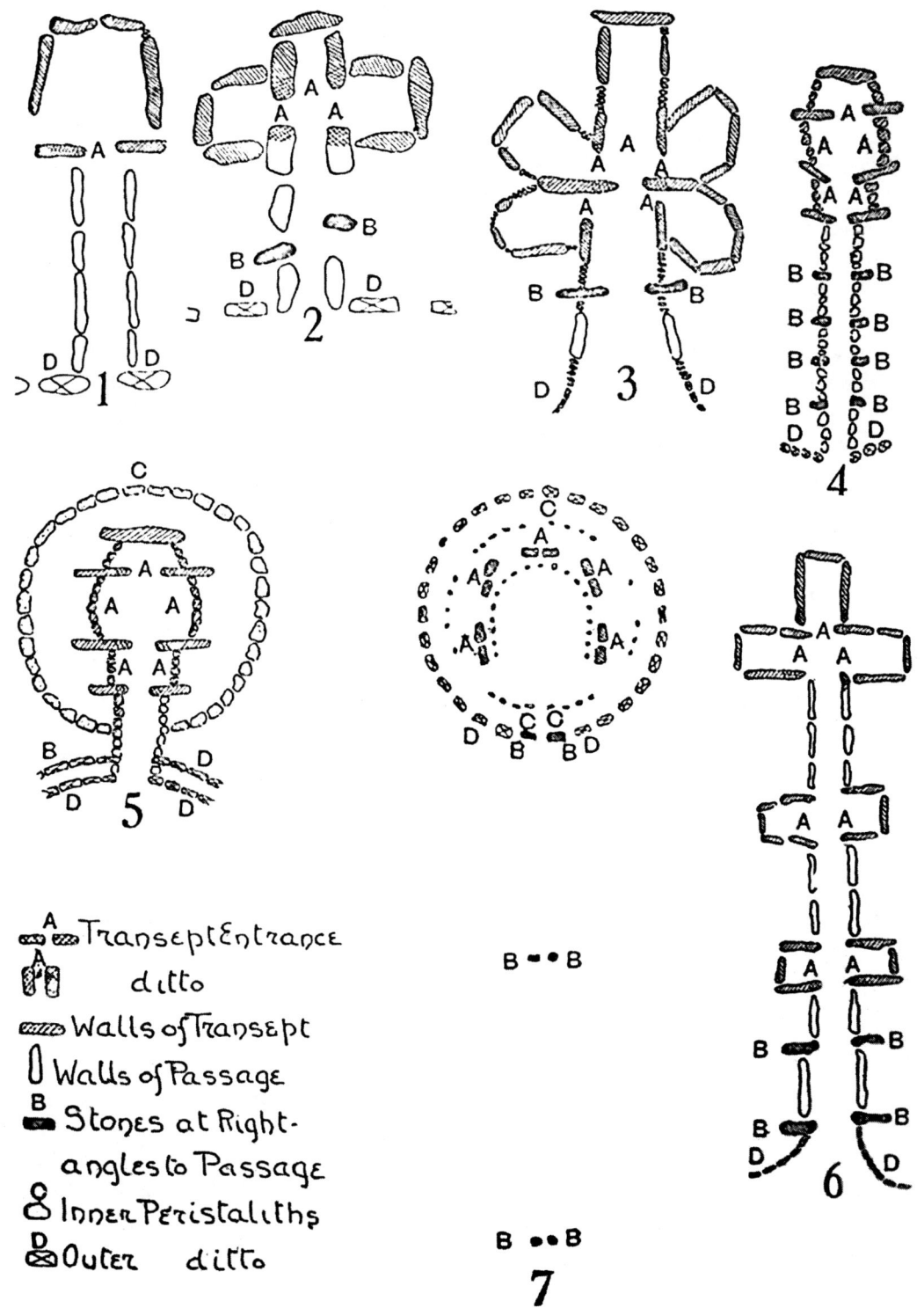

Fig. 46. *Stonehenge compared to the ground plans of a variety of chambered tombs; from Newall 1929.*

noted, Stonehenge is a freestanding chambered tomb with its earthen mound "modified away."

To spell out Newall's visual argument, the first thing to notice is that the great sarsen stones at the center of the monument are arranged in two groups, the sarsen ring and the five trilithons within (Evans calls them triliths). In plan only the uprights are indicated. Although their lintels are unique to Stonehenge, the ground plan of their pillars clearly offers a basis for making systematic comparisons.

Looking at the Stonehenge schematic in this light, the ring of sarsen stones at letter D represents a typical circle of outer peristoliths, the ring of stones bordering some earthen mounds. In other cases these outer peristoliths are abbreviated to crescent horns curving outward from the tomb's entrance. They completely encircle the mound at Bryn Celli Dhu, my favorite example in fig. 43. At Stonehenge there is a complicated play on the basic idea, in which two of the 30 pillars are tagged letter B for a pair of stones typically set at right angles in the galleried entrance to passage graves. Newall's reasoning is that these two pillars are set one foot further apart than the others, indicating the sarsen ring's doorway facing the Avenue.

Down the Avenue itself are two pairs of stones also tagged letter B. Nearest is the Slaughter Stone and its lost twin, and the Heel Stone and *its* lost twin. The virtue of this analysis is that Newall recognizes the importance of the socket holes in which the missing stones were set. That demolishes the fanciful theory that the Heel Stone (now slightly pushed over toward the center) was used to observe the rising of the midsummer sun: a theory which also requires that the Slaughter Stone had always lain recumbent. Both stones, however, had once been fully upright, and had been paired with two others like them.

Letter C indicates what Newall calls inner peristoliths, which are common enough in all his examples. At Stonehenge they constitute the bluestone circle, although it is not clear whether he so designates the bluestone horseshoe within the matching array of trilithons. Whatever, his concept of inner peristoliths complements the view at fig. 22 that the bluestones are statue menhirs. Both ideas, after all, subserve the grand scheme first articulated by Sir Arthur Evans.

Finally, and most importantly, Newall at letter A designates the towering trilithons as modified transept entrances. In his other examples the same type of uprights help define galleries as well. At Stonehenge the five trilithons alone are marked letter A: freestanding versions of transept entrances visible in the isometric drawing of burial chambers inside West Kennet Long Barrow (fig. 42). This completes the picture of Stonehenge as an open air monument with obvious connections to the sepulchral architecture of chambered tombs hidden beneath their massive mounds of earth.

If the trilithons are indeed figurative transept entrances, the logic of what follows in this book is transparent. To lay out the story I shall later unfold in detail, the trilithons are taken as memorials to the honored lineages of the royal and vice-regal authorities who ruled the Stonehenge region and four subordinate regions nearby. Five trilithons, five regions: the biggest one for the overking, the four lesser sized for his underkings. Five trilithons representing as many royal families, whose lineages are validated by the public imagery of collective tombs: memories of Neolithic egalitarianism used as a political cover story for a Bronze Age hierarchy of kings and subjects. That is the short of it. From there, inspired by Dr. Charleton, I go on to the reconstruction of Stonehenge as an election court, remembering that dynastic kingship is much later than elective kingship, and remembering also that elected kings always were elevated not by the general public but by their own peers, a warrior nobility. Hence the trilithons as family monuments to nobles living and dead.

What goes unexplained in Newall's brilliant theory is the placement of lintels atop pillars of the sarsen ring (letter C) and of the trilithon horseshoe (letter A). There is not a single instance of lintels attached to prehistoric monuments anywhere else in all of Europe. They are radically unique to Stonehenge. They may very well express the overbearing load of earth upon the underground model, or in the special case of the trilithons, the roofing slabs over burial chambers as in West Kennet. Whoever designed Stonehenge had a profound knowledge of sepulchral architecture. Druids (or proto–Druids)?

The answer to the above question is yes. In the next chapter, "The Builders," a survey of Bronze Age burials in the Stonehenge cemetery reveals a hierarchical society, a tripartite society of priests, warriors, and producers. It was a caste-like system introduced by the Indo-European invaders (= Battle-ax Folk) who swept into Old Europe and transformed it, other places as well. The few burials that survived the random looting of grave robbers were excavated by amateur archaeologists, whose finds are now housed in local museums. Everything known about the builders derives from the study of these precious artifacts.

The burials fall into a number of categories. Rarest are the royal graves, most common the warrior graves, from whose ranks kings evidently were elected. Some are female graves, the significance of which is reserved for chapter 3. Right now attention is drawn to what are called archaic graves.

These archaic graves are so called because the artifacts taken from them predate the Bronze Age, relics of a much older cultural tradition. Since religion is the most conservative aspect of human culture, professional archaeologists with some knowledge of anthropology conclude that these are the graves of shamanistic adepts, religious specialists who mediate between the natural and supernatural worlds, foretell the future, and by magic cure illness. The term shaman comes from the Evenki word *šamān* by Russian ethnologists to name such specialists they found among a variety of Siberian tribes. The same is true for similar adepts among some North American tribes that used to be called medicine men, now shamans in accord with a widely used cross-cultural term.

This insight is astute enough when applied to the archaic graves at Stonehenge, so far as it goes. Shamanism, however, is a part-time practice of freelance individuals in tribal societies, and the Bronze Age order underlying Stonehenge City is far from that condition. Shaman burials in the surrounding cemetery must rather be seen as the graves of a class or caste of priests belonging to a tripartite society headed by a royal figure. Hence I do not hesitate to tag these entombed shamans as proto-Druids, continuous with the Druidic clerisy of Iron Age Europe, commented on by Greek and Roman observers.

Granted that proto-Druids designed Stonehenge, where did they get their sepulchral model? It is unlikely they were inspired by the long barrows in the Stonehenge I cemetery, whose timber mortuary houses are today known archaeologically only by soil analysis indicating the former presence of wooden beams. There are plenty of stone-built chambered tombs nearby that could not have escaped notice, principally West Kennet, to which we now return.

Julius Caesar in his commentaries (51 B.C.) on the Gallic wars has interesting things to say about the Druids in Gaul. What he knows from observation and what from Greek ethnographers like Posidonius is not clear, except when the latter is directly quoted. He reports that Druids from all over Celtic Gaul met annually at Cenabum (present-day Orléans in France), and then goes on to say they got their priestly training in Britain, home of Druidic learning. This is possible given a memory of Stonehenge as a power center once dominating all of continental Europe, and *not* for any religious mystique it carried abroad. The brutal fact of the matter is that Stonehenge held sway because its kings, merchants of death, exported arms to the rest of Europe. They controlled the manufacture of bronze ax-heads, battle weapons (as already mentioned) inscribed all over almost every sarsen upright, so far as can be seen after much erosion. This weapons industry was uniquely possible to the Stonehenge kings because they sat on a rare Bronze Age resource: tin. Tin alloyed with more commonly available copper makes bronze, and one of two then-known tin mines was near the Stonehenge region. More on this military-industrial business later.

Meanwhile it is important, for all that, to say more about the role of proto-Druids in designing Stonehenge III. They surely had little to go on for their sepulchral model from the Neolithic long barrows of Stonehenge I, with their sod-and-timber mortuary houses inside. These proto-Druids, however, did have a chance to inspect a rich density of easily enterable chambered tombs nearby, above all the supreme West Kennet Long Barrow. Combined with oral tradition from Neolithic times, they formulated the collective ideology they built into the election court for their masters. It is a monument to Bronze Age kings who gained their wealth from trade in weapons, their elevation to power from religion: the funerary symbolism brought to the monument by its proto-Druidic designers. It is their lore and learning remembered by Gaulish Druids at the time of Caesar's conquest of Gaul.

The day I visited West Kennet, after a long hike far from any refreshing pub, I packed a picnic lunch and ate it atop the mound. Looking down the sides there was no trace of the mighty curbstones (= outer peristoliths) that originally bordered it. That they once existed, before being quarried for local building material, is evident from drawings made by John Aubrey (1665). In other cases, much smaller long barrows, nothing remains *but* the curbstones. Their destruction is due not alone to the plough agriculture of recent centuries but to the much longer sustained kitchen-gardening of Neolithic farmers. West Kennet is massive enough to have survived nearly intact, except for a nineteenth-century wagon road cut into the mound (see the aerial view in fig. 39).

Construction of West Kennet probably began before 2500 B.C. and remained in use for about a thousand years, judging by radiocarbon dating and the typological dating of pottery shards. This overlaps the time of the Stonehenge I cemetery and a little beyond. The proto–Druidic wisemen could not have missed its nearby presence, nor its architectural significance.

While eating sandwiches on top of the mound, it was possible to look down on another picnic area below: a crescent-shaped forecourt laid out in front of the tomb's entrance. Here the ancients held something like church socials, with something like barbecue roasts on the menu. Charred cattle bones have been excavated all over the place, for the many generations the tomb was open. After a long time it was closed with the blocking stones indicated in fig. 42.

For a thousand years the tomb was open for a succession of burials, the forecourt serving as a place for nothing short of ancestor worship. But who were the ancestors enchambered there? Surely not all members of the Neolithic community who built it and maintained it. The best answer is offered by Ashbee (1978), who thinks long barrows of all sorts in southern England mark tribal territories, divisions of pastureland, their leading persons and families therein consecrated.

The burials within, however, are not whole bodies laid to rest; they rather consist of disarticulated skulls and long bones. Somewhere outside, at some hypothetical mortuary temple, corpses were exposed and allowed to rot away and be picked clean by carrion crows or whatever. Then the skulls and long bones were deposited in one or another of the mortuary chambers.* At that time, probably, feasting in the forecourt took place, or perhaps annually on a certain date scheduled for ancestor worship.

Each of the five mortuary chambers was most likely dedicated to a single family line or clan whose leading lights were important figures in their respective territories, all of which may have been loosely allied and so represented in West Kennet.

It is therefore easy to conclude that the proto–Druids who designed Stone-

---

The long bones are mainly hefty femurs (thigh bones). Perhaps they suggested to the ancients a nearness to the generative organs. Curiously enough, this reminds of the reverse imagery emblemized in the skull and crossbones flag flown on death-dealing pirate ships and later on the labels of bottled poisons. The locution goes back to about 1820–1830. The only conclusion to be drawn is that the same bones mean different things in different times. What they meant for the Neolithic British cannot be recovered, except to say they were selected for collective burials.

henge III got their idea for the monumental trilithons from the transept entrances in chambered tombs like West Kennet. These trilithons, as figurative transepts, thus represent the royal lineages of the five elected kings: one overking of the Stonehenge region and four underkings of as many local satrapies.

It may be only a coincidence that the five trilithons match the number of collective burial chambers in West Kennet, but it is well to remember that five is a magic number in Celtic mythology. For example the five directions: north, east, south, west and *here*, the center. The five kingdoms of ancient Ireland were based on the same cosmology: one overking at the capital city of Tara, the center, four underkings ruling the other directions. The locations of these kingdoms were not actually distributed on points of the compass, their political geography being determined by cosmic considerations.

Looking back on Bronze Age Stonehenge from the Celtic Iron Age is a useful exercise, laid out and justified in the Epilogue. The discontinuities of prehistory and history are obvious to see, continuities less obvious but no less real. Suggested here in this chapter are continuities running from Neolithic long barrows to the sepulchral design of the election court at Stonehenge.

The problem with looking forward from West Kennet is that its five mortuary chambers are not typical of other chambered tombs, which may contain only one (like Bryn Celli Dhu), or six (like Stoney Littleton), or four or other numbers in other cases. This strongly suggests that West Kennet must have been the sepulchral model for the Stonehenge trilithons, while allowing for the monument's other funerary features to be derived from yet other sources known to the monument's proto–Druidic designers.

The designers also built into the monument the mythic political geography of the five kingdoms its election court represented. Fig. 47 shows how the four Station Stones, located just inside the circular embankment, indicate four of the five cardinal directions. Stone number 91 = North, 92 = East, 93 = South, 94 = West. Lines connecting the arrows given there pass through the four lesser trilithons, and cross in the middle of the election court (fig. 48). Here the fifth direction, Center, is established, perhaps reified by the so-called Altar Stone. But remember, as mentioned in chapter 2, the original placement of that stone was in a socket hole behind the principal trilithon, whose pillars are marked 55 and 56. The Altar Stone's appearance and mineral composition is like no other stone on the site. Located where it belongs, it is not just another inner peristolith, or statue menhir. Most likely it is a collective representation of the divine race or royal lineage from which the Stonehenge overking was elected. His trilithon, a stylized transept entrance derived from chambered tombs, shelters his figurative ancestors, whose genealogy the proto–Druids were commissioned to recite, just like the Celtic Druids of Iron Age Ireland did for the high king installed at Tara.

Opposite: Fig. 47, top. *Plan of Stonehenge with arrows indicating the directions to which the Station Stones point (HMSO).* Fig. 48, bottom. *The five directions at Stonehenge (drawing by the author).*

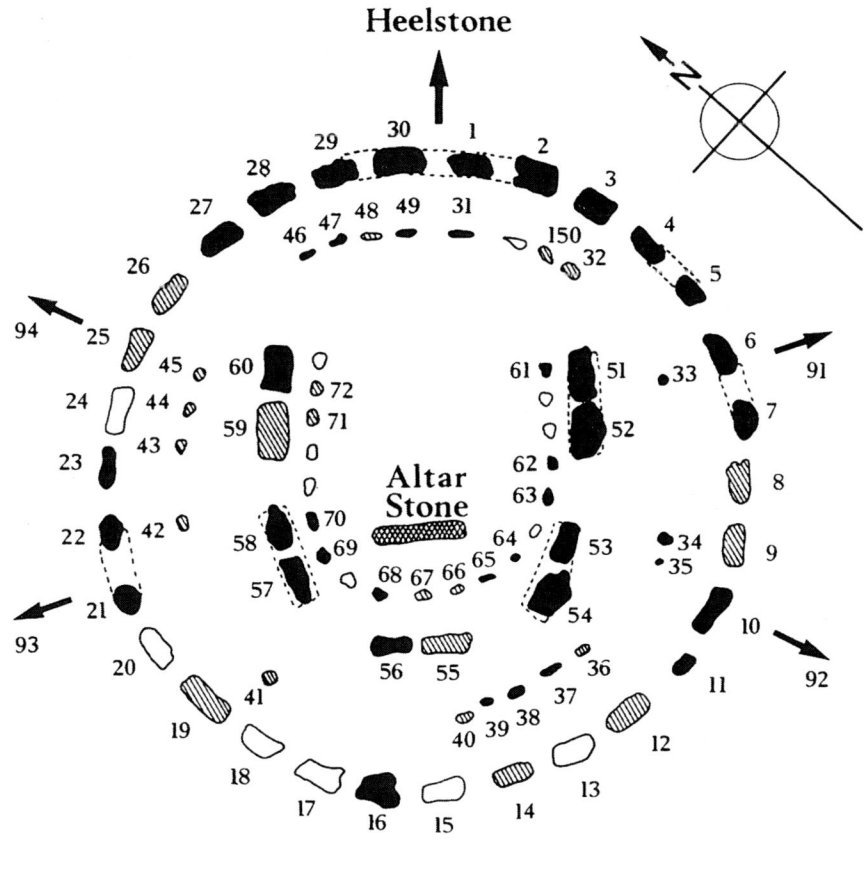

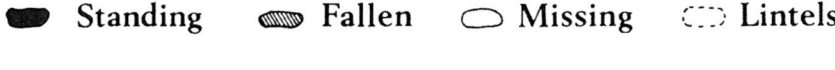

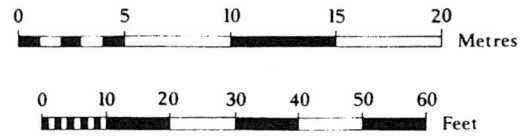

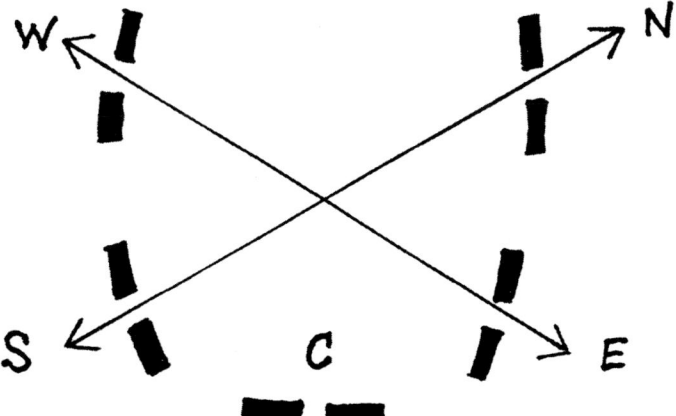

The notion advanced by Gerald Hawkins (1965) and others that Stonehenge served as an astronomical observatory traces back to an early book done by the famous English astronomer, discoverer by spectroscopy of elemental helium in the sun, Sir Norman Lockyer (1906). The present work rejects that notion, but does accommodate a related cosmological theory. The proto–Druids who designed Stonehenge were not academic astronomers, but they did dwell on matters of cosmology in the prescientific or mythic sense.

I:1, top. *Ax-head and dagger carvings on stone 53.* I:2, bottom. *Casting bronze ax-head in flat mold.*

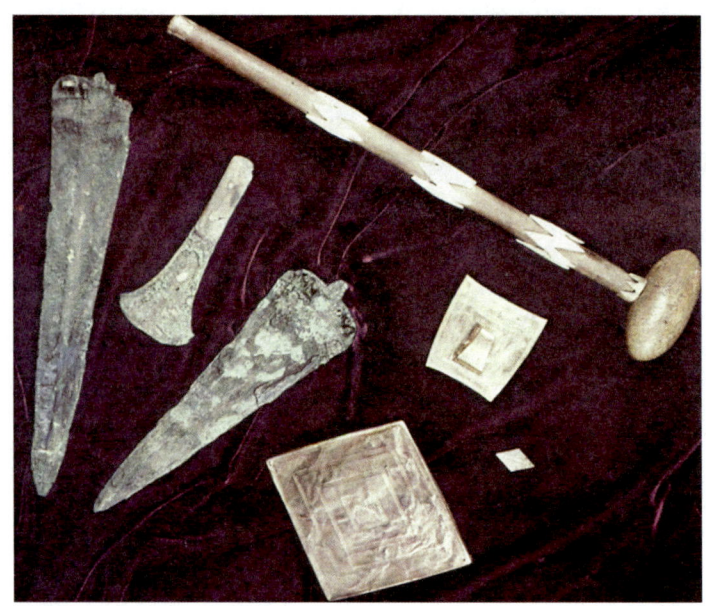

II:2. *Flat ax left, flanged ax right.*

II:1, top left. *Bush Barrow grave furniture.* II:3, bottom. *View into royal grave, Bush Barrow.*

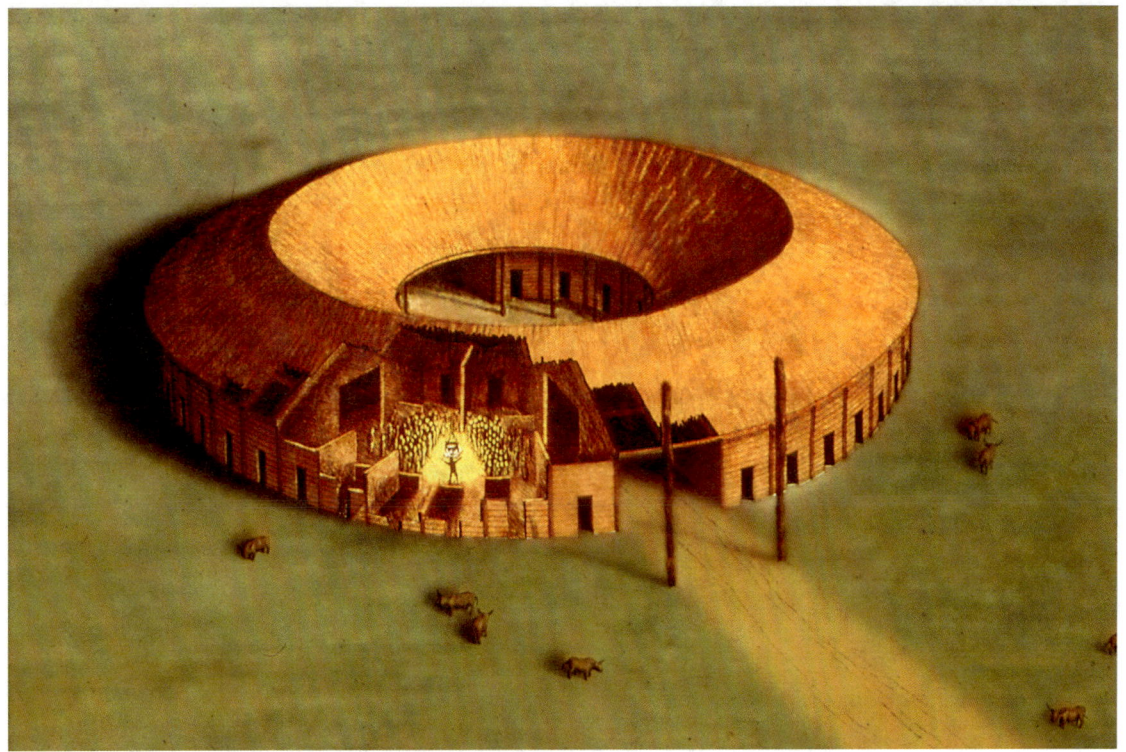

III:1, top. *Cutaway view of Tara Hall.* III:2, bottom. *Cutaway view of Stonehenge Hall.*

IV:1, top. *Cross section of Bush Barrow.* IV:2, bottom. *Cutaway of Stonehenge palace.*

V:1, top. *Footrace at the Cursus.* V:2, bottom. *Stonehenge election court.*

VI:1, top. *Sacrificial arrow-shooting at election court.* VI:2, bottom. *Sacrificial impaling in election court.*

VII:1, top. *Burning of wicker man, election time.* VII:2, bottom. *Detailed view of Stonehenge electors.*

VIII:1, top. *Raising a trilithon upright.* VIII:2, bottom. *Election stone at Tara.*

3

The Builders

My Stonehenge of the kings, first explained in Stover 1978, is no longer unrealistic speculation. In 1985, the International Edinburgh Festival mounted a spectacular exhibit of Stonehenge III artifacts drawn from the British Museum and all local holdings. The Festival issued a handsome catalogue, *Symbols of Power at the Time of Stonehenge* (D.V. Clarke *et al.* 1985), with magnificent color plates and a number of thoughtful essays reflecting on the cross-cultural realities of power, others on Bronze Age craftsmanship and court artisans, and on organized trade run by the Stonehenge kings.

In 1999 the European Council launched a traveling exhibition in Copenhagen, Bonn, Paris and Athens under the title *Gods and Heroes of the European Bronze Age*. Its lush catalogue (Demakopoulou *et al.* 1999) pictures and captions more than 250 museum items from 23 European countries. The point of its analytical essays is to establish that the present-day European Union had its cultural foundations laid down from 2500 B.C. in the Bronze Age, with a realistic emphasis on continuities into the pre–Roman Iron Age and beyond. Stonehenge, without a doubt, was integral to that process.

Already sensing that some years earlier, I designated the builders of Stonehenge as proto–Celts. What other term is possible? Happily it has now entered the literature (Gantz 1981:3). This should comfort readers of the present book when they come across proto–Druids and Celtic mythology and other legendary material as recorded by Christianized Druids in ancient Ireland. Ireland is important because Roman legions never reached its shores, although from about A.D. 500 missionaries of the Roman church did. They conquered Ireland for Christianity, just as the Roman Empire expired. The historical figure (among others unknown) credited with the victory is St. Patrick. Recognized as the patron saint of Ireland, a towering statue of his imagined likeness stands at Tara, where he is said to have converted the high king and his chief Druid. Thereafter all Druidic wise men took to the new religion with a special interest in lore and learning. They founded monasteries and scriptoriums which conserved and copied Greek and Roman classics otherwise lost when the Roman Empire fell to barbarian invasions. They also wrote down native oral traditions.

These Druids turned monastic scholars thus provide the earliest voice from the dawn of western European civilization. After Caesar's conquest of Gaul, nothing of Gaulish literature survived, if ever there was any. More than a thousand years passed before Latin evolved into medieval French, and only then did French literature begin. By contrast, Irish literature began much earlier, written in a Latin-derived script adapted to the Gaelic vernacular, called Ancient Irish by linguists.

This Gaelic literature, started up in the eighth century, comprises not only numerous religious and legal writings but also a large body of lyric poetry and a long list of epic hero tales written in prose alternating with passages in verse, very like the Homeric epics remembering the Mycenaean Bronze Age. For that reason it is useful to look at ancient Irish literature for any reminders of the European Iron Age, which may reflect something of the preceding Bronze Age and the culture of the proto–Celtic builders of Stonehenge.

As good Christians, altogether pious, the Irish monks nonetheless never forgot their pagan heritage. At the end of their manuscripts recording the hero tales of old, they would add a disclaimer apologizing for such ungodly stuff. Yet with equal piety they *did* preserve it. Above all their scriptoriums were given to copying and disseminating the Gospels, always done with elegant calligraphy. The most famous example is the Book of Kells (now in the British Museum), dating to the eighth century and named after a town in Ireland near a former monastery. It is illuminated with colorful motifs taken from late Bronze Age and early Iron Age art work (see Megan 1970).

By a wonderful turn of events, it was Irish monks who returned to Britain (St. Patrick's home) and continental Europe during the Dark Age after barbarian invaders overwhelmed it. The monks established new monasteries and brought back all the lost learning and enlightenment of classical antiquity, to the salvation of Western civilization (see Cahill 1995 and Fletchner 1997). This is a dramatic instance of the cultural continuities bespoken here.

The builders of Stonehenge III are buried all about. An inventory of their grave goods, in distinctive types of burial, is itemized below. It summarizes evidence prolixly documented in Stover 1978, thus allowing the present work's argument to lead the move directly into its reconstruction of Stonehenge City in the next and decisive chapter.

- **Royal Graves.** Only one burial of a Stonehenge king survived looting by gold seekers: the famous Bush Barrow. Its rich grave goods are now on display in the British Museum, transferred from the Salisbury and South Wiltshire Museum. Some vice-regal graves of the Bush Barrow type were also missed by tomb robbers. They contain as emblems of office short bronze daggers with gold pointillé ornament in their hilts.

Vice-regal graves represent the four underkings of the Stonehenge overking. The Stonehenge III cemetery is above all a royal cemetery, in part translocal in its burials. An apt comparison might be Arlington National Cemetery, which not only honors military heroes but also United States senators if they so choose to be buried there. If not they may choose a family plot in their home states. Some states maintain a public cemetery for their senators, another choice. This familiar model may help explain why at least one vice-regal burial is known, outside the royal cemetery, from one of the four regions ruled by Stonehenge underkings.

- **Female Graves.** Burials in so-called disc barrows. They contain ladies of noble birth, consorts of the royal house. Their grave goods consist of small gold-plated shale cones (buttons?), and tiny halberd pendants from central Europe. Also miniature pottery vessels, small bronze knives, gold-edged discs of Baltic amber, bone awls, and beads of faïence from trade with Egypt. Skeletal remains of their female attendants are probably sacrificial victims.
- **Warrior Graves.** Always stone battle-axes are present, together with short wide-shouldered bronze daggers whose hilts are ornamented with gold pointillé, others not. But since the Stonehenge regime based its wealth and power on extensive trade and not on military conquest, its honored warriors must rather represent the king's militia for the keeping of internal order.

  Not that stone battle-axes would have been deployed as functional weapons, now but dim echoes of sweeping Indo-European conquests of old. The real thing in weaponry are the bronze daggers, if they are not merely badges of authority. Higher ranking members of the militia were armed, and buried with bronze ax-heads of the sort exported by the regime to warring kingdoms or lesser chiefdoms in continental Europe.
- **Simple Graves.** These appear to inter lower ranking warriors and female consorts. Burials of the former are characterized by belt hooks and dagger-pendants of bone; the latter by a few shale, bone or amber beads, with bone pins and at times with miniature bronze knives.
- **Archaic Graves.** In the literature these are said to suggest the burials of shamanist medicine-men (proto–Druids in the present work). They are called archaic graves because they contain relics of a time before the age of Stonehenge, as appropriate to the conservative temper of religious specialists. Here the grave goods consist of

Fig. 49. *Archaic grave goods on display in the Devizes Museum. Note pair of boar's tusks at top in this best preserved example of this burial type (HMSO).*

necklaces of wolves' teeth or of animal bones neatly graduated in size. Also out-of-date chipped flint tools and arrow points, together with ornaments that may have fringed ceremonial garments, not unknown among Siberian shamans. In some cases miniature stone battle-axes are present, indicating that these ranking Druidic figures, like the militia, served at the king's pleasure (see fig. 49). They themselves, however, no doubt conceived of their priestly caste as the leading one in charge of everything: the dominant note struck in every surviving remnant of Indo-European mythology.

The above classification of burial types and their grave goods makes plain as can be the hierarchical social order of the living affirmed in death. No such status burials are evidenced in Neolithic long barrows: undecorated pottery for all and nothing else. Collective tombs are just that. By comparison to the individuated round barrows of the Stonehenge III cemetery they do indeed tell of a more communal, unstratified social order. Yet people of the Wessex Neolithic were able to organize labor for massive building projects: Silbury Hill and West Kennet Long Barrow. The builders, however, are not stratified in death as are the builders of

3. The Builders

Stonehenge. Its architecture, derived from the chambered tomb, was devised by the clerisy to mystify royal power, to put executive authority in a good light: the king rules for the common good. Who is to say his political double-talk, drawing on collective imagery built into his election court, was not effective, or to the ultimate benefit of the citizens of Stonehenge City?

Southern England thus was elevated to a level of civilization unknown to the rest of barbarian Europe. Is it too much to claim that Stonehenge, with its monumental election court, set the pattern for the cult of electoral kingship in Anglo-Saxon England (see Chaney 1970), and then on to the world's first parliamentary democracy? Long horizons in history, going back to prehistory, cannot be ignored, however little they are understood.

In 1922, in the Valley of the Kings, the English Egyptologist Howard Carter discovered the only unrobbed pharaonic burial: the tomb of Tutankhamen, 14th century B.C., 18th dynasty. Were it not for grave goods recovered from Bush Barrow, the only unrobbed tomb of a Stonehenge king, archaeologists would never know there was such a thing as kingship at Stonehenge, since there are no written records to document that prehistoric fact.

As far as gold goes, the Bush Barrow treasure is nothing compared to the Tutankhamen find (see plate II:1 for the full display). The main object is a lozenge-shaped breastplate, together with a little one of the same design, and a gold-plated belt hook. Nor are the two sword-like daggers remarkable, except they are longer than those in warrior graves. More interesting is the fact that the shorter one is made of copper, not of bronze, as if the king's ancestral patrimony spanned a time from the Copper Age to the Bronze Age.

The giveaway, revealing kingship, is the scepter of royal authority: a polished-stone mace head mounted on a shaft decorated with jagged bone ornaments resembling lightning flashes (the shaft itself long vanished). This reminds, with blinding clarity, of King Agamemnon's "lightning sceptre" in Homer's *Iliad*.

This introduces a question: How much of Indo-European mythology, later recorded, was brought into southern Britain by the Indo-European invaders who established the Bronze Age Wessex Culture there? What irresistibly comes to mind is the god of thunder and lightning, Thor, in Norse mythology. Its origins must trace back to the preliterate ancestors of the Vikings and of the Mycenaean Greeks alike, as is evident in similar theological formulas from India to Ireland, the eastern and western wings of the ancient Indo-European cultural domain with literary relics left behind for comparative study: a vast subject to be touched upon in due course.

Meanwhile let us not lose sight of the lightning sceptre once held by the Agamemnon of Stonehenge, another high king. A related symbol of power belonging to one of his four underkings is known from Clandon Barrow, Dorset, in the southernmost kingdom. See fig. 50. Its mace head is of polished jet or shale, with five gold studs inset, two in front, two in back, one on top: the Five Directions indicated, with Center at Stonehenge. As if to affirm this association, the underking entombed in Clandon Barrow was also buried with a gold breastplate exactly like the one from Bush Barrow in every detail: same size, same pin holes for sewing on some garment, same lozenge-shaped lines inscribed on it. Each region, however, had its own local artistic motifs marked on ordinary artifacts, and these are evidenced in heroic burials at Stonehenge: Arlington National Cemetery again.

With kingship now unambiguously in the picture, it is time to look at the stratified society it implies. Stonehenge City, then, would be a small city-state typical of the ancient world, including Mycenaean Greece: a palace town and surrounding countryside. The extensive cemetery, as already profiled, has buried in its round barrows of Stonehenge III a fair sample of the city's population. Some archaeologists, on scanty ploughed-over evidence, believe that the cemetery housed not only the dead, but homes of living grave-tenders. Just as scanty is evidence for housing of the population at large, although it surely existed. My reconstructions in the next chapter confine to more substantial buildings.

Fig. 50. *Head of vice-regal sceptor from Clandon Barrow in Dorchester Museum (HMSO).*

Contents of the Stonehenge necropolis foreshadow, as nothing else, the layered ordering of Celtic society. Julius Caesar outlined it as a tripartite order, with two dominant estates holding joint sovereignty over a subjected one.

> *Tripartite Society in Gaul*
> 1. *equites* (warriors)
> 2. *druides* (priests)
> 3. *plebs* (husbandmen)

Caesar's first and third terms are Latin. *Equites* (usually translated as "knights") are the wielders of force, *plebs* (alluding to the Roman underclass) do the productive work. The second term, *druides*, is borrowed from the Greek ethnographers.

Druides (always in the plural) presupposes a Gaulish form something like *druwids*, meaning "very wise men." I take this to mean those men who are "thrice wise," taking *dru-* for *tri-*, an intensifier as in the French adjective *très* from the same Indo-European root. Elsewhere in the most ancient texts of Indo-European

3. The Builders

oral literature warrior heroes are termed "thrice strong" (Lincoln 1981:104). As for *-wid* (= wit = wise = seers), this also has far-reaching Indo-European cognates. Most interesting, from the viewpoint of linguistic continuity, is our term *video*, derived from this same root, for something we see on video. This is the same word titling the *Rig-Veda* (*veda* = wisdom), the sacred text, or wisdom book, of the Hindus, based on oral tradition going back to the Aryan (= Indo-European) invasion of India in about 1500 B.C. Written down in Sanskrit somewhere in the 18th century, it remains the bible of the superior caste of Brahmins: Druides to the letter and law.

The *Rig-Veda* is typical of Indo-European literary relics assigning the priestly caste to the highest rank. Caesar, a military man with political ambitions, took a more realistic view of things in Gaul. Priests may write themselves into the top ranking caste in the mythology they generate, but Caesar knew better. He saw that Druids in Gaul were subservient to warriors and the kings who presided over both. Select warriors of the royal kin served as electors, while Druids were expected to recite the genealogy of each new king at election time. So it happened in Stonehenge times, if a retrospective from the Iron Age rings true. I think it does.

As the reader well knows, I have all along been stressing that the Stonehenge election court is located in the middle of a monumental cemetery. A topical study of ancient Ireland by Ellen Ettlinger is highly relevant. She finds that popular assemblies were held in graveyards, associated with fairs and horse racing (still a favorite Irish sport). At the same time and in the same five provinces the election of kings took place, as required. The time was 1 November, Samain (sä'-win), the Celtic New Year's, our Halloween.

Samain was the most festive event on the Celtic calendar, lasting from a week before and a week after 1 November. Pope Boniface IV Christianized this pagan holiday in the seventh century to All Hallows' Day to commemorate the lives of the saints. Actually it is All Hallows' Eve (Halloween) on the church calendar, an interesting reminder that the Celts counted by nights, not days. The same relic is echoed in New Year's Eve, Christmas Eve, and the measure of two weeks as a fortnight.

Halloween at Stonehenge? Looking back from the Celtic experience it is quite reasonable to suppose. The proto–Celts who inhabited Stonehenge City must have held similar festive events at the same time of year, not just when kings or underkings were elected by a warrior nobility. The idea of popular assemblies (like the Viking *thing* [*ting*]) should not imply that the common folk who attended them were among the electors; certainly they did not come to vote, or to participate in any way in the election ceremonies except as a crowd to witness a public spectacle. Otherwise they no doubt had the fun of the fair ground, dealing in interregional trade, gossip, and marriage arrangements. Kingship was the business only of the royal race, a pool of candidates whose ancestral lineage was enshrined in the sepulchral architecture of the election court. Its public interest would lie in the communal symbolism of collective tombs, as if the Stonehenge kings ruled for the common good, the wanted perception.

If the Celtic connection holds up, Halloween at Stonehenge would have no astronomical significance whatsoever. Samain was not held to celebrate the rising of the midsummer sun, much less the setting of the midwinter sun; nor is there any relationship to the celestial equinoxes. The Celts had their eyes on the ground. What they observed there was pastureland grass turning sere: a sign of the onset of the cold season: time to bring the cows home. Watch the skies? No; watch the grass. The Celts were settled pastoralists, with a mixed economy of agriculture and cattle raising. Since they had contrived no barns for keeping these animals over the winter, they slaughtered the most of them for Samain feasting, while preserving a breeding stock in their own homes for release come the onset of the warm season (Beltaine on 1 May). So it must have been in Stonehenge times.

Celtic references abound in this book. Fortunately a huge literature on the subject has been consolidated in one comprehensive *Dictionary of Celtic Mythology* (MacKillop 1998), complete with pronunciation guide and extensive bibliography. Another useful work is the richly illustrated *Dictionary of Celtic Myth and Legend* (Green 1992). One thing to be learned from these two works and their sources is that the social order described by Caesar for Gaul has its parallel in ancient Ireland.

This is important because, as already mentioned, Ireland remained outside the Roman Empire. In conquered Gaul the native language drifted into sort of pigeon Latin that later became French. But in Ireland the native language, Old Irish (modern Gaelic), persisted long after missionaries of the Roman church from A.D. 500 introduced the Latin script. Christianized Druids, now monks, then recorded their own oral heritage going back who knows how long. The two dictionaries named above draw upon all these records together with archaeological matter, under systematic cross-referenced topics: the ultimate in Celtic studies.

These priceless records document many aspects of untouched Celtic culture, most basically its ideal picture of social stratification. It exactly matches what Caesar observed in pre-conquest Gaul.

Tripartite Society in Ancient Ireland
1. *ri* (warriors)
2. *drui* (priests)
3. *aire* (husbandmen)

See pronunciation guide in MacKillop 1998.

Meanwhile, in the Eastern wing of the ancient Indo-European domain the same social order obtained, as remembered in the *Rig-Veda*. This Hindu classic recalls the Aryan invasion of the Punjab region in northwestern India and is acknowledged as the sacred text validating the basics of the Indian caste system. It is no longer fashionable to speak of Aryan invaders. The great archaeologist and philosopher of prehistory, V. Gordon Childe, once wrote a masterful book on Indo-European origins, *The Aryans* (1926), no longer polite to mention. (It is now proper etiquette to speak of the Battle-ax Folk.) The term Aryan was coined by nineteenth-century philologists to name a widespread family of languages with a supposed common origin. Not without reason did they take the cue from the language and literature of Iran (= Aryan): a place with more literary sources than anywhere else.

The big question in Indo-European studies is how much related-language families correspond to the spread of a common culture. Leaving that controversial question aside for the moment, it will be helpful to look at the three original Hindu castes. Even more enlightening is the trinity of major gods associated with this system. The gods in question suggest a cosmological theory that the divine order above models earthly affairs. As it is in heaven, so it is below.

Tripartite Society in Aryan India
1. *Brahmin* (priests)
2. *Kshatriya* (warriors)
3. *Vaishva* (husbandmen)

Note that the caste of Brahmins comes first, considering it is they who formulated the system. After all, in their theology *their* guiding divinity heads the Hindu trinity, as outlined below. Each of these gods represent one of the cardinal forces of the universe.

The Hindu Trinity
1. Brahma (creation, wisdom)
2. Siva (destruction, force)
3. Vishnu (possession, desire, lust)

In the divine scheme, Brahma joins with Siva for the creative destruction of Vishnu's possessiveness, the selfish motives of common folk. The struggle is to subordinate them to a social order modeled after cosmic harmony: Brahma's creative idea.

How amazingly powerful and persistent is this Indo-European scheme Plato carries forward in the *Republic* (4th century B.C.). His philosopher king rules an ideal city-state dominated by two castes of Guardians, whose combined mission is to browbeat common citizens (farmers and artisans) into sharing their produce for the sake of a creative state-idea.

Tripartite Society in Plato
1. Teachers, or Perfect Guardians.
    Wisdom, propaganda.
2. Soldiers, or Auxiliary
    Guardians. Coercion.
3. Citizens, or producers.
    Obedience.

More amazing, the same schema persisted into medieval Europe. To be sure, this in reality was no more than the idea of a would-be theocracy (Lopez 1966: chapter 2, "The Tripartite Society"). All the same, it is interesting to note how long the ancient ideal survived.

Tripartite Society in Medieval Europe
1. clerics
2. nobles
3. serfs

The social reality, of course, was nothing like this. Real enough to the historian of ideas, however, is its continuity with a long-lasting ancient model.

Another striking example is the mythology of the Norsemen, fragments of a once more coherent cosmology. Its written evidence is in the *Verse Edda* and the *Prose Edda* and the Sagas, composed in eleventh century Iceland, then a Christianized Viking colony (see Branston 1980 and Davidson 1964). However localized these Icelandic compositions, Old Norse transcribed in Latin script, they give voice to venerable oral traditions once current throughout the prehistoric Scandinavian and Germanic world, apart from the Celtic world yet not unrelated.

The many divinities in Norse mythology reduce to three not unlike those in the Hindu trinity, and with the same functions.

The Norse Trinity
1. Odin or Woden — high
2. Thor or Thunor — just as high
3. Frig or Frey and Freya — third

Although it is interesting to note they give name to three days of the week — Wednesday, Thursday, Friday*— it is even more interesting to speculate if related gods go back to Stonehenge times. How tantalizing is the Thor-like lightning sceptre found in Bush Barrow, not unlike Agamemnon's in Homer. The comparison strongly suggests a common Indo-European culture of great antiquity, as old as Stonehenge or even older, going to its proto–Indo-European heritage.

In 1796 the English jurist and linguist Sir William Jones first suggested that Sanskrit originated from the same sources as Latin and Greek, and thus laid the foundations for modern comparative philology. The vast geographical reach of related Indo-European language families is displayed in fig. 51. From that linguists were led to consider one single source, proto–Indo-European (PIE), going back thousands of years. So successful has this research been that recent editions of the *American Heritage Dictionary* have been confident enough to add PIE roots to its etymologies. The most discursive dictionary on the PIE roots of English words is that done by Shipley (1984), a thrillingly erudite work.

Through complicated reasoning, the proto–Indo-European homeland has been

---

The seven-day week itself is the heritage of ancient Egypt. Sunday and Monday passed into Old English as sunnandæg and monandæg from Latin solis dies and lunae dies. Tuesday, Old English tiwesdæg, is from the German god of war Tiw (= Norse Thor = Roman Mars). Saturday is from the day of Saturn, on which the Roman festival Saturnalia was held. The romance languages all use derivatives of these names. Frey and Freya are incestuous brother and sister who represent the fertility of plants and animals: function 3 incarnate.

identified with the Black Sea steppes of southern Russia, then inhabited by warrior herdsmen. It is further reasoned that elements of this population, in successive waves, began about 4000 B.C. to move into Europe and India and elsewhere. Those who did not migrate out later became known as the Scythians, a widely dispersed group of nomadic and seminomadic stockbreeders and horsemen in the first millennium B.C. Their spectacular monuments are some 40 single-grave round barrows of heroic size located at Pazirik in the High Altai, where freak conditions preserved everything, each entombing a warrior chieftain in a roomy wooden burial chamber with all his prize goods, himself richly laid out in his treasure-hauling wagon. Most exciting to students of Scythian art is the wild variety of its stylized animal motifs. They apply not only to objects of gold and other metals — vessels, horse-trappings, personal ornaments — but also to woodwork, textiles and garments, and even (by tattooing) the human body. Soon after Soviet archaeologists released a detailed study of Pazirik, its barbaric splendor was conveyed by the jangling and dissonant music of Prokofiev's *Scythian Suite*.

Anatolian		Hittite*
Baltic		Latvian
		Lithuanian
		Old Prussian*
Celtic		
	Brythonic	Breton
		Cornish*
		Welsh
	Continental	Gaulish*
	Goidelic	Old Irish*
		modern Irish
		Manx*
		Scots Gaeolic
Germanic		
	East Germanic	Gothic*
	North Germanic	Old Norse*
		Icelandic
		Norwegian
		Swedish
		Danish
	West Germanic	High German
		Dutch
		Frisian
		Anglo-Saxon*
		English
Greek		Ionian (Homeric Greek)*
		modern Greek
Indo-Iranian		
	Iranian	Persian
	Indo-Aryan	Sanskrit*
		Kasmiri
		Punjabi
		Urdu
		Hindi
		and other modern languages of India
Italic		Latin*
		French
		Spanish
		Italian
		Portuguese
		Rumanian
Slavic		
	East Slavic	Russian
		Ukrainian
	South Slavic	Slovene
		Serbo-Croatian
		Bulgarian
	West Slavic	Czeck
		Polish
		Slovak

Fig. 51. *Major Indo-European language families (boldface) with some representatives, an asterisk indicating a dead language; from Stover 1978.*

Scythian conquests extended all across the Euroasian steppes, from the Danube to China, a vast stretch of grassland interrupted by mountain ranges, like the Altai massif, but with passable corridors between them. The Greek historian Herodotus (5th century B.C.), ever interested in distant places, did a lengthy ethnography of the Scyths (his term), even longer than the account of his visit to Egypt. Looking back from that, it is not unreasonable to suppose that proto–Indo-European ancestors were warrior herdsmen of a like sort: mobile, aggressive, invasive.

How warrior herdsmen moved out of the PIE homeland to fill all areas of the Indo-European domain is hugely controversial. On the one hand it is held that no migration of any peoples ever took place, certainly no "Celtic coming" in Europe; it is all a matter of cultural diffusion (Renfrew 1987). On the other hand it is said that small groups of mobile marauders were responsible for the cultural unity of the Indo-European domain (Mallory 1989). Such contentions repeat arguments made after V. Gordon Childe (1926) first connected the spread of Indo-European languages with archaeological evidence for cultural traits in common. The debate rages on.

Where does the present work stand? It sides with the most radical thesis of all, that of outright invasion, military incursions, a thesis espoused by Maria Gimbutus, professor of European archaeology at the University of California, Los Angeles. Because I cited her work with approval she, as a matter of academic courtesy, wrote an approving statement for mine of 1978. She said of the book that it succeeds

> in breadth of reference and ingenuity of exposition to present a realistic and convincing account of events through several millennia, and to recreate the social life and mentality of the Wessex people and their parents. It is the rare combination of two approaches — anthropological and historical — which makes this book outstanding and especially valuable.

Her work is not very much appreciated by many other archaeologists and anthropologists, but for my own part I trust her insights.

Professor Gimbutus has done systematic work on the archaeology of Old Europe (her term, 1973) and what happened to it after the Indo-European invasions (1974). Most obviously was the transformation of the old Neolithic order by the imposition of a tripartite social order. In two cases invasions entailed the pretty horrible city-smashing of literate civilizations, the Mycenaean in the Argolid and the Harappan in the Indus River valley. The former fell into darkness and then recovered in classical Greece at the start of the Iron Age there. The latter conquest is remembered in the *Rig-Veda*, later the sacral basis for a new civilization.

But everywhere a tripartite society emerged, the common particular of Indo-European culture. More, there is a common ideology behind it (see Dumézil 1958). Each god and caste of that layered society is color-coded exactly the same way. Indeed, every nation of Indo-European heritage flies a flag with some variant of the same tripartite colors. Nothing could better illustrate long horizons of cultural continuity.

3. The Builders 75

This excursive look at the color-coding of certain national flags may seem a far-fetched diversion. Not so. The short distance between the proto–Celtic builders of Stonehenge is nothing compared to the longer-term continuities connecting the whole Indo-European domain with the color symbolism of modern nations.

The oldest record of Indo-European color coding comes from the *Rig-Veda*, whose oral composition surely goes back to the entrance phase of the Aryan invasion of India. The text that has come down written in Sanskrit (no longer a living language) is very explicit about the *varnas* or colors assigned to each god in the Hindu trinity and its associated castes: the starting point for any comparisons.

Varnas in the Hindu Trinity
(with variants in flag colors)
1. Brahma — white (gold, yellow)
2. Siva — red
3. Vishnu — blue (green, black)

Evidence for similar color coding in the Norse trinity is more indirect (main divinities).

Varnas in the Norse Trinity
1. Odin — white robe
2. Thor — red beard
3. Frey and Freya — greenish-blue garments

At the western extreme of the ancient Indo-European domain, half a world away from Aryan India, is Ireland. Yet its Christianized Druids (*drui*) were moved to record its heathenish oral literature in Old Irish, like Sanskrit another dead language. That record, however, is not as doctrinally systematic as the *Rig-Veda*: no theologically crafted trinity. Nonetheless the hero tales evince a tripartite society color-coded like the Hindu caste system.

Varnas in Ancient Ireland
1. *drui* — white
2. *ri* — red
3. *aire* — green

The same varnas persist to this day in the color symbolism of all national flags whose nations are recent products of the Indo-European heritage — not surprising except to those who think change is the only constant in history.

In the examples below, listed alphabetically, the first two functions are sometimes reversed as they were in ancient times. Green and blue are variants, as is black, the extra varna for slaves (*sudra*), a subcaste in the Hindu scheme that somehow got confused with function 3.

- France. Red, white and blue in three vertical stripes, the famous tricolor of the French Revolution. Its colors descend from those assigned to the three functions of the Three Estates of medieval France, as does the *bleu de travail* of workers' clothing.

- Germany. Yellow (= white), red and black in three horizontal stripes. Even the flag of Nazi Germany was colored the same but with a different design: red field, white circle with black swastika within.
- India. Red, white and green (= blue).
- Iran. Red, white and green.
- Italy. Red, white and green. This flag still flew even during the period of the Fascist dictatorship.
- Russia. Red, white and blue. Vertical stripes, flown during Czarist times and then again in the post–Soviet Russian Republic. During the Soviet era, the flag of the ruling Communist Party had a red field (= force) with hammer-and-sickle emblems of industrial and agriculture in gold (= white) in upper left hand corner. There is no blue (= function 3) in the flag, as if the sovereign state* owned the peoples' instruments of production.
- United Kingdom. Red, white and black, the complex union jack.
- United States. Red, white and blue, the "stars and stripes." A truly

---

Actually a party-state. In the vocabulary of political science this designates the dual structure of the Soviet regime: the party commands, the government administers. Its flag perfectly emblematizes the Platonic ideal, as explained by Heller and Nekrich in Utopia in Power *(1986). Plato's utopian command-and-administer state is the model. His teachers are the party (= white), his soldiers the enforcing government (= red). The absence of blue in the flag seems to indicate that producers are simply taken for granted: only the two ranks of Guardians are represented. Given this example, it is hard to ignore the lasting imagery of the ancient Indo-European color code. In the stars and stripes of the American flag, blue is redefined democratically: function 3 is a participant in government, no longer its object of control and abject exploitation.*

The Indo-European color code is not the only aspect of tripartite ideology to persist; similarly enduring is the idea of triplisms with third term different: "high, just as high, and third" in the words of one Norse poet (Snorri Sturluson). The striking examples, far apart in time, come from St. Augustine and Freud: three sins and three psychic levels.

St. Augustine	Freud
1. libido scienti (lust for knowledge)	superego
2. libido dominandi (lust for power)	ego
3. libido sesnorium (sexual lust)	id

In St. Augustine the first two sins correspond with the two virtues of Plato's ranked Guardians, knowledge and direction, while the third sin corresponds with the Vishnu-like desires of his third function deserving of suppression. The same in Freud's psychoanalytic theory. The superego internalizes moral rules, while the ego mediates between directives of the knowing conscience and the instinctual but unconscious impulses of the primitive id, needful to control if any social order or civilization is to be maintained. Indeed, the Christian doctrine of the Trinity (fourth century A.D.*) is not dissimilar: father, son, and holy ghost: third term different in a mystical way. God the father (1) is like Plato's perfect Guardians, while Jesus Christ the son (2) is like his auxiliary Guardians, instrumental to God's purpose. The holy ghost (3) inspirits the church of believers, not unlike the spirit of obedience Plato would have instilled in accord with his ideal state-idea.*

Another worthy example is the children's classic, The Wonderful Wizard of Oz *by L. Frank Baum (1900), in which three characters each embody the very opposite of the function they represent. The Scarecrow (knowledge) lacks brains (1), the Cowardly Lion (power) lacks courage (2), and the Tin Woodman (love) lacks a heart (3).*

3. The Builders

revolutionary flag, it symbolizes the equality of all three functions of the ancient color-coded Indo-European scheme, in which blue (function 3) subserved the two functions above it and held joint sovereignty over its productive work. Of the three branches of government, red = executive, white = judicial, and blue = legislative, representing people power.

None of the above is meant to suggest that the color-coding of tripartite society extends back to Stonehenge. But there *is* one feature, in the Stonehenge cemetery, that goes all the way back to the proto–Indo-European origins of the invasive transformation of Old Europe. This is a basic matter considered in the next section.

The Stonehenge story begins in the proto–Indo-European homeland, identified with what Gimbutus (1974) calls the Kurgan culture. *Kurgan* is a Russian word for the culture's characteristic single-grave burials in round barrows, the same type of round barrow that defines the Stonehenge cemetery in its final two Bronze Age phases. The trail of such extends all the way across Europe, from southern Russia to southern England: the trail of Kurgan migrants. Their stay-at-home descendants, the Scythians, built huge versions of same at Paziric. The Kurgan migrants are otherwise known as the Battle-ax Folk, whose stone ax-heads found in Stonehenge barrows are yet another trace of continuity to PIE beginnings.

At about the same time, in the fifth millennium B.C., that Kurgan migrants departed the PIE homeland, migrants from Old Europe entered southern England and introduced the Wessex Neolithic. They brought with them the practice of building collective tombs, the sort of long barrows associated with Stonehenge I. That monument is a type of circular earthwork altogether unique to Britain: the *henge* monument (see Wainwright 1989). The term, a back-formation from Stonehenge, applies to a number of examples ranging from 150 to 1,700 feet across, the biggest being Avebury. Many have extra features such as burials, pits, circles of upright stones or of timber posts.

The Wessex Neolithic, said before, derives from that part of Old Europe that built long houses and long barrows in a forested setting, while practicing slash-and-burn agriculture (swidden). This was the swidden of the so-called Danubian culture, which depended on the regrowth of forest cover after its cutting down and burning over: the clearing for crops, the ashes for fertilizer. What made this possible were particulars of the soil and the species of trees native to it, conditions not everywhere the same.

When farmers of the Wessex Neolithic moved into southern England, they too practiced swidden but, trees and soil being different, the regrowth was not forest cover but grass. The same thing happened when mixed farming by diffusion from the Near East reached the Kurgan homeland, whereupon the resulting grassland was exploited for nomadic pastoralism. The windswept downs at Stonehenge are an artifact of the Wessex Neolithic, a ready-made environment for Indo-European pastoralists to move into. The difference here is they became settled pastoralists (Stover 1978:32–34).

In the history of anthropology, the Three Age system (another Indo-European triplism) was the first evolutionary scheme: from stone to bronze to iron. With refinements it has remained a fixture. By the nineteenth century there were considered to be three stages of social evolution — savagery (hunting and gathering), barbarism (pastoralism), and civilization (neolithic farming + urbanism).* But this has turned out to be grossly misconceived.

Pastoralism is *not* a stage, it is a specialized derivative of mixed farming, the animal side of the original Neolithic: plant cultigens and barnyard domesticates like cattle, sheep and pigs. The Kurgans, in the PIE homeland denuded of trees and turned grassy, were the first pastoralists, emphasis on cattle.† They also domesticated the horse, which gave them the mobility to act as warrior herdsmen.

Quite apart from Kurgan intrusions into Harappan India and Old Europe, they set in train the horrific scourges of horseback-riding Huns and Mongols all across the Eurasian steppes. The steppe and the sown were at odds all this time, a recurrent threat to urban civilization.

Not only domesticated horses but the war chariot was a Kurgan development. In ancient Sumeria a heavy solid-wheeled war wagon drawn by onagers (asses) was in use, but it had not the swift striking power of the light spoke-wheeled chariot. This device enabled them to invade Anatolia and Greece as ancestors of the Hittite and Mycenaean rulers, into Egypt as the Hyksos, into Mesopotamia as the Kassites who conquered Babylon, and into India as the Aryan wreckers of Harappā (Vlahos 1968).

Chariot warfare, however, does not figure in the Kurgan conquest of northern Europe and the Stonehenge region in southern England. To be sure, Caesar meets with charioteers when, after vanquishing Gaul, he next invades Britain. But his Celtic foes there got their chariots during the pre–Roman Iron Age long after their disuse in the eastern Mediterranean: Egypt, the Levant, Mycenae. By about 1200 B.C., massed infantry formations had replaced chariots on the battlefield, a military change that effectively ended the Bronze Age in its greatest power centers (Drews 1993). Homer remembered chariots only dimly when he has his warriors brought to the battlefield in them like so many taxis, not as war weapons to fight with. The Romans seem to have used chariots only for hippodrome racing and as parade vehicles.

The scheme's most influential theorist was the American ethnologist Lewis H. Morgan in Ancient Society: Researches in the Lines of Human Progress from Savagery through Barbarism to Civilization *(1877). Curiously this became a canonical text of Marxist thought, in which the culminating stage of progress was to be socialism: a miraculous future that ends history.*

†*In the* Rig-Veda, *for example, chariot-driving leaders of the Aryan invasion are called "cow chiefs." In Homer's* Iliad *the worth of bronze armor captured in battle is calculated in so many head of cattle. In the Irish hero tales cattle reaving is the chiefest subject. The king of Stonehenge surely was the biggest cattle owner in the region, but it is likely his increase of wealth and power came more from his regime's export of bronze ax-heads to continental Europe.*

3. The Builders

The builders of Stonehenge II did not even bring horses with them, much less chariots. They did, however, raise their Kurgan-derived round barrows next to the long barrows of Stonehenge I, as they did next to the long barrows of northern Europe. Within the henge monument itself they started to erect two concentric circles of bluestones. Soon after, this project was abandoned, the bluestones put aside, and the great sarsens of Stonehenge III erected. The big question is, was this merely a change of plan or the sign of a new plan introduced by another incoming population of Indo-European warriors? A fierce debate revolves around this question.

Where do I stand? For the sake of argument let us assume a second wave of Indo-European invaders, already established in the literature as the Wessex Warriors. The first wave, if it be such, is likewise well established as the Beaker Folk, a subject of immense confusion in the archaeological literature. At last there is a definitive book untangling this mess, *The Beaker Folk* by Richard J. Harrison (1980), the distinguished British archaeologist who has devoted his career to this vexing problem.

The Beaker Folk are so called after the characteristic ceramic drinking vessels buried with them. Three basic types are illustrated in fig. 52. Their many varieties, distributed from central to western Europe, from Slovakia to Portugal, have for almost two centuries set off rival typological schemes, all of them indicating contradictory movements of the Beaker Folk. One scheme even had them originating in Portugal! It is easy, therefore, to make fun of archaeologists for their heavy reliance on pottery. Whole or in fragments it is the most consistently reliable of imperishable Neolithic evidence. During a university dig in southeastern New Mexico, I myself got caught up in the excruciating analysis of potsherds. It was a dangerous business and we went armed against pot hunters: collectors of unbroken vessels for which there is immense profit in the illegal antiquities trade. One night in a gunfight we had to drive off a determined gang of pot hunters who thought our camp shel-

Fig. 52. *Basic types of Beaker pottery: bell, long-necked, and short-necked; from Bray and Trump 1970.*

tered a store of already excavated pots, intact and richly painted examples of early Pueblo ceramic ware. It did not; we had only lots of tiny sherds to classify.

The two types of Beaker pottery found in the Stonehenge II burials are the long-necked and the short-necked. Chemical analysis of residue in their bottoms tell of beer supplied for the afterlife. Given beer pots in association with stone battle axes as grave goods, one is irresistibly reminded of the Viking heaven in Norse mythology, Valhalla, the hall of the chosen slain, in which the fallen are treated to eternal drinking and fighting. In the Celtic ethnography of Posidonius, the Iron Age Celts of pre-conquest Gaul are said to have traded their war captives as slaves to Rome in exchange for wine. The continued importance of drinking for warriors certainly is evident in the elegant wine flagons buried with their hospitality-giving chiefs: the most lavishly artistic items of the European Iron Age (Megaw 1970).

The Beaker Folk, as the advance wave of Kurgan migrants/invaders into Old Europe, brought decisive changes there: the introduction of metallurgy (copper) and a stratified tripartite society. Their principal metal artifacts, copper arrowheads, give rise in the archaeological literature to a so-called Copper Age preceding the Bronze Age: not a very useful distinction. Beaker smiths did indeed work copper before the advent of bronze (an alloy of copper and tin), but the copper deposits they worked were themselves naturally alloyed with metallic arsenic. The bones of Beaker smiths show evidence of poisoning by arsenic fumes; but at the same they learned that another metal, eventually tin, served to harden the softness of elemental copper.

The Beaker Folk were archers, as tanged arrowheads of copper (unintentionally hardened with arsenic) and slate wristguards in their graves indicate. A rare settlement site in central Europe, strewn with horse bones together with those of sheep, pigs and cattle, indicates the presence of warrior herdsmen right out of the PIE homeland. Although their copper metallurgy does not trace back to that source, their Kurgan round barrows do. Another feature picked up along the way is the stone battle ax, associated with a different ceramic tradition, beakers called Corded Ware for the decor impressed on their long necks with some kind of rope (see fig. 53). So, it is not possible to speak of this or that definite wave of Kurgan migrants. The Indo-European transformation of Old Europe was a complicated series of related movements not easy to sort out.

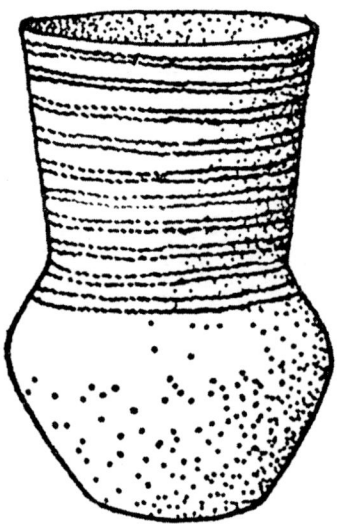

Fig. 53. *Corded-ware beaker from Saxo-Thuringa in Germany; from Bray and Trump 1970.*

The outcome was a widespread use of the alloy bronze that gives the European age its name. More importantly it superimposed a layered tripartite society on the native, unstratified Neolithic order. That radical transformation is the result of a real conquest.

3. The Builders

It may very well be remembered in Norse mythology as the war of the Æsir and the Vanir (see Dumézil 1973). The Æsir are all the gods of functions 1 and 2 (not just Odin and Thor), the Vanir are the many more gods and goddesses of function 3 (not just Frey and Freya). The Æsir won and the Vanir thereafter remained subject to them, an arrangement not unlike Plato's.

Tripartite Society Revisited

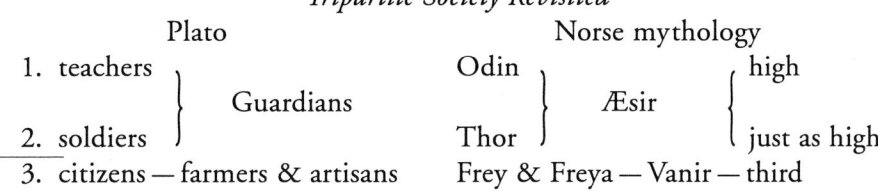

The builders of Stonehenge III are everywhere in the literature called the Wessex Warriors, as members of the early Bronze Age Wessex Culture in Wiltshire (not to be confused with the Wessex Neolithic). Buried in round barrows (= Kurgan mounds) exactly like those of the Beaker Folk of Stonehenge II, their grave goods, apart from stone battle-ax heads, are quite distinct. Take pottery for instance. Instead of highly decorated long-necked and short-necked beakers we find rather plain vessels with whipped-cord ornament on their high collars, somewhat reminiscent of Corded Ware beakers, as well as miniature drinking cups with a knobby surface in high relief decor (see fig. 54).

The Wessex Warriors, however, were not warriors like their ancestral battle-ax conquerors of Old Europe. They now had become industrialists, producers of bronze weapons for export, making Stonehenge the power center of a mighty kingdom. A fortune of geography made this possible. Stonehenge is located near sources of tin which, anciently, were the most plentiful anywhere in Bronze Age Europe — sources that eventually attracted the attention of the Mycenaeans, that other great Bronze

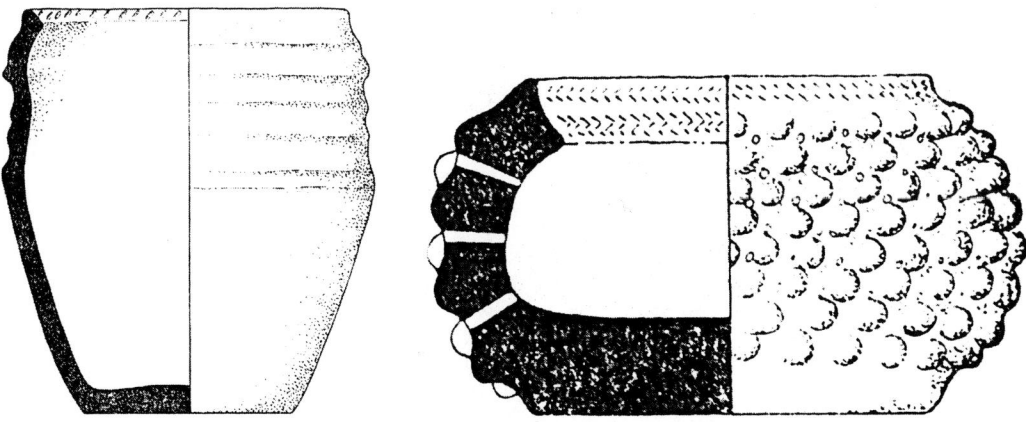

Fig. 54. *Collared Wessex vessel and so-called "grape-cup" from the Stonehenge III cemetery; from Crittall 1973.*

Age power in pre–Classical Greece. In the next section we shall see how Mycenae made its presence felt at Stonehenge III, after it was built, in circa 1500 B.C.

The ratio of tin and copper in bronze is about 1 to 9, worked out by early bronze smiths determined to harden copper without making it too brittle. The same ratio obtains among modern sculptors who make bronze statues and other creations of that metal. This is the lasting legacy of the Beaker Folk, whose copper smiths first experimented with alloys. They were not only smiths but also far-traveling prospectors and mineralogical explorers. We moderns should never forget that prehistoric ancients, absent jet planes, were also well traveled and just as interested in what became the sciences of geology and metallurgy (see Adams 1938).

No tin, no bronze. While copper deposits are widely available, those of tin or its compounds are not. When and where these two elemental metals were originally alloyed are questions not easily answered. Influential books by V. Gordon Childe (1942, 1957) had it that bronze was the indigenous development of ancient Mesopotamia, the first Bronze Age civilization. This turns out to be far wide of the mark.

In my reading of the evidence (Stover 1978:36,60–63), bronze making began north of Mesopotamia in the Caucasus region between the Kuro and Araxes rivers in about 4500 B.C. I call it the Kuro-Araxes culture, using the term culture in the archaeological sense to refer to any assembly of artifacts assumed to belong to a local people or related peoples. The vague Kuro-Araxes culture is known only by a few artifacts, at first ornamental pins, later weapons, the technique of casting them transferred by trade to Mesopotamia. The weapons were from the start open-mold castings of ax-heads, eventually bivalve castings of shaft-holed axes, in the imitation of shaft-holed stone ax-heads associated with the Battle-ax Folk. These smiths, in turn, are associated with the Beaker Folk who seemed to have worked as independent craftsmen for trade and profit. Later bronze smiths worked as craftsmen subserving a royal court not unlike the one at Stonehenge.

The Kuro-Araxes culture invented the bivalve mold, a complicated technical advance over open-mold casting. But this matter is far from settled. The origins and development of bronze metallurgy are perhaps unknowable, but all suppositions now agree that Gordon Childe's thesis no longer holds. A case for the Caucasus region, quite apart from its rich copper deposits, rests on the early dating of a few bronze ornaments and ax-heads. Totally unknown is the source of tin for these products. It may have been as distant as the tin-bearing mountain slopes of the Eastern Alps, not a bar to ambitious prospectors. For a distribution map of tin and copper ores in central and eastern Europe see Gimbutus 1965.

Not much about early bronze making shows itself in the archaeological record, not even later developments insofar as workshops are concerned. A rare and spectacular find of that sort was uncovered by the Soviet archaeologist A.L. Mongait at Kalinovka (near then–Stalingrad, now Volgograd). In a round barrow there he found a complete bronze maker's kit, the smith himself with pestle in hand (Mongait 1961). Fig. 55 reproduces his drawings. At left are bivalve molds for shaft-holed

3. The Builders

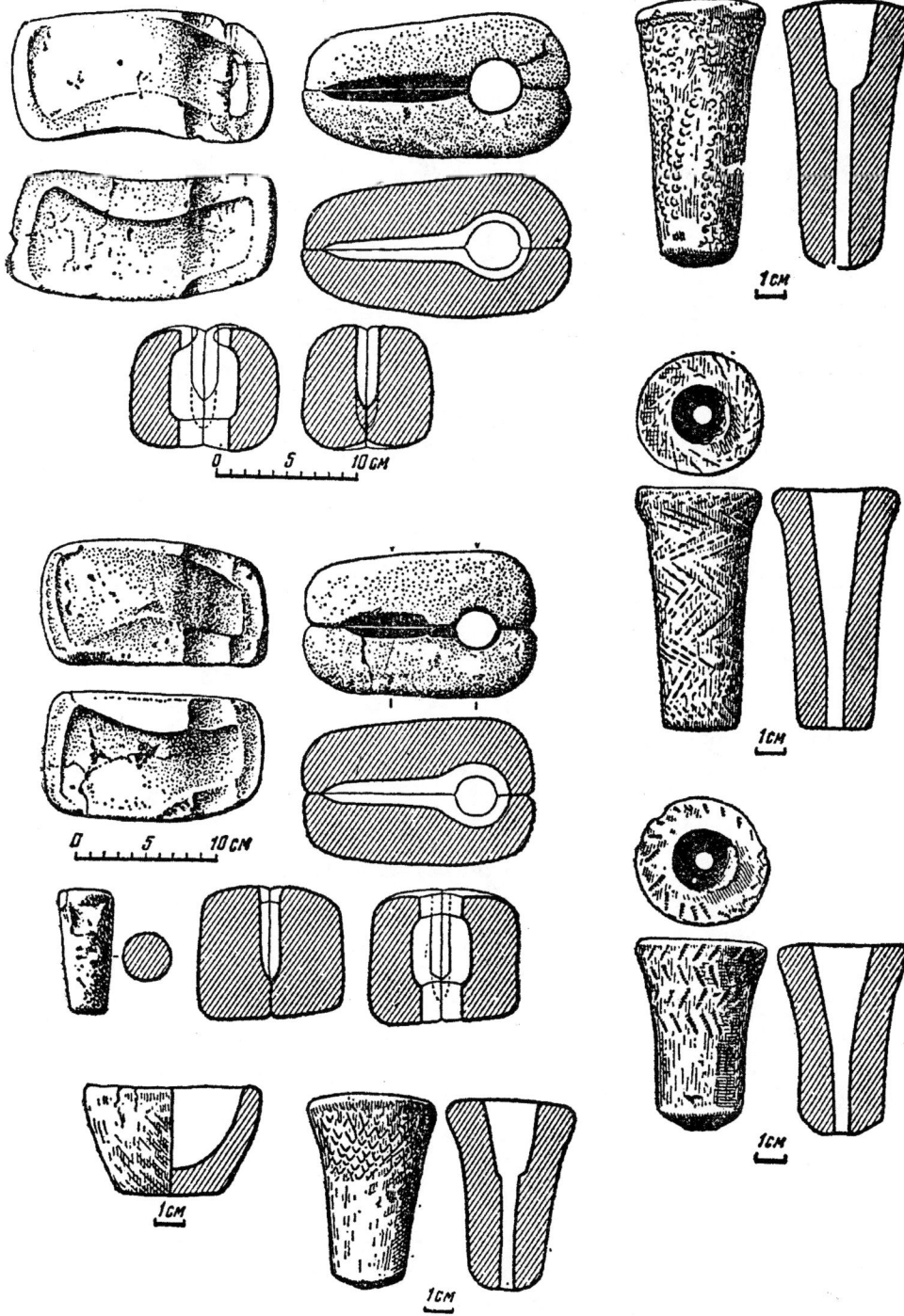

Fig. 55. *Bronze worker's kit at Kalinovka in the Caucasus region, not far north of the Kuro-Araxes site where bronze casting began; from Mongait 1961.*

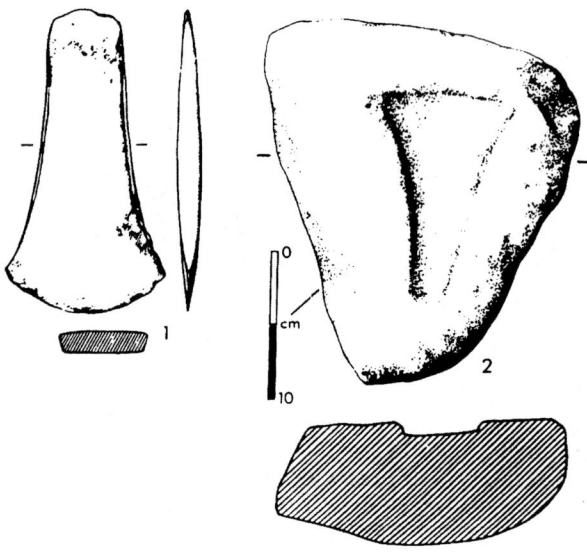

Fig. 56. *Flat ax from northern Scotland (left) and corresponding open mold from Ireland (right); from* Inventaria Archaeologica GB *26.*

ax-heads, at bottom the smith's mortar and pestle. At right are ceramic funnels for pouring molten metal. Mongait dates this find anywhere from 1200 to 400 B.C. The one book that would have a radio-carbon date for the site (Coles and Harding 1979) does not. It is certain, however, that the site dates later than Stonehenge III: a reminder that Bronze Age technology was not everywhere a uniform development.

At Stonehenge, to be sure, bronze was big business but its technology did not nearly approach that evolved by the foundry at Kalinovka—a lucky find. No such weapon shop has been revealed anywhere else, and certainly not in the Stonehenge region, nor at the royal tin mines, nearby in Western England. The only evidence is the product itself, ax-heads and long daggers (or short swords) found as grave goods.

In plate I:2 the artist imagines a Stonehenge smith casting flat axes. He pours molten bronze into an open mold of carved stone like the one pictured in foreground at bottom left; at bottom right are finished products. This method of open-mold casting preceded the development of ever more complex bivalve molds. Fig. 56 at left illustrates the same type of flat ax from northern Scotland, while at right is a corresponding open mold from County Cork in Ireland.

It would seem that the already-mentioned ax carvings all over the sarsen stones at Stonehenge were reproductions of open molds, as in stone 54 shown in page I:1 and in fig. 28. But this is not quite the case, even though the Stonehenge kingdom gained its wealth from the manufacture and export of weapons very like flat axes, but flanged at the haft. See plate II:2 for the difference.

Fig. 57 shows a sample ax-head found in the round barrow of the Stonehenge III cemetery. It is like a flat ax, except that its edges are slightly flanged at the narrow end where it attaches to some kind of handle, a blade castable only in a bivalve mold, however simple. To the right is a shaft-holed stone ax from the same grave, the Kurgan weapon that gives the Battle-ax Folk their name, and that modeled the shaft-holed bronze axes cast in complex bivalve molds at Kalinovka. The typical flanged ax at Stonehenge had to be mounted the same way flat axes were. My drawings in fig. 58 show three possible ways these were hafted. The middle one suggests how a flanged ax may have been hafted more securely.

More important, however, is the question of a source for tin. Where did Stonehenge smiths get it at a time when tin ores were a very scarce resource, not widely known to prospectors ever on the lookout for it. Gold, in the ancient world, was far less a valuable commodity than tin. Tin meant bronze, and bronze meant power and great wealth, above all at Stonehenge. Upon tin the Stonehenge kings raised their impressive monument, from which radiated their great influence abroad. To this day Stonehenge is the most fabled monument of antiquity.

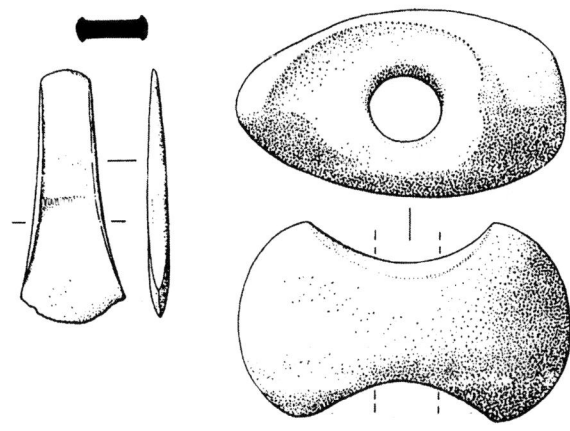

Fig. 57. *Flanged bronze ax-head (left) and stone ax-head from Stonehenge; from Crittal 1973.*

Fig. 58. *Possible ways of hafting flat axes (drawings by the author).*

The Stonehenge tin mines locate to the southwest in the drainage system between Cornwall and Devon. This region is today littered with slag heaps and the remains of engine sheds for the pumping of water out of deeply sunk mine shafts. At one site in Cornwall I have seen a museum exhibit featuring a magnificent Victorian steam engine serving that purpose, and then went on to visit other local museums housing prehistoric exhibits. In Stonehenge times nothing like modern mining methods were used, no digging into the ground at all.

Indeed, nothing remains of how Stonehenge metallurgists exploited the region's tin ores because they did *not* dig. The assumption has to be they collected surface finds of cassiterite, nodules of tin dioxide (SnO_2) naturally occurring in tin streams, dried river beds, long ago picked clean (Fox 1964). But not before this ancient resource caught the attention of far-ranging Mycenaean prospectors.

When in 1953 Professor Atkinson revealed the carving of a royal Mycenaean dagger on the inside face of stone 53, he deduced, by typological dating, that the

Fig. 59, left. *Mycenaean dagger carving next to native ax-head carving (drawing by the author)*. Fig. 60, above. *Flat ax (4³⁄₁₀ inches long) and hilt (4¼ inches) of Mycenaean short sword from same barrow in Cornwall; in Truro Museum.*

monument was built in 1500 B.C. He even suggested that it may have been constructed at Mycenaean initiative, a startling idea I played with in an often reprinted and a widely translated historical novel (see Appendix III). Later radiocarbon dating, however, proved me wrong.

Fig. 59 (to repeat the image) indicates the dagger carving in question next to one of a native ax-head. Mycenaeans *were* indeed there in 1500 B.C., 500 years after the monument was raised in 2000 B.C. It obviously still was active, Stonehenge kings still a power in the region. The question then is why Mycenae reached that far at that time. The answer is equally obvious: tin. But to get at it, agents from Bronze Age Greece had to gain access to Cornish tin stones under the control of another Bronze Age kingdom. The dagger carving on stone 53 may very well be the sign or signature of some kind of royal trade agreement.

Indeed, evidence of high-level trade relations is visible in Cornwall itself, where Stonehenge smiths probably worked. From the same burial near Truro are two related artifacts illustrated in fig. 60. To the left is a native-made flat ax, to the right the remains of an important Mycenaean short sword. Another trade good is the famous Rillaton cup, a corrugated gold cup like those found in the royal Shaft Graves at Mycenae (see fig. 61).

On the other side of the trade equation is a rare example of tin ingots cast for export. Fig. 62 shows the one dredged from the mouth of the River Fal off the Cornish coast, no doubt cast by resident Mycenaean smiths who smelted tin ore on the spot. The ingot's H shape is practical for securing it by rope aboard a sea-going

Fig. 61, top. *Mycenaean cup of corrugated gold (height 3¼ inches) from a barrow near Rillaton in East Cornwall; electrotype in Devizes Museum, original in British Museum.* Fig. 62, bottom. *Tin ingot cast by Mycenaean smiths in Cornwall; length 2 feet 10 inches, weight 158 pounds; in Truro Museum, photograph courtesy Cornwall County Museum.*

vessel, one of which evidently sunk in Cornwall waters. But the shape also suggests a stretched-out cow hide, recalling Homer's calculation of wealth in terms of so many cattle. In fact ingots like these were anciently called "hides."

The Mycenaean dagger carving, significantly, is next to that of a bronze axhead of the sort decorating all faces of the sarsen uprights at Stonehenge. These decorations, I would say, were actually intaglio settings for hammered-in copper or gold. Such a gleaming display of wealth and power surely was intended to impress the mass of spectators who attended election ceremonies. No doubt the dagger carving was also inlaid with gold, the better to glorify the Stonehenge kings whose reach extended not alone through their weapons trade but through the export of tin to another great kingdom far, far away.

4

The Reconstructions

Now for the main event, the color plates found between pages 62 and 63. These are imaginative paintings that make graphic my vision of Stonehenge City. Let it be said at the outset, however, that they represent *ideas*; they are conceptual statements for which details are offered only for the sake of something concrete for the artist to visualize. At every point I am careful to specify the visual associations each detail is meant to convey: details that reflect on very real cultural continuities. The reader is therefore asked to judge the reconstructions with critical thoughtfulness.

As for my constant reference to the seat of a high king at Tara in ancient Ireland, my rationale must await the Epilogue: "Looking Back from the Iron Age." Meanwhile let us get on with the instructive comparison between Iron Age Tara and Stonehenge of the Bronze Age kings.

The first thing to be done here, then, is to lay out the plot of my comparative analysis, Tara and Stonehenge. This comes down to five equivalent features:

1. Election court
2. King's palace
3. Banquet hall
4. Cemetery
5. Race course

These places are numbered in the following two maps.

Fig. 63 is a map of the Stonehenge region, enumerating the above features. Fig. 64 is a map of the Tara site, numbered the same. Everything that follows plays on this comparative topography.

First the Stonehenge region —

1. *Election court.* The great sarsen stones of Stonehenge III.
2. *King's palace.* Reconstructed from a series of concentric postholes at a site quaintly named Woodhenge.

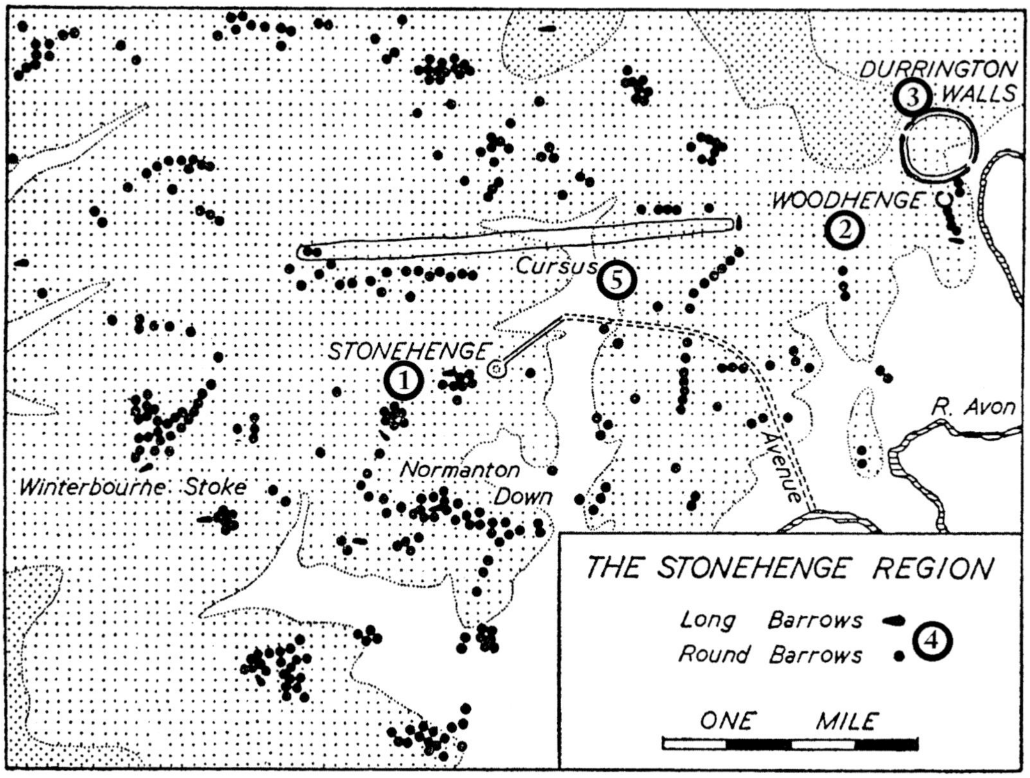

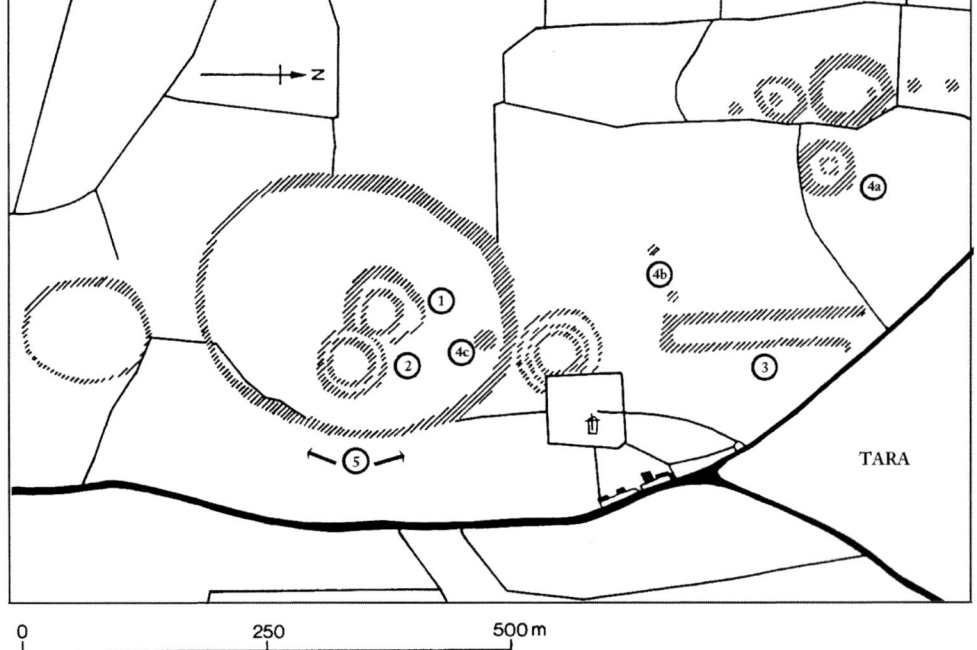

Fig. 63, top. *The five main features of the Stonehenge landscape; adapted from Atkinson 1956.* Fig. 64, bottom. *Five similar features at Tara; adapted from Raftery 1994.*

4. The Reconstructions

3. *Banquet hall.* Reconstructed from a circular array of postholes located within the large henge monument called Durrington Walls.
4. *Cemetery.* Includes Neolithic long barrows from the founding of Stonehenge I to the Bronze Age round barrows of Stonehenge II and III.
5. *Race course.* Elongated earthwork called the Cursus by William Stukeley (1740). Reconstructed as a track for foot races (when not in use as a fairground and camping site for tourists attending election ceremonies).

Next Tara —

1. *Election court.* Centered within a double ring of circular earthworks.
2. *King's palace.* Located within a palisaded earthwork. Seat of the high kings of pagan Ireland.
3. *Banquet hall.* Bounded by a rectangular earthwork, whose interior is well documented in Irish literature.
4. *Cemetery.* Much eroded by plough architecture. Traces of it remain at 4a, 4b, and 4c of fig. 64. As at Stonehenge, it starts with a Neolithic graveyard. (At 4e is a Neolithic chambered tomb called the Mound of Hostages.)
5. *Race course.* A track for horse racing running around a vast earthwork called the Royal Enclosure.

1. Election Court

STONEHENGE

Once again Dr. Walter Charleton must be credited for the startling originality of this fertile idea. He was, of course, quite wrong in dating the monument and attributing it to an election court erected by Viking invaders. But he did grasp the essential concept of pre-dynastic kingship, which lasted in Europe until 1356, when Holy Roman Emperor Charles IV abrogated its last vestige in Denmark with his famous Golden Bull *De Electione Imperatorum* (see page 150 in Appendix II).

Significantly, Charleton's advisor, Dr. Olaus Wormius, made the history of Denmark his life work. His precocious field studies of prehistoric monuments include a type he calls *comitalia loca*, election places. At their grandest they feature a circle of stones upon which stood the electors, while the prince or king being elected stood on a higher stone at the center. From the specifics and interpretations provided by Dr. Wormius, Dr. Charleton drew up a systematic point by point comparison with Stonehenge (see excerpt 5, page 152, in Appendix II). Surprisingly it works out very well, for all the wild anachronisms entailed. But on the other hand, real continuities come into play here. Norse mythology, recorded by Christianized poets and saga composers in the Viking colony in Iceland, seem to recall a similar institution when they describe annual assemblies at a local *thing* (*ting*), at which law cases were heard and kings elected at the national *althing* (see Wilson 1980:179). The same persistence of lore and legend obtains in Irish literature recorded by Christianized Druids.

Plate V:2 displays my reconstruction of the royal Stonehenge election court. At center stage is the high king being elevated to office as he stands on the lintel of the main trilithon, joined by his four underkings atop the four lesser trilithons. Ranged around lintels of the sarsen ring are celebratory electors drawn from the royal clan. Their way up there is indicated at top left, where one of the pillars of the sarsen ring (stone 11) is half-sized, a convenient place for the artist to imagine a set of wooden stairs.

Note that I have excluded the bluestones, the better to keep unobstructed a view of exotic events on the ground and of paintings on the sarsen stones. These latter, however, do not in the least in my depictions intend to imagine or recreate such paintings. They suggest only the fact that the stones were indeed decorated with something. In the event they were covered with ax-head carvings, probably inlaid with gleaming copper or gold. Time and strong hilltop winds have eroded most of these, but enough remain to indicate a former profusion of them.

To start with paintings on uprights of the sarsen ring. These echo a splendiferous profusion of rock carvings in Bronze Age Scandinavia, dating from the time of Stonehenge to about 500 B.C. Their motifs survived in the region until the eleventh century of the Christian era — an unbroken tradition unmatched elsewhere in all Europe (see Gelling and Davidson 1969).

One rock carving of enticing relevance is represented in fig. 65. It pictures three (three!) warriors prancing about with weapons held high, battle axes crudely hafted with bronze blades of the flat ax type (refer back to fig. 58). The warriors also bear round shields emblazoned with a symbol of the sun, as all authorities agree. They also agree that the sun is emblematic of the shiny metal bronze itself. The conspicuous phallic projections indicate the warrior's virility in battle: warriors "thrice strong" in later Celtic mythology. One of them has a foot linked to a circular design that may very well indicate a stone circle, as in Norse mythology, upon which Viking

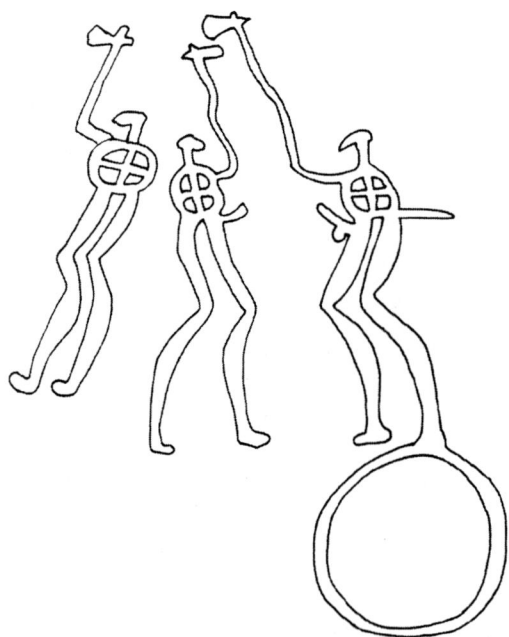

Fig. 65. *Bronze Age rock carving in Scandinavia (drawing by the author after Gelling and Davidson 1969).*

4. The Reconstructions

warriors stood when convened at some *althing* to elect their kings. I have dared to suggest that the warrior-electors dancing on the lintels of the sarsen ring relate to this lasting tradition (see details in plate VII:2). If the Scandinavian rock engravings do indeed date back to 2000–1500 B.C., their symbology most certainly reflects a culture also current in prehistoric Denmark, whose now-vanished monuments (proto–Viking?) were described for Dr. Charleton by Dr. Wormius, notably his *comitalia loca* interpreted by him as election courts: the crucial idea driving the present work.

As for paintings on the trilithons, they too merely suggest something else. They do, however, illustrate a very real archaeological fact. The Stonehenge election court, everywhere inscribed with ax-head carvings, brought together five regions under the sway of one overking. His trilithon is decorated with a lozenge design taken from the large gold plate found in his royal burial (see fig. 66), together with a smaller one of the same design. Because this one grave, Bush Barrow, is the only royal burial to have escaped looting by tomb robbers, the lozenge motive in gold is not otherwise represented in the Stonehenge cemetery. It is, however, unique to that site and so I use it to decorate the overking's trilithon.

Accordingly, the lesser trilithons of the four underkings are decorated with artistic motifs, known mainly from pottery, derived from those four other regions. Significantly, these elements show up in some round barrows in the Stonehenge cemetery: proof that it served as a kind of Arlington National Cemetery for noble warriors from all regions. This, to be sure, is pretty slim evidence for my five-kingdoms thesis. Prehistoric geography, however, adds considerable support.

Look at the map of southern England in fig. 67. The black areas are lowland forests, the white areas are windswept high downs, treeless and open for pasturage. It simplifies a complex cartographic survey done by L.V. Grinsell in *The Archaeology of Wessex* (1958), detailing for the age of Stonehenge everything from geology, soil types and vegetation to every archaeological site. Fig. 67 reduces all this to the black and white areas and to the five most significant prehistoric centers of barrow cemeteries, henge monuments, and raised megaliths, none lintelled except Stonehenge: seat of the overking who united all five regions.

Apart from a panoramic view of the election court, showing instal-

Fig. 66. *Line drawing of large gold plate, 8½ inches across, from Bush Barrow.*

Fig. 67. *Map of the five regions comprising the five Stonehenge kingdoms; simplified in Stover 1978 from Grinsell 1958, map II.*

lation ceremonies for the overking in progress, three other color plates are closeups of some horrific sacrificial practices of the sort attributed to Celtic Druids by classical writers hostile to them. In a contrary tradition, beginning with William Stukeley (1740), Druids are regarded as wise men far too philosophical to indulge the barbarism of human sacrifice (Piggott 1968). Even more controversial, if possible, is the reading back of Druids into the proto–Druids of Stonehenge times. To me, this is reasonable enough to speculate on in the following three plates.

Plate VII:1 focuses on the famous wicker man reported by Julius Caesar in *De Bello Gallico* (51 B.C.; Book VI). Caesar writes,

> Some tribes build enormous images with limbs of interwoven branches which they fill with live men; the images are set alight and the men die in a sea of flame.

This theatrical account inspired Aylett Sammes, the seventeenth century antiquary, to illustrate it in his early translation of Caesar's text. See fig. 68, drawn from volume 1 of his *Britannia Antiqua Illustrata* (London 1676). His fanciful engraving, titled Wicker Image, rapidly became a popular favorite with subsequent writers who loved to stress the barbarity of the Druids. I have selected it, among others, because it is so memorable.

Sammes also loosely translated and freely illustrated portions of other classical writers on early Celtic society, including Strabo the Greek geographer, a citi-

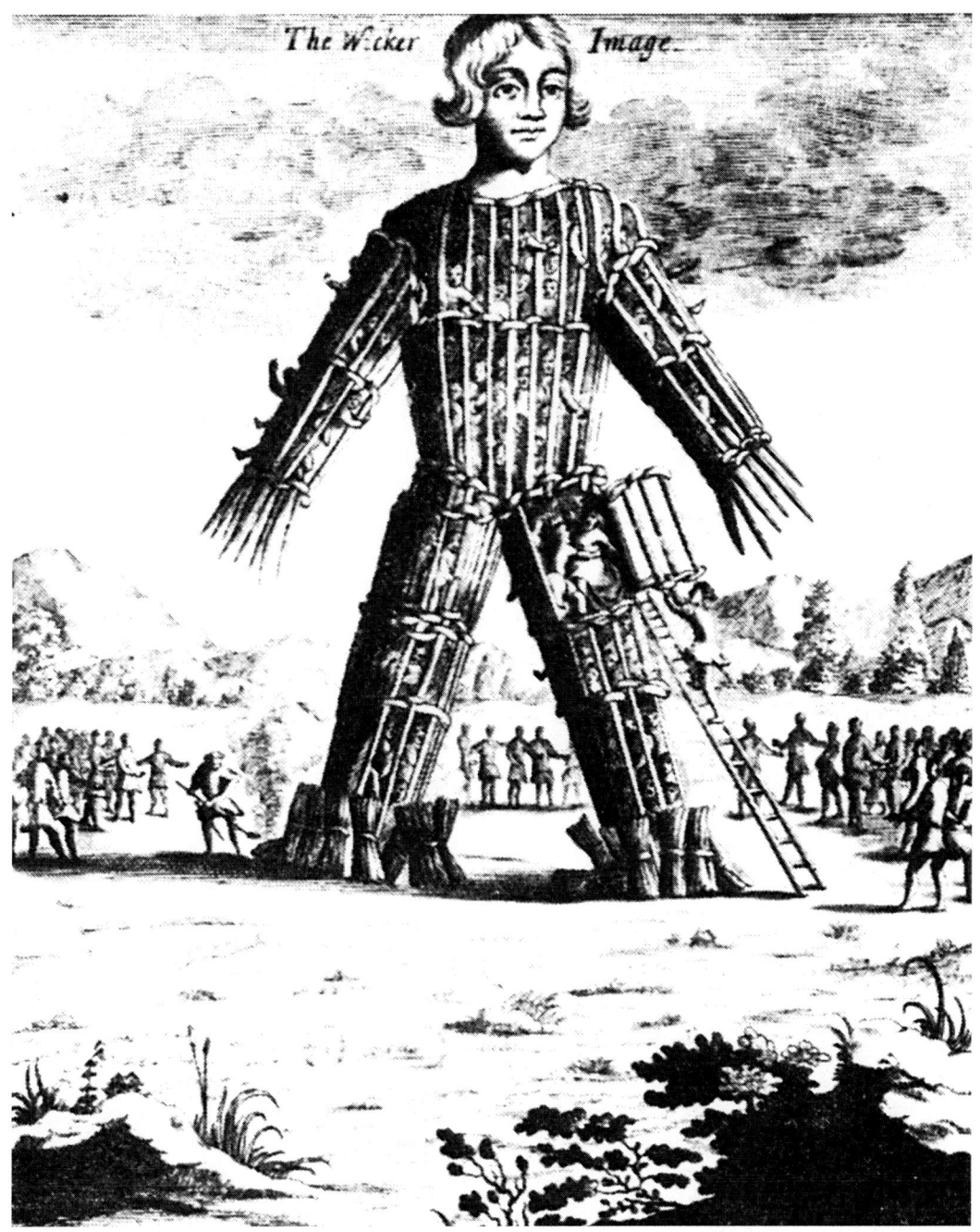

Fig. 68. *"Wicker Image" from Aylett Sammes,* Britannia Antiqua Illustrata *(1676).*

zen of Augustan Rome who, in his library research, obviously drew upon the lost ethnographic books of Posidonius. In his *Geographica* (A.D. 20), Strabo writes of the Druids,

> They used to stab a human being whom they had devoted to death, in the back with a dagger, and foretell the future from his convulsions. They offered their sacrifices

not without a Druid. There are also other accounts of their human sacrifices; for they used to shoot men down with arrows; and impale them in their temples, or making a large statue of straw and wood, throw into it cattle and all sorts of wild animals and human beings, and thus make a burnt offering.

The wicker man again figures, as in Caesar, as well as other forms of human sacrifice, all illustrated by Sammes. None, however, are nearly as famous as the fanciful Wicker Image.

Plate VI:1 centers on the arrow-shooting mentioned by Strabo. The victims, like those torched in the wicker man, are assumed to be war captives or else criminals, as reported for Celtic Gaul by observers from the classical world. One of these practices actually diffused to that world, notably the arrow-shooting of the third-century Christian martyr, St. Sebastian, in the Roman arena: the favorite subject of many sacred paintings. That the same tradition extends back to Stonehenge times is evidenced archaeologically at one of the round-barrow sites. Many of these have secondary burials deposited in the outer earthwork. In one case a body is riddled with arrowheads, and near it is the posthole of the stake to which the victim was tied. In another case the skeletal remains of a similar victim, arrowhead embedded in his spine, has been recovered from the silted-over ditch of the earthen henge monument itself (Ashbee 1960, 1978).

Even more grotesque is the impalement scene in plate VI:2. It derives from the Sammes illustration of Strabo's reference to such. This has a curious resemblance to fig. 69, a 1499 German woodcut from Nuremberg. It shows Vlad IV (1455–1462),

Fig. 69. *Vlad the Impaler and his grisly work, from a German woodcut of 1499.*

the bloodthirsty prince of Walachia in present-day Romania, supping on the entrails of the victims of his punishment, spies and other trespassers. He left a name in history as Vlad the Impaler or as *Dracul* (= the Devil), and in horror fiction as Count Dracula. Ashbee (1960) thinks a posthole just outside one of the Stonehenge round barrows indicates a place of sacrificial impalement. So, maybe plate VI:2 is not wholly speculative.

Tara

In the map of Tara at fig. 64, the election court is indicated by numeral 1. The center of it is a single pillar, the "Stone of Fal," which may not always have been where it now is. One tradition says it used to stand near the so-called Mound of Hostages at 4b, once part of an area-wide cemetery mostly erased by centuries of plough agriculture. The barrows of the Stonehenge cemetery, in which its Bronze Age election is located, remains largely intact because the land since then long was used for grazing cattle, then sheep. Another tradition has the Stone of Fal located within earthworks said to be within the remains of an earlier royal palace, later enlarged at map number 2. Whatever, the Stone of Fal to this day is emblematic of Ireland itself, surely a memory of the stone's importance to the election of pagan Ireland's high kings: the Iron Age as Golden Age.

Plate VIII:2 recreates an election ceremony, absent the crowd of spectators completing the scene of a typically Celtic popular assembly. The newly elected high king stands on the rounded top of the Stone of Fal (surely a feat of agility that may have been part of the test), while warriors from the royal clan, standing in a circle around him, acclaim their approval with raised swords. The Stone of Fal, all traditions agree, was called the "stone penis," a term that suggests the virile warrior-electors pictured in the Scandinavian rock carving at fig. 65.

Another ancient connection also comes to mind, not from the Bronze Age but from the Roman Iron Age. I am thinking of the famous account of Cornelius Tacitus in his *Germania* (A.D. 98). He says of the election of Teutonic chieftains that encircled warriors signaled their selection by the clashing of their spears. "No form of approval can carry more honor than praise expressed by arms." It should be noted that Tacitus is the most reliable of classical writers on "barbarian" Europe. He saw little difference between the Celts of Gaul and the Teutons of Germania. On the other hand Caesar, for political reasons, exaggerated the difference when he drew the boundary line along the Rhine River (see Tacitus 1948).

2. *King's Palace*

Stonehenge

Two miles northeast of Stonehenge is the obscure henge monument grandly named Woodhenge. Few if any tourists ever visit the site because nothing is to be

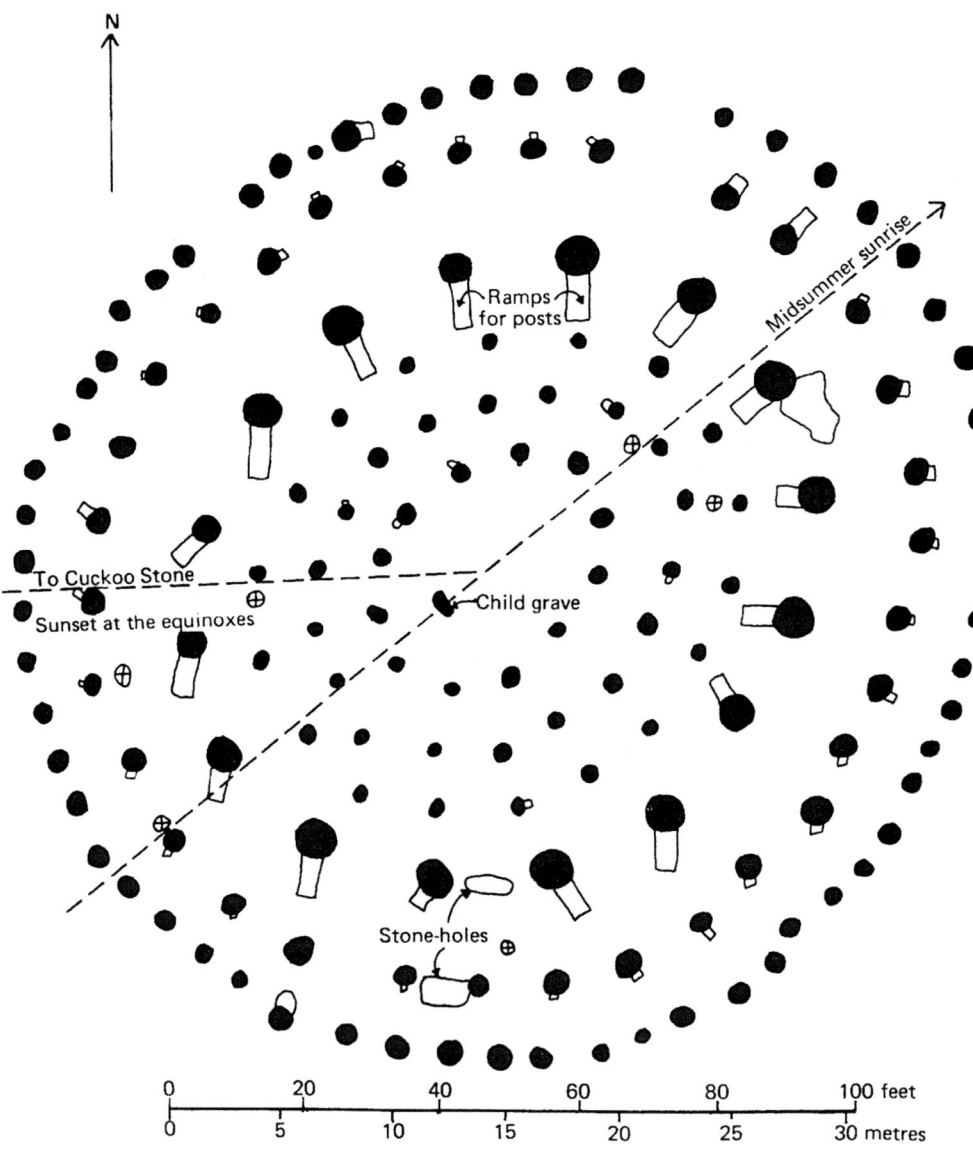

Fig. 70. *Plan of Woodhenge; from Cunnington 1929.*

seen there, save a worn-down embankment and a silted-over ditch. What lies within is known only to archaeologists familiar with the excavation report by M.E. Cunnington (1929): six concentric rings of postholes. The Cunningtons, husband and wife, were interested in the astronomical approach to Woodhenge, and concluded that the long axis of its slightly oblate circles pointed to midsummer sunrise (see fig. 70).

Other archaeologists are not like-minded. They endorse the official government pamphlet, on sale at the Stonehenge souvenir shop, which reconstructs Wood-

4. The Reconstructions 99

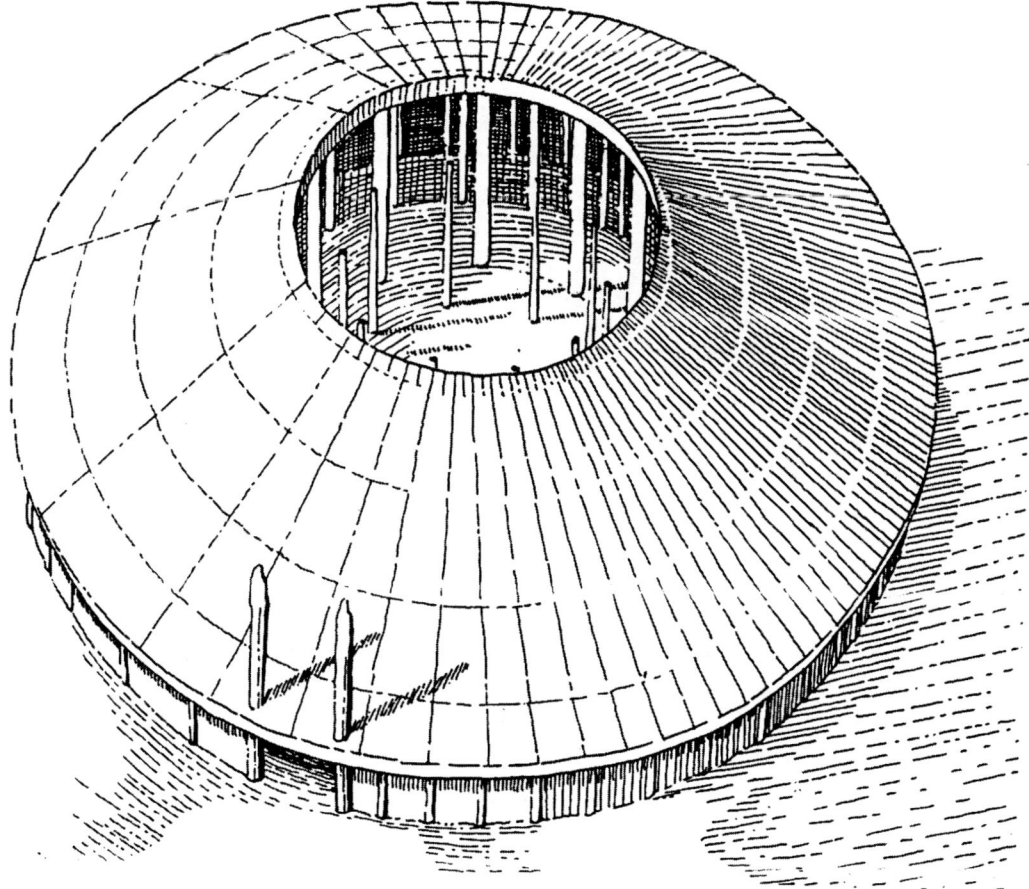

Fig. 71. *Official reconstruction of Woodhenge as a temple (HMSO).*

henge as a doughnut-shaped temple. See fig. 71. The hole in the center figures because no way could be found to roof over the inner space absent a sizeable center post.

My own reconstruction, which so astonished Professor Atkinson with its obvious plausibility, directly addresses the roofing problem. See plate IV:2. The problem interested a student of architecture in my Stonehenge course, who then came up with a solution. But not just technically. He already was aware that his architectural solution had to be consistent with the Indo-European cultural heritage of the Stonehenge builders.

Accordingly, the result is that in fig. 72, the Stonehenge king's royal palace shown in elevation. The roofing derives from the crown of tent-like yurts built even today by Turkic and Mongol peoples. See fig. 73. The yurt has long been the mobile home of these nomadic herdsmen on the Eurasian steppelands. They are what was left behind after their proto–Indo-European ancestors moved into Europe, eventually Britain, and became settled pastoralists. The luminous and translucent

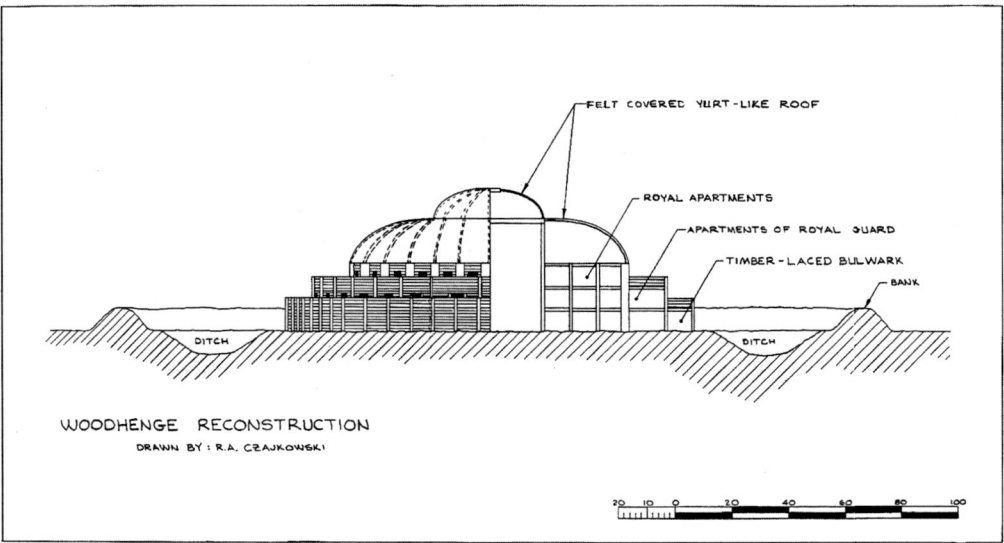

Fig. 72. *Architectural drawing of the restored palace shown in elevation, with scale in feet; student drawing.*

roofing in plate IV:2 is meant to convey the skinned animal hides or felt that cover Mongol yurts.

Before saying a few more words about the roofing, the reader needs consult fig. 70, M.E. Cunnington's plan of his Woodhenge excavations. He lettered the six rings of postholes A to F, outer to inner. The C ring has postholes about 60 inches in diameter, twice that of the two outer and three inner rings, indicating massive timber posts erected in those C ring holes. The ramps next to them suggest very heavy timbers that had to be raised the same way the great sarsens at Stonehenge were.

The trouble with the official Woodhenge reconstruction is that it is too easy and simplistic. It misprizes the skills of the Stonehenge builders, who were well versed in both woodworking techniques and large scale construction. My restoration shrinks not from a sophisticated complexity. The expansive roofing is of two yurt-like structures, with the E ring providing support for the rim of the outermost crown, that of the F ring the inner crown.

For example, the timber-laced bulwark in fig. 72 recalls the architecture of Celtic hill forts, stone-built with cut timber beams holding the unmortared stones in place: a dry walling technique. The royal palace, after all, is a fortified place as indicated by the earthen embankment around and which very well may have been palisaded. Typical of other henge monuments in Britain, the bank is breached and the ditch bridged with a causeway, a single one in this case (some others, like Stonehenge, have more than one).

Turning now to the bottom of the structure, it is again useful to look back from the Celtic Iron Age.

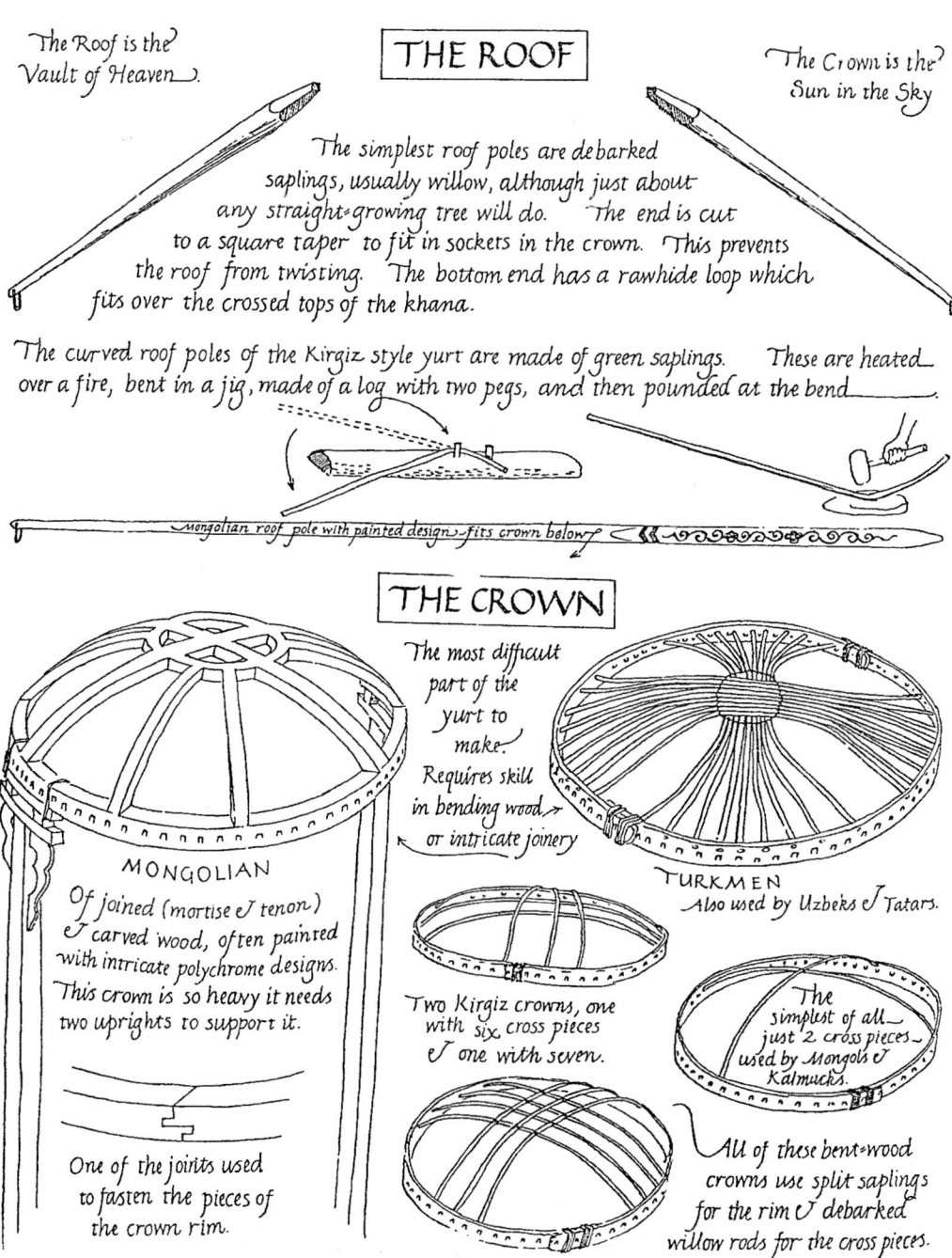

Fig. 73. *Architecture of the yurt as built by steppe peoples (from a source provided by the student who did fig. 72).*

If the need for defense, then palace guards. Quarters for them are provided in fig. 72 on the lower floor, as is a rampart for them to walk and keep watch. While the security of the king would of course have been important, so also would be the security of his livestock housed in the basement, given that favorite war-sport of the Celts, cattle reaving. After all, the great Homeric epic of the north, the *Iliad* of Irish letters, is none other than the *Táin Bó Cúalnge* ("Cooley's Cattle Raid").

Basement housing for cattle is another Celtic practice. So far as Celtic homesteads are known from archaeology and Irish literature, the practice was to keep a few cows downstairs during the winter months, then release them for breeding at the beginning of the warm season when pasturage again turned green. The rest were slaughtered for feasting on Samain. The Stonehenge king did no differently, as indicated in plate IV:2.

A good archaeological example comes from northern Scotland at Clickhimin, where stone not timber was the main building material. The reconstructed site in fig. 74 shows a fortified Celtic homestead. Inside the circular walling, at left and right, are two-storied apartments. Fig. 75 illustrates the interior view of one of these: living quarters upstairs, cattle pens downstairs. These images very much influenced my reconstruction of Woodhenge.

One more detail. At the center of Woodhenge is a grave, the burial of a child with its skull split by an ax blow: another service of the proto–Druids. Nothing remarkable about this, given the ancient practice of foundation sacrifices. So likewise do we place mementoes in the cornerstones of public buildings, a secular consecration.

TARA

For the King's Palace at Tara I have no reconstruction to offer, because there are no archaeological reports able to verify what the site amounts to. Plentiful tradition, however, has much to say about the remains, those two circular earthworks on the map at fig. 64. Irish literature insists that they form part of the Royal Seat, itself located within the so-called Royal Enclosure. This extensive earthwork proves, by excavation, to have been heavily palisaded: a massive security precaution.

The richest tradition concerning these remains is that of the eleventh century manuscript *Dindshenchas*, or lore of prominent places. It collects, in prose and verse, recorded legends going back to the ninth century and even longer in oral tradition. Above all it preserves the memory of a once powerful kingship in Ireland's golden Iron Age.

3. Banquet Hall

STONEHENGE

When digging with a team of archaeologists in the American Southwest, we tagged any artifact of unknown utility a "ceremonial object." It is a common prac-

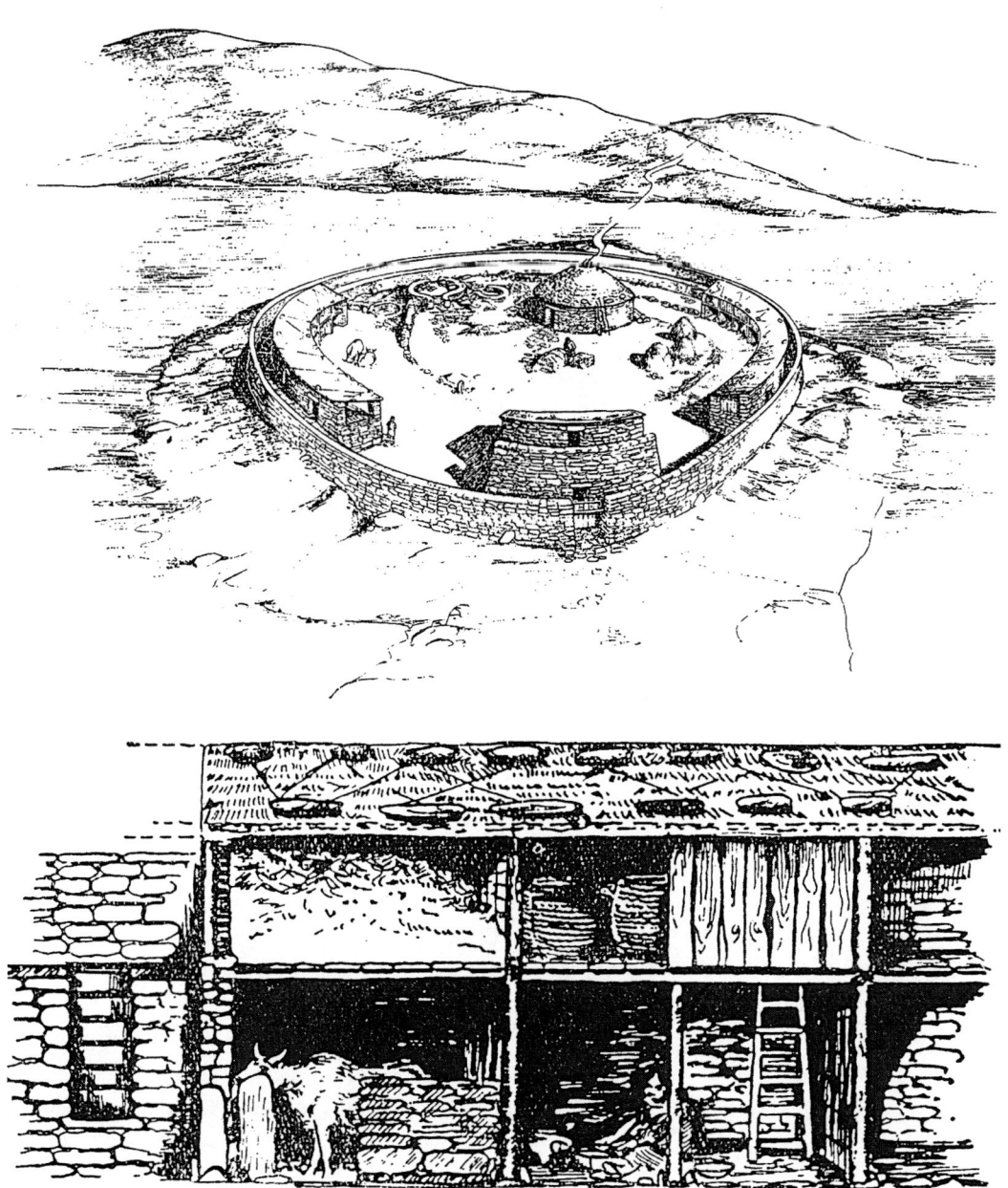

Fig. 74, top. *Reconstruction of Iron Age fort in northern Scotland; from Hamilton 1968, HMSO.* Fig. 75, bottom. *Cross-section of two-story housing depicted from the outside in fig. 74.*

tice in the field: if puzzled or in doubt, appeal to religion. So it has been with the ruins of Stonehenge, deemed a "temple" by all the premodern antiquaries save Dr. Charleton with his political approach. And so with Woodhenge: another temple. And so yet again with the timber circles here constructed as the king's banquet hall.

The site in question is Durrington Walls, a partially excavated henge monument about 1,600 feet in diameter, the length of two football fields. See fig. 76 for

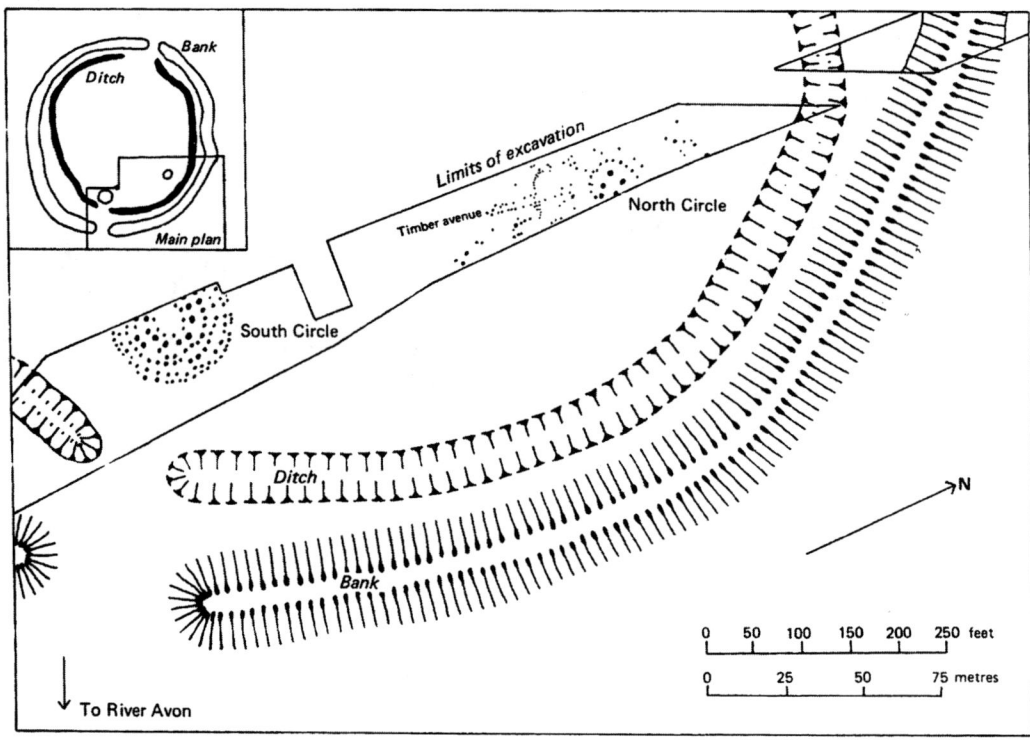

Fig. 76. *Excavated portion of Durrington Walls; from Wainright and Longworth, 1968.*

the archaeological record. The henge has two openings, one at the top of the inset, the other at bottom. The latter is only 80 yards from the king's palace at number 2 on the map in fig. 63. How convenient it would be if the South Circle is indeed the king's palace of my reconstruction and not a "temple," as the smaller North Circle also is supposed to be. Temples, temples everywhere, and not a hint of political realism.

To begin with the reconstruction in plate III:2. I have borrowed the architectural model of Woodhenge-as-temple in fig. 71, although to a radically different purpose. Consonant with this, the expansive henge monument that includes the South Circle, five timber rings 128 feet in diameter, is here a cattle pen. Its enclosed livestock, taken from free-ranging pasturage, would then have been slaughtered and served up in the king's feasting hall. (That would make the North Circle a kind of kitchen facility.)

Royal feasting halls always figure in Hollywood movies about medieval times, and they always feature scenes of combat in them. As a 9-year-old boy I thrilled to the epic sword fight, in *Robin Hood* (1938), that took place in King Richard's castle, usurped by Prince John. Later I came to think that the fight amidst banquet tables was no more than Hollywood hokum. Later still I witnessed a similarly disordered feast of eating and drinking in *The Vikings* (1958), and found it credible.

By then, some historical literature had begun to sink in: *Beowulf*, the *Iliad*, and the Irish hero tales, not to mention classical sources on Celtic society in pre-conquest Gaul.

The reconstruction of the Stonehenge king's banquet hall is not without some convergent literary associations. The Greek ethnographer Posidonius is without a doubt the only trustworthy witness to Celtic life in pre-conquest Gaul. Alas, most of his voluminous books recounting his travels and firsthand observations are lost, with only fragments quoted in Caesar and Strabo and others.

This reconstruction of the Stonehenge banquet hall does not trouble to provide a roof over the wide interior space (as done for the king's palace), but leaves it open to the sky. The ground below, a central courtyard, serves as a combat arena, one that was viewable by all within, each with a ringside seat. I surmise they would see a championship fight between the overking's champion and one or another put up by one of the four underkings. Like medieval tournaments (another favorite subject of historical movies), such public combats in Stonehenge times would have celebrated warrior heroes. The heroic is a highly rated virtue in Homer, as in Celtic tradition.

The reconstructed banquet hall presupposes yet another incipient Celtic tradition. Feasting at the time of Samain, the Celtic New Year, was carnival time because that was the season when cattle were brought home from pasturage and slaughtered for feasting, allowing some animals to shelter until the next warm season. In this light the king of Stonehenge gathered his excess into that great cattle pen, Durrington Walls, butchered them (the site is littered with cattle bones) and served them up in his banquet hall. Here assembled his underkings and nobles and warriors, his generous hospitality serving to cement all five kingdoms: redistribution as the key to power.

The hall's interior, shown in the cutaway part of plate III:2, suggests feasting booths for the various guests from each kingdom. They would not only eat and drink there for days at a time, but also sleep there on rushes laid on furs and rugs, if details authenticated for the banquet hall at Tara (next section) is any guide. The Irish hero tales describe episodes of individual combat taking place within the hall, fought out in the midst of blazing hearths and roasting pigs.

Athenaeus, the Greek compiler of voluminous miscellanea on almost every aspect of ancient life and customs, quotes a lost work of Posidonius:

> The Celts sometimes engage in single combat at dinner. Assembling in arms they engage in a mock battle-drill, and mutual thrust-and-parry, but sometimes wounds are inflicted, and the irritation caused by this may lead even to the slaying of the opponent unless the bystanders hold them back. And in former times, when the hindquarters were served up the bravest hero took the thigh piece, and if another man claimed it they stood up and fought in single combat to the death.

It is a scene often repeated in the Irish hero tales and in a variety of works of the classical authors.

Diodorus Siculus in his *Bibliotheca Historica* (Library of History, 1st century

B.C.) has much to say about the Celts, especially the northern Gauls nearest Britain. In the following passage, significantly, he quotes a relevant line from Homer. Speaking of feasting halls and their revelers,

> Beside them are hearths blazing with fire, with cauldrons and spits containing large pieces of meat. Brave warriors they honor with the finest portions of meat, just as Homer introduces Ajax, honored by the chieftains, when he conquered Hector in single combat: "He honored Ajax with the full-length chine."

It was the right of the best hero present to carve the chief carcass and give himself the best joint of meat, the "champion's portion." But who *was* the bravest hero present?: the original bone of contention.

All of the above feeds into plate III:2. The central courtyard suggests a more formalized arena for such combats.

The exterior wall of my reconstruction, with its many doors leading into the various guest booths, is meant to suggest a powerful mythic image that elevates the feasting hall to a veritable heaven on earth. In Viking mythology the warrior's paradise of feasting and fighting was Valhalla, Odin's great hall in the sky. Hung with shields and roofed with spears, it was entered through 640 doors. Each heavenly day the chosen slain (chosen from the battlefield by Valkyries) feast on Odin's beef and pork, then go outside to fight and kill each other all over again, then return to start another round of same.

TARA

Like the Stonehenge banquet hall, the one at Tara is located hard by a royal palace. The high king in both cases would naturally prefer to be near his redistribution center, when at Samain he lavished hospitality on his underkings and their retinues. Nothing is more basic to kingship than distributing rewards for some measure of loyalty. The king always risks death (the only way to usurp his power) by ambitious rivals, a common theme in Irish epics like *Táin Bó Cúalnge*. Indeed, cattle raids are portrayed there as but a cover for just such attempts.

Nothing remains of the Tara hall save a much eroded rectangular earthwork, one end completely ploughed under. Fortunately a copious literary tradition relates to it, more so than for details of the royal palace. This most certainly indicates where the overking's power really lay, in his hospitality center. Herein he provided that impressive and resplendent heaven on earth so much echoed in heroic literature everywhere.

One might even say the king was the master of a fantasy world, which he manipulated to good political effect: the secret of Irish nostalgia for Celtic magic. Could the Stonehenge hall have been any different?

The most detailed memory trace of the Tara hall is recorded in the Yellow Book of Lecan (ninth century), named after the monastic scriptorium at Lecan that produced it. See fig. 77 for the seating plan given therein. The text, elaborated in the *Dindshenchas* (eleventh century), explains the complex protocol involved. Two rows

4. The Reconstructions

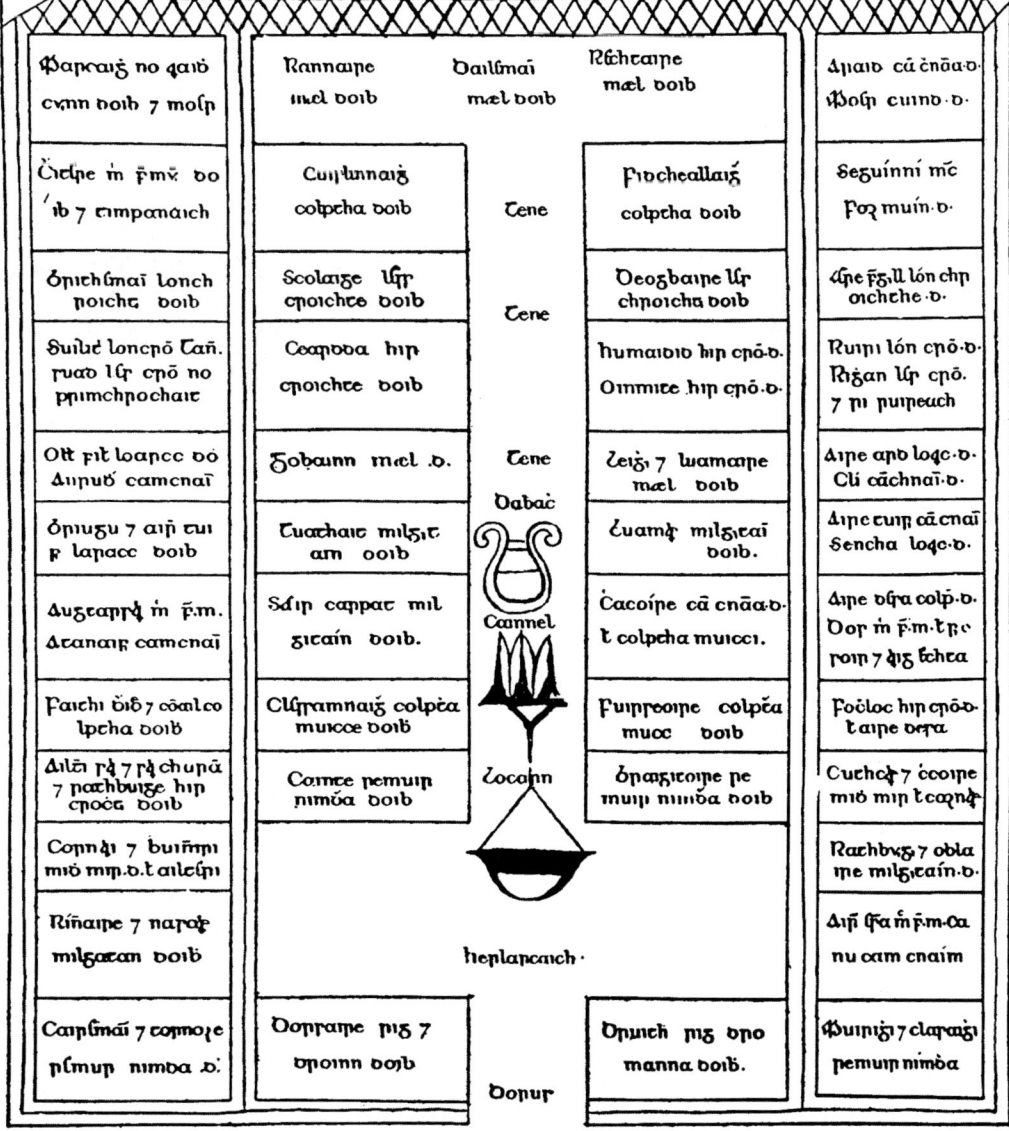

Fig. 77. *Layout of the Tara hall from the Yellow Book of Lecan; after Petrie 1839.*

of booths fitted with benches run down either side of the central aisle, arranged with burning hearths and cauldrons of boiling meat. Favored booths nearest the aisle are at ground level, those along the walls are raised. The open space at the top of the diagram (to the south) is reserved for a select few commoners sitting on the ground. In all, 15 different cuts of meat are said to have coordinated with 42 seating positions among 50 ranked occupations, from king to court fools and lowly leather workers.

Fig. 78 numbers the booths in the above diagram. The royal hall is here rep-

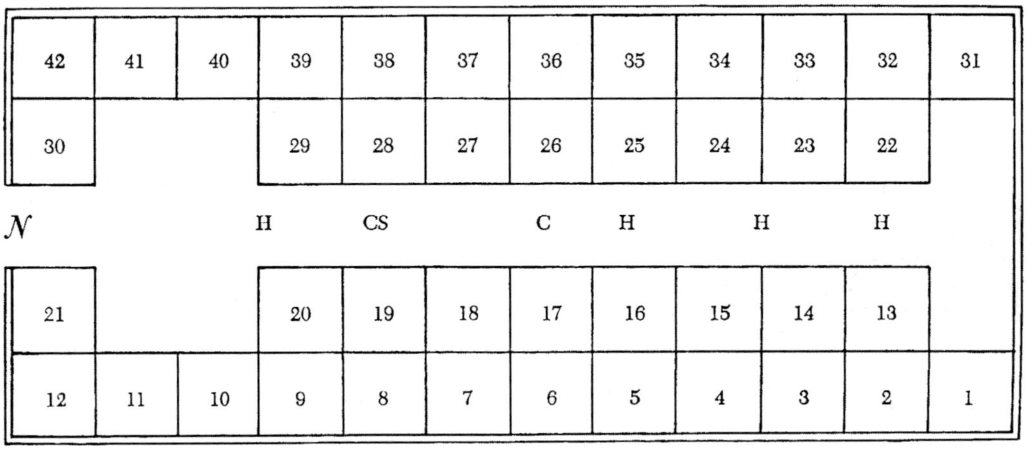

42	41	40	39	38	37	36	35	34	33	32	31
30			29	28	27	26	25	24	23	22	
			H	CS		C	H		H	H	
21			20	19	18	17	16	15	14	13	
12	11	10	9	8	7	6	5	4	3	2	1

N

Fig. 78. *Seating arrangements in the Tara hall diagrammed by MacAlister (1931): C = cauldron, H = hearth.*

resented as 700 feet long by about 70 wide, with one main entrance at the north end. The original text mentions six or seven doors on each side. Below is a translation of the 42 designated booths.

1. Charioteers and Stewards
2. Deer-stalkers
3. Nobles of the first rank
4. King and Queen
5. Third-grade nobles and Third-grade poets
6. Second-grade nobles and Historians (no grade mentioned)
7. Fourth-grade nobles and Fifth-grade poets
8. Sixth-grade poets
9. Cooks
10. Fort-builders
11. King's champions and Fourth-grade poets
12. Sappers
13. Chess players
14. Spencers (keepers of larders)
15. Braziers (bronzesmiths)
16. Physicians
17. Pilots
18. Merchants
19. Jesters
20. Buffoons
21. King's fools
22. Flute-players
23. Schoolteachers
24. Goldsmiths
25. Blacksmiths
26. Shield-makers
27. Chariot-builders
28. Conjurors
29. Satirists
30. Doorkeepers
31. Horsemen
32. Harpers and drummers
33. Judges (Druids)
34. Chief Druids (doctors of letters) and their Understudies
35. Chief poets and Second-grade poets
36. Hospitalers (men who have charge of public hostels)
37. Master wrights and their Understudies
38. Soothsayers and Ordinary Druids
39. Builders and wrights
40. Horners and pipers
41. Engravers (men who decorate metal objects)
42. Cordwainers (leather-workers)

In practice, the king sat in booth number 11 along with fourth-grade poets, not because he belonged with them in rank, but to be near the door in case of trouble. Also with him were four armed guards, each ready to act as the king's champion. Other persons with him, as always, were a noble, a judge, a Druid (later a bishop), a doctor of laws,* a poet, a historian, a musician, and three servants. The king's part in hall festivities was to receive tribute in food and country products from his underkings (and their subkings), while he in return made them presents of deluxe objects, such as weapons, armor, and ceremonial drinking horns. The exact list of all tributes and presents expected of this exchange was recited by the king's chief Druid, and refusal to accept a present signaled rebellion.

Some archaeologists argue that the rectangular earthwork cannot be the banquet hall assigned by tradition because it has no cuts for doorways. My reconstruction addresses that problem directly. Plate III:1 shows the main door and side doors reached by stairways. Looking inside at the center aisle one can imagine cauldrons of boiling beef and spits of roasting pig, the literary place where fights over the champion's portion took place, as in the graphic tale of "MacDatho's Pig." The reader can now see why I draw upon Celtic elements for reconstructing the Stonehenge hall, on the assumption of Bronze Age precedent for Iron Age developments.

4. *Cemetery*

STONEHENGE

The Stonehenge cemetery is notable above all for its one surviving royal burial. This is the famed Bush Barrow find, so named after eight or nine thorn trees planted on it in the eighteenth century. Their roots may have defeated the grave robbers who plundered so many barrows, who knows how many tombs of other kings. The roots almost defeated William Cunnington, who finally opened Bush Barrow in 1808 at considerable cost. Cunnington was a wealthy wool merchant who busied himself excavating Stonehenge barrows from 1800, almost reaching professional standards. He kept extensive notebooks, carefully labeled and described each artifact, and kept all finds from each barrow together in his private museum (Grinsell 1978). His collection from Bush Barrow is now in the British Museum after a long stay in Devizes Museum.

---

*This "doctor of laws" is MacAlister's (1931) translation of the Old Irish in fig. 77, an obvious anachronism reading back from the medieval university system. The translator means to convey that this degree-holding lawyer is a high-ranking Druid well memorized in oral tradition relating to law and custom, to whom the king would turn as we might consult a jurist. Same with the "historian," another Druid versed in legendary use and wont. What is truly amazing is how complex was Iron Age civilization in pre-literate Ireland, as made tangible in the banquet hall's elaborate protocol. The king's authority very much depended on the prestigious lore and learning of his loyal Druids. Others, not so loyal, sided with rebellious factions. Politics, always a muddle as Aristotle wisely observed.

What is most interesting about the king's grave furniture (laid out in plate II:3) is not the finely worked items of gold but the ornaments of plain ordinary bone once inlaid in the handle of his royal scepter. Its mace head of polished shale (fossil *Stromatoporoid*, common enough in the tin mining area of South Devon) is perforated to accommodate the now perished wooden handle. Around its hole are traces of a bronze ring with which it was attached to its shaft with a bronze pin, the work of a skilled craftsman, as are the three perfectly cut bone cylindrical mounts of zig-zag form.

A similar royal scepter with zig-zag bone mounts (the whiteness of bone for lightning flashes) is known from shaft grave Iota in Grave Circle B at Mycenae (Mylonas 1966). As already mentioned, Homer remembered something like that when he spoke of King Agamemnon's "lightning scepter." Even more interesting, zig-zag gold mounts for some *bâton de commandement* is known from a dolmen at Kerlagat in the Morbihan, a department in western France (Taylor 1978). Some authorities suspect Mycenaean influence, but this is not possible because Mycenae did not arise until 500 years after the construction of Stonehenge III. A true explanation has to lie in the foundations of Indo-European cosmology, which everywhere posited a thunder-and-lightning god not unlike the well-attested Thor of Norse mythology.

My reconstruction of the Stonehenge king's burial in Bush Barrow begins with a cross section of a typical round barrow, a complicated mound of earth or chalk rubble interlaced with cut turfs (Ashbee 1960). In this case (plate IV:1) the burial chamber is that of a stone cist, while others are rotted-away wooden chambers. None of these may be considered chambered tombs because there is no access to them from the outside. Plate II:3 looks down into the king's tomb, where he is laid out with the grave furniture buried with him. His skeletal remains indicate a man about 6 feet 4 inches tall, a dominating figure for the time.

I have decorated the stone slabs walling the cist with the Stonehenge art motive, after the lozenge-shaped design inscribed on the king's gold breastplate, but no evidence for such exists. The intention is rather to evoke something of the immaterial idea behind the burial. Most suggestive is a kingly tomb from Kivik in Sweden. See fig. 79. Kivik is in Scania, the ancient name for the southern tip of the Scandinavian peninsula, now famous for its prehistoric carvings on the sloping face of the bare rock scoured by glaciers. Pictured in fig. 79, from a 1784 engraving, is a huge round barrow formed of piled up stones. When these were being removed in the eighteenth century for local building material the stone cist within was exposed. All the walling slabs of the cist are inscribed with elaborate designs. The one shown here depicts fancy bronze axes, which probably date to about 1000 B.C., but no one really knows.

Drawings of this and other slab inscriptions are given in fig. 80. The one at top left outlines the axes, with stylized boat below. Top right depicts some horses, bottom left two four-spoked sun discs. Bottom right looks like a funeral ceremony, including chariot racing (from Gelling and Davidson 1969:98). All repeat features

4. The Reconstructions 111

Fig. 79. *Burial mound at Kivik; from a Swedish engraving published in the 1780s.*

of the Scanian rock carvings: disk, ship, ax, horse. In decorating slabs of the Stonehenge king's cist I had these other images in mind, but with much more abstract designs.

Tara

Although the cemetery on the hill of Tara is largely obliterated, what remains of it indicates a once expansive reach not unlike the one at Stonehenge, and with

Fig. 80. *Drawings of carvings on slabs lining stone cist at Kivik; from Gelling and Davidson 1969.*

the same contextual meaning. Certainly no royal burials are to be found there comparable to Bush Barrow. But the poet of Tara in the metrical *Dindshenchas* says,

> On these high beloved grounds,
> Many are the burial mounds,
> Where, with fame that never dies,
> Many a king and noble lies.

Moreover a rich tradition records the names, personalities and feats of a whole succession of Tara overkings. Indeed, some Irish families even today trace their ancestry to the O'Neills, a long line of them, traditionally elected by special families like the O'Hagans and O'Cahans who had that hereditary right.

5. Race Track

STONEHENGE

When kings were elected by members of the royal clan, no rule of primogeniture applied as with much later dynastic kingship. Elections were not finally ruled out until the Holy Roman Emperor Charles IV so decreed in the fourteenth century, the last holdout being Denmark. The pre-dynastic method entailed formal election courts, as Dr. Wormius presupposed for the prehistoric *comitalia loca* he surveyed in his homeland. Although kingship itself was not hereditary, the pool of electors belonged to a hereditary nobility. They kept royalty contained within their exclusive group of kinsmen.

The race track at Stonehenge, I propose, served the purpose of disposing of defunct kings' property, no more inheritable than royal power. The solution to this ancient problem is quite simple: put the property up for grabs in athletic contests. The Stonehenge solution is not unusual, given other examples actually documented, as we shall see. Had not professional archaeologists been so quick to judge the antiquarian William Stukeley a rank amateur, they may have been led to the conclusion he reached in *Stonehenge* (1740). See fig. 81.

His drawing of the site in question he named the Cursus. The immensely elongated enclosure, just north of Stonehenge, runs west and east for a distance of a mile and three-quarters, with parallel sides 300 feet apart, each marked by a low bank and ditch. The western end is closed by a rounded continuation of the same

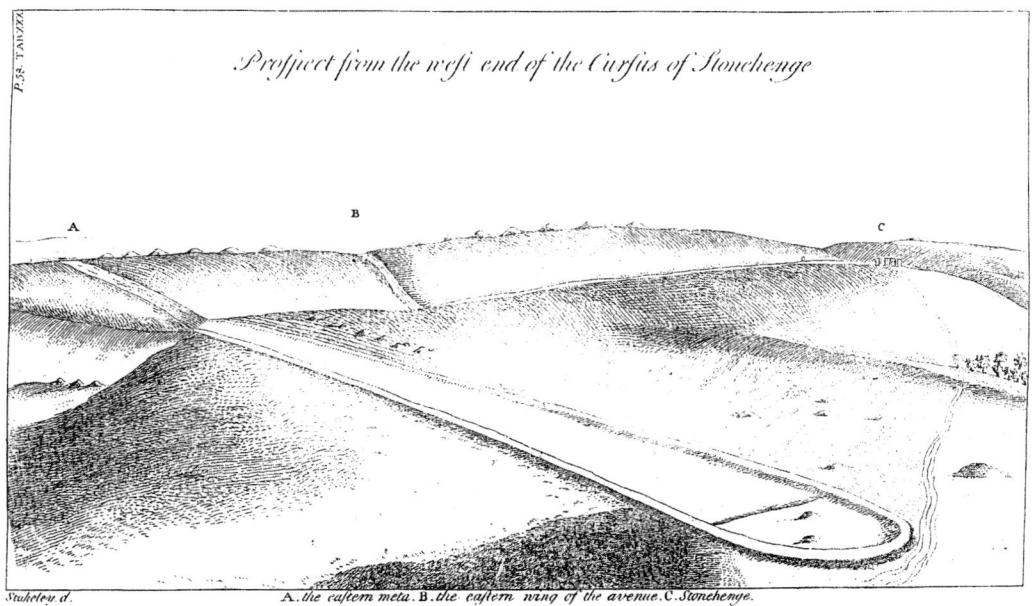

Fig. 81. *The Cursus, looking east; from Stukeley 1740.*

bank and ditch, marked off with a line of demarcation. Within that terminal area are two long barrows. This might suggest a construction of the late Neolithic, but not necessarily so. Maybe the Cursus was designed to so enclose those two barrows at its terminus. The eastern end is also rounded, but without the same internal features.

Stukeley, versed in classical letters, named the Cursus after the example of Roman race tracks. But he went further to suggest that the one at Stonehenge was intended for the celebration of funeral games. He could not know how right he was. My reconstruction of a foot-racing scene at Stonehenge builds on Stukeley's insight into such as an athletic funeral game. Add to that a reference to good evidence from Bronze Age Mycenae and from a remote corner of continental Europe at the time of King Alfred: a convincing relic of ancient custom.

In Mycenaean Greece, according to Homer, King Agamemnon initiated funeral games in honor of Patroclus. Agamemnon's purpose was to bring warring parties within his ambitiously-conceived empire under a periodic sword-truce, during which the parties fought not for war-booty but for prizes won in sports events. The prizes were at first the goods of deceased kings or of fallen battle heroes. The athletic trophies were symbolic vessels called "eared tripods," the ancestor of today's loving-cup with its two ear-shaped handles. These games eventually became the Olympiads of classical Greece, held at Olympia from 776 B.C. From the evidence of Greek vase paintings, funeral games (usually a fight to the death) consisted of five events — chariot racing, boxing, wrestling, footracing, and fighting in armor (Thomson 1949). The Romans elaborated this last into the gladiatorial games. Indeed, gladiators were first known as *bustarii*, "funeral men," because they once performed on private estates of the wealthy to honor a deceased relative (Pearson 1973).

The next evidence relating to Stonehenge funeral games, even more telling, comes from the pen of King Alfred in a ninth-century work on the geography of Europe. It reports a voyage he sent out to explore the Baltic coast, reported back by one Wolfstan. The most interesting observation concerns a geographical area somewhere east of what is now Gdansk, a Polish seaport. Alfred says, digesting Wolfstan, that when a wealthy man dies his corpse is preserved until the annual assembly and then his possessions are laid out at the finish line of a race track. Here the corpse lies with his worldly goods, the prize for the swiftest horse rider.

> Then all those are to be summoned together who have the fleetest horses in the land, for a wager of skill, within the distance of from five or six miles from these heaps; and they all ride a race toward the substance of the deceased [Ingram 1807:83].

Although the wealthy man in question is not designated as a kingly figure, who else could he be? No capitalist economy then existed to concentrate wealth apart from the robberies of war.

Now for my reconstruction of a racing scene on the Cursus near Stonehenge. In plate V:1 are depicted five footracers approaching the finish line marked by a dead king's personal goods. Their bodies are tattooed with art motifs representing the five different kingdoms ruled by the Stonehenge overking, on whose home ground this event takes place. The tattooes are not inconsistent with the Celtic practice of so marking warriors with family or clan designs, a custom that surely traces back to the steppe warriors buried at Pazirik. Standing at the finish line are some shamanistic proto–Druids, organizers of the event. They are dressed with as much imagination as may be applied to their archaic graves.

One last thing is worth noting. Stukeley not only discovered and first described the Cursus, he also discovered the faint remains of what he called the "Cursus Avenue." This leads directly from Stonehenge to the race track, a significant connection relating to the whole business of elective kingship.

Tara

No archaeological evidence for anything like the Cursus is evident here. All we have is traditional testimony that a circular track for horse racing ran around the Royal Enclosure. Later historical records are replete with accounts of horse racing at all annual assemblies and fairs, or *óenachs*, at every political level (Ettlinger 1952). The conclusion must be that all five features of Stonehenge City — election court, king's palace, banquet hall, cemetery, race track — are the same integral components at Tara when it flourished as the seat of Celtic Ireland's high kings.

Epilogue

Looking Back from the Iron Age

In reconstructing the five main features of Stonehenge City, the capital of a Bronze Age kingdom, I have to a qualified degree modeled it after Tara, the metropolitan center of an Iron Age empire in ancient Ireland. How justify this retrospective look at southern England another age away? For one thing, the caesuras or breaks in the Three Age system tend to overemphasize culture change at the expense of underlying and even more fundamental continuities.

For a really long perspective on the Western world as it evolved, one should find it worth reflecting on how the ancient world, reaching into prehistory, shaped it. Tara is such a rich example for marking the passing of the ages because it shows just how elaborate the culture of the old Celtic civilization could develop under pre-literate circumstances. That of the Gauls whom Caesar conquered was much the same as that of the Irish; the Germanic system, described by Tacitus, was no less complex. The northern peoples who invaded Roman territories and set up the medieval feudal system were barbarous only in the eyes of those peoples they conquered. The main line of cultural development from which current Western practice derives undeniably draws from both sources.

The Iron Age itself overlaps with the industrial revolution and the age of steam followed by the age of petroleum, and now the atomic age. In all this time, however, nothing has changed in the basic design of hand tools still used by today's carpenters and other craftsmen; all of them in their plenteous variety, from handsaws and planes to shears and files, were established by Celtic ironsmiths: every wood- and metal-working tool except the screwdriver (no screws until Britain's industrial revolution). Iron smelting began as a sword-making secret of the Hittites, but it got out when their Anatolian empire collapsed, a matter of historical record. Bronze Age peoples of central and western Europe (archaeologically the proto–Celts) picked up on it. Iron-working then flourished beyond mere weaponry during two rapidly expanding phases, Hallstatt and La Tène, from about 700 to after 100 B.C. when Roman provinces replaced the native order.

Iron (and its carbonized derivative steel) is such a commonplace material of industrial usage that little romance attaches to the discovery of the Iron Age as a prehistoric horizon. But that story is as exotic as any. In 1846, on the shores of Lake Hallstatt in Austria, amid magnificent mountain country, the director of Austrian state mines uncovered a prehistoric village. He called in the Vienna Academy of Sciences to further excavate (the site dates to the first half of the first millennium B.C.). Later (in 1876) Academy archaeologists investigated a prehistoric salt mine nearby. Their finds were spectacular, not for their wealth (precious goods) but for the remarkable degree to which common things had been preserved in salt-laden soil: protective clothing of the miners, the framed leather sacks they used to carry the rock-salt product and their wooden tools.

At that point a Hallstatt culture was established in the literature, one with wider geographical ramifications. Meanwhile important discoveries were being made at La Tène on the shores of Lake Neuchâtel in Switzerland. When in 1858 the lake waters lowered, museum authorities from Zurich went to investigate a number of exposed settlements. The Swiss archaeologists recovered a vast quantity of metalwork: iron swords in their decorated sheaths, spears, shield bosses, horse gear, tools of all kinds together with ornaments, coins, and many other objects. Now the Hallstatt–La Tène type sites connected as phases of a rapidly evolving Iron Age. Soon the two phases in Europe were subdivided into Hallstatt A, B, C, D, and La Tène I, II and III. By now the literature is replete with any number of even more refined typologies.

To generalize all this proliferation, Hallstatt A and B date to the late Bronze Age, C and D to the earliest phase of the Iron Age from 700 B.C. La Tène, from about 500 B.C. spread throughout western Europe and into the British Isles including Ireland. The whole spread coincides with the world of the Celts. After Caesar's conquest of Gaul, La Tène culture disappeared into a Romano-Gallic culture, much as the native order in Britain was absorbed into the Roman empire. Ireland, of course, remained outside the scope of the Roman imperium over northern "barbarians." It alone preserved La Tène culture intact (artwork and all) until the coming of Christianity brought by missionaries of the Roman church from about A.D. 500. That is why ancient Ireland is such a significant relic important to understanding the early transition from Bronze Age to Iron Age.

This brings me at last to explain the logic of looking back from the Iron Age, the Irish Iron Age in particular. The distance from Stonehenge to Tara is not all that far, all things considered. Cultural continuities over lengthy periods of time are too regular to be ignored.

The Iron Age, in its Roman development, includes not only cheap iron for weapons and tools, but also the alphabet, coinage, free craftsmen organized in guilds, and a state tied together with a system of horseback-riding postmen. Cheap, mass produced swords and armor destroyed the monopoly on force held by the old

Bronze Age nobility equipped with expensive metals, and made organized armies possible; alphabetic writing destroyed the monopoly on literacy held by priestly scribes serving Bronze Age kings; and coinage made small business possible, beyond that of kingly dealings in bullion, as did cheap tools make possible the guild-protected independence of artisans. Taken together these features made for a new kind of polity for Iron Age rulers to administer, imperial in scope.

Ancient Ireland, fixed at the La Tène horizon, came remarkably close to full-fledged empire despite the absence of three crucial features: writing of any kind, money, and guilds. Yet evidence remains of an empire-wide network of highways (Raftery 1994), all roads leading to Tara. Traveling them would be couriers bearing oral messages and tribute-giving delegates from the provinces to the capital. Tradition speaks of four underkings subserving the high king at Tara, but a close examination of the record indicates more than that, plus any number of subkings. Tradition rightly praises a succession of high kings for their political skills in holding all this together by creating the majesty and glory and eternal mystique of Tara. Great men they certainly were. No less the Stonehenge kings.

If my analysis at figs. 47 and 48 of the ground plan of the Stonehenge election court is correct, the basic idea behind its layout expresses a cosmological reading of the kingdom's political geography. This anticipates a feature of Celtic mythology, the notion of five cardinal directions: north, east, south, west, and center or *axis mundi*. These mystic directions apply irrespective of actuality. Four of the five kingdoms led by the Stonehenge overking lie directly north and south of the *axis mundi*. At Tara, metropolitan center of a pre-literate Iron Age empire, the myth of five directions is even more fictitious. More than five kingdoms existed; the high king's imperial capital at Tara was situated near Ireland's eastern seaboard; and the many sub-kingdoms he ruled were pretty much aligned north and south along that coast, few located inland to the west. Yet the geographic mythos of five directions dominated political reality. What is most interesting about this aspect of Celtic cosmology is that the proto–Celtic builders of Stonehenge first made it visible. It surely contributed to a mythos manipulated by the high kings of Tara, from which vantage, in a circular way, this book looks back.

Appendix *I*

"To My Honour'd Friend, Dr. Charleton" by John Dryden (1663)

Walter Charleton's esoteric Stonehenge book, more than a treatise by a founding member of the Royal Society, was also a notable literary event, as witnessed by the two ranking poets who each wrote a "commendatory epistle" to it.

The first is by Sir Robert Howard (1626–1698), today judged a minor poet and playwright. As the son of the Earl of Berkshire, imprisoned during the Commonwealth and honored after the Restoration, his name carried political weight. After 1688 he himself entered politics.

The other is by John Dryden (1631–1700), Poet Laureate. Today his verse dramas and occasional poems are canonical. Among the latter is the one dedicated to Dr. Charleton. It is here reproduced, with annotations. Its political significance is as a tribute to England strong and free under the newly restored king, Charles II, whose chartering of the Royal Society of London for Improving Natural Knowledge made London the world capital of modern science. The poem celebrates its most distinguished members, above all Dr. Charleton who had advised the king how and why to organize it.

Interestingly, Dryden's poem opens with an attack on Aristotle, that exemplar of false classical science whose only authority comes by consecrated tradition: no longer enough. He pays especial tribute to Sir Francis Bacon (1561–1626), rightly estimated as the most eloquent propagandist for the new science, now the established norm with its experimental protocol for testable (and practical!) results.

Also noteworthy, the poem reflects a view that literature and science are as one to cultivated minds, a sensibility no longer current: our loss. Indeed, Dr. Charleton saw to it that Dryden was brought into the Royal Society as a poet understanding its mission to advance "free-born *Reason*."

Despite his endorsement of Charleton's work, the Inigo Jones thesis it confutes did not vanish. Jones's pupil John Webb come back at Charleton with a garbled *Vindication* (Webb 1665), remarkable for its hateful *ad hominem* rhetoric. Today Charleton is dismissed as just another in a long line of ignorant antiquarians. He is, however, the very soul of reason arguing from available evidence.

To My Honour'd Friend, Dr. Charleton
on his learned and useful Works; and more particular
this of Stone-Heng, by him Restored to the true Founders

> The longest Tyranny that ever sway'd,
> Was that wherein our Ancestors betray'd
> Their free-born *Reason* to the *Stagirite*,[1]
> And made his Torch their universal Light.
> So *Truth*, while onely one suppli'd the State,
> Grew scarce, and dear, and yet sophisticate,[2]
> Until 'twas bought, like Emp'rique Wares, or Charms,
> Hard words seal'd up with *Aristotle*'s Armes.
> *Columbus* was the first that shook his Throne;
> And found a *Temp'rate* in a *Torrid* Zone:
> The fevrish aire fann'd by a cooling breez,
> The fruitful Vales set round with shady Trees;
> And guiltless *Men*, who danc'd away their time,
> *Fresh* as their *Groves*, and *Happy* as their *Clime*.
> Had we still paid that homage to a *Name*,[3]
> Which onely *God* and *Nature* justly claim;
> The *Western* Seas had been our utmost bound,
> Where *Poets* still might dream the *Sun* was drown'd:
> And all the *Starrs*, that shine in *Southern* Skies,
> Had been admir'd by none but *Salvage*[4] Eyes.
>
> Among th' *Assertors* of free Reason's claim,
> Th' *English* are not the least in Worth, or Fame.
> The World to *Bacon*[5] does not onely owe
> Its *present* Knowledge, but its *future* too.
> *Gilbert*[6] shall live, till *Load-stones* cease to draw,
> Or *British* Fleets the boundless Ocean awe.
> And noble *Boyle*,[7] not less in *Nature* seen,
> Than his great *Brother*[8] read in *States* and *Men*.

1. *Aristotle.* **2.** *Rarified.* **3.** *Aristotle again.* **4.** *Savage.* **5.** *Sir Francis Bacon, mentioned in the headnote. His* Novum organum *(1620) set the program for modern research.* **6.** *Sir William Gilbert (1540–1603), who did decisive work on the properties of magnetism.* **7.** *Robert Boyle (1627–1691), of Boyle's Law on the nature of gasses. For students of chemistry today it is the outstanding example of deduction from observed laboratory experiments.* **8.** *Sir Roger Boyle (1621–1679), Irish brother of Robert Boyle, a politician "read in States and Men." At first he had sided with the Cromwellians against the royalists in the English Civil War, then changed his mind after the Restoration, having been*

The *Circling* streams, once thought but pools, of blood
(Whether Life's fewel, or the Bodie's food)
From dark Oblivion *Harvey*'s[9] name shall save;
While *Ent*[10] keeps all the honour that he gave.
Nor are *You*, Learned Friend, the least renown'd;
Whose Fame, not circumscrib'd with *English* ground,
Flies like the nimble journeys of the *Light*;
And is, like that, unspent too in its flight.
What ever *Truths* have been, by *Art*, or *Chance*,
Redeem'd from *Error*, or from *Ignorance*,
Thin in their *Authors*, (like rich veins of Ore)
Your Works unite, and still discover more.
Such is the healing virtue of Your Pen,
To perfect Cures on *Books*, as well as *Men*.
Nor is This Work the least: You well may give
To *Men* new vigour, who make *Stones* to live.
Through You, the *DANES* (their short Dominion lost)
A longer Conquest than the *Saxons* boast.
STONE-HENG, once thought a *Temple*, You have found
A *Throne*, where Kings, our Earthly Gods, were Crown'd
Where by their wondring Subjects They were seen,
Joy'd with their Stature, and their Princely meen.
Our *Soveraign* here above the rest might stand;
And here be chose again to rule the Land.

   These Ruines sheltered once *His* Sacred Head,[11]
Then when from *Wor'sters* fatal Field *He* fled;
Watch'd by the Genius[12] of this Royal place,
And mighty Visions of the *Danish* Race.
His *Refuge* then was for a *Temple* shown:
But, *He* Restor'd, 'tis now become a *Throne*.[13]

convinced that Oliver Cromwell's Commonwealth was a tyranny for its brutal war against the independence movement in Ireland. When the Restoration of Charles II seemed inevitable, he as a member of Parliament secured peace with Ireland for the king, gaining him the title 1st Earl of Orrey. **9.** *William Harvey (1578–1657), who discovered the circulation of the blood.* **10.** *Sir George Ent (1604–1689), friend and champion of Harvey.* **11.** *The reference here of course is to Charles II, son of Charles I who was executed by Cromwell. Charles II then fled to exile in France. On the way he hid himself among the ruins of Stonehenge, following the battle of Worcester (1651), in which his avenging army was defeated. His victorious return, with the aid of French soldiers, is the Restoration in English history. This explains the king's interest in Stonehenge, and his commissioning his learned physician to study it. Dryden's poem ties the Restoration with the restoring of Stonehenge to a royal seat of power, not as a Roman temple of classical design seen in it by Inigo Jones, the royal architect to James I. That king was the last of the execrable absolutists. By comparison Charles II was more enlightened for his chartering of the Royal Society in the spirit of free and rational inquiry, much appreciated by intellectuals of the time.* **12.** *Presiding spirit.* **13.** *These last two lines make clear that Charleton's work refutes Inigo Jones, who proposed Stonehenge as a temple of classical design in Roman times. This equates with the absolutism of James I, served by Jones as the royal architect, and with the outworn tradition of classical science exemplified by Aristotle: the point of Dryden's attack on him in the opening lines.*

CHOREA GIGANTUM,

OR,

The most Famous Antiquity of

GREAT-BRITAN,

Vulgarly called

STONE-HENG,

Standing on *Salisbury* Plain,

Restored to the

DANES.

By *Walter Charleton*, Dr in Physic, and Physician in Ordinary to His Majesty.

Quæ per constructionem lapidum, & marmoreas moles, aut terrenos tumulos in magnam eductos altitudinem, constant; non propagabunt longam diem: quippe & ipsa intereunt.

Seneca, de Consolat. ad Polyb.

LONDON,
Printed for *Henry Herringman*, at the Sign of the *Anchor* in the Lower Walk of the *New Exchange*. 1663.

Appendix *II*

Excerpts from *Stone-heng* by Walter Charleton (1663)

It is only fitting that Dr. Charleton's own words be recalled in a book dedicated to his worthy memory. His theory of Stonehenge is of course very wide of the mark in attributing the monument's construction to the Vikings. More insightful is his *political* concept of the place as a court royal for the election of pre-dynastic kings: the very idea inspiring the present work.

Generous excerpts from Charleton form this appendix. They amply illustrate the temper of his argument. As a charter member and chief organizer of the Royal Society, he more than any one man first institutionalized the spirit of modern science. His book on Stonehenge exhibits that spirit, reasonably argued from the evidence, even as he leaves open revision of his theory by others. He is not dogmatic.

This appendix includes five excerpts, each with its own headnote. Some quaint differences in seventeenth-century typography have been modernized, but otherwise the text is as published. The style of writing is as plain and direct and lucid as can be for the time, similar to the best scientific monographs done for the Royal Society. What comes through, if the reader allow for locutional differences, is hardheaded reasoning and logical discourse.

Excerpt 1. Charleton begins by reviewing the extant literature on Stonehenge. First is Geoffrey of Monmouth's ever-popular account of Merlin's magic and witchcraft, which is "absurd and ridiculous." Besides, Geoffrey leaves in doubt "not only what King, Prince, or General, but also what Nation it was, that bequeathed this Wonder for a Legacy."

Next Charleton turns his attention to William Camden's entry on Stonehenge in his encyclopedic *Britannia* of 1586. Camden was the chief historian and antiquarian of Elizabethan times. His massive work went through six editions and achieved such a scholarly repute that it set the model for the lasting authority of the *Encyclopædia Britannica*, whose first edition (three thick volumes) appeared in 1771.

The sixth edition (1607) of Camden's renowned encyclopedia reproduced an otherwise lost print of Stonehenge by William Rogers titled "The Giants' Dance." This keeps Geoffrey's Latin tag *Chorea Gigantum*, the very title of Charleton's book. Rogers humanizes the monument by picturing many of the sarsen uprights as writhing giants. This contrasts with Charleton's realistic depiction in fig. 3. The Rogers print (fig. 82) he attaches to the following quotation from, and comment on, Camden's encyclopedia entry.

You, perhaps, have not yet beheld this Monument, or at least not taken a survey of it in its stately ruines; and, therefore, it behoveth me to prepare you the better to judge of its Antiquity, and Design, by entertaining you in the first place with the

Description of Stone-heng, by Mr. Camden.

"About six miles from *Salisbury*, northward (saith He) on *Salisbury* Plain, is to be seen a huge and monstrous piece of work, such as *Cicero* termeth *insanam substructionem*. For, within the circuit of a ditch, there are erected, in a manner of a Crown, in three ranks or courses, one within another, certain mighty and unwrought stones; whereof some are twenty eight foot high, and seven foot broad: upon the heads of which others, like overthwart pieces, do bear and rest crosswise, with small tenents and mortescies, so as the whole frame seemeth to hang; whereof we call it STONE-HENG, like as our old Historians termed it, for the greatness, *Chorea Gigantum*, the Giants Dance."

Then, to illustrate his description, He subjoyns this Draught, or *Figure*.
Where *A*. denoteth the Perpendicular stones, called Corse-stones, weighing twelve Tunn, carrying in hight twenty four Foot, in breadth seven Foot, and in compass sixteen: and
B. the Overthwart stones, called Cronets, or six or seven Tunn weight.

Here in all likelihood, You will a little wonder, both by what way *Mr. Camden* could attain to the weight of these so ponderous masses, so as to be positive in the assignment of it: and why, having first made the altitude of the Erected stones, or Columns to be twenty eight foot, he immediately, in the explication of his pourtraict, brings it down to onely twenty four foot. Nor, indeed, can I ease you of that wonder; otherwise than by referring the former to his meer Conjecture, and the other to his Forgetfulness. But this transitory remarque is of as small importance to our main scrutiny; as His description comes short of that satisfaction, which is required to an exact survey of all parts of the wonder. Let us pass, therefore, if your curiosity and leisure permit, to the more ample [excerpt 2].

Excerpt 2. Although Camden's brief account of Stonehenge seems insignificant, Charleton quotes it because in his day it carried the authoritative weight of Camden's impeccable scholarship on every subject covered by his encyclopedia. What Stonehenge looks like is a common enough perception today, but that was not always so. Charleton refers to Camden's description for the simple reason that he had to establish the true features of the monument before he went on to advance

Fig. 82. *Old print of Stonehenge in Camden's encyclopedia reproduced by Charleton.*

his theory of it. His realistic drawing in fig. 3 was unprecedented and forms the most basic element of his argument.

We today can scarcely imagine how difficult was the historical struggle to arrive at even the most obvious description of what Stonehenge actually looks like. The struggle to explain it still goes on. The explanation offered by Inigo Jones (1655) is faulted by Charleton in the first place because even Jones, a professional architect, failed to see what was there; he drafted a totally unreal representation.

Today's reader will find tedious Charleton's detailed architectural critique, but he had more than the monument's visual appearance to deal with. Jones had been Architect-General to James I, under whom he brought about the great and glorious classical revival. For that he was celebrated as the English Vitruvius, a reference to Marcus Vitruvius Pollio, the first century B.C. Roman architect and author of *De Architectura*, a ten-volume work consulted by Italian Renaissance architects. Jones did the same for the classical revival in England. His triumph he then imposed on his restoration of Stonehenge to the Romans in the time of Agricola in A.D. 79. No less specifically he named it a temple "inscribed to Coelus [Uranus], the Senior of the Heathen Gods, and built after the Tuscan Order." At the same time he celebrated the monarch, James I, who commissioned the study.

In the first sentence of excerpt 2 below, Charleton refers to John Webb, who actually authored the Jones book from "some few indigested notes" and published it posthumously for him in 1655 (Jones died at age 80 in 1652). Webb took offense at Charleton's disproof of the Vitruvian symmetry Jones claimed for the monument. Two years later he came back with a spiteful, not to say hateful personal attack on Charleton in *A Vindication* (1665). He had no other ground to stand on since the Jones restoration is indefensible in every detail. But look behind this personalized bitterness and you will see the unmistakable factional politics of Jacobites versus the House of Stuart to which Charles II belonged and whom Charleton served. Webb is clearly a die-hard Jacobite, or apologist for the absolutist monarchy of James I whom Webb's father-in-law served (see Kenyon 1981 under Jacobites and Stuart, house of).

The reference to Webb is to his Preface to the text ostensibly written by Jones himself, although it is in fact Webb's done from his master's notes. Charleton quotes key passages he intends to explicate for their misperception of reality. Among the features he touches upon is what Jones calls the "Greater Hexagon." My fig. 83 illustrates that imaginary configuration of the trilithons. Later Charleton goes on to discredit even Jones's typing of his own restoration as a structure built to the Tuscan Order. Because Jones was the first to do a book-length study of Stonehenge, Charleton perforce had to analyze it in detail before advancing his radical revision.

Description of Stone-heng, by Mr. Inigo Jones.

Who being, and not unworthily, called by *Mr. Web* (in his preface to *Mr. Jones* his Book, entituled *Stone-heng Restored*) the *English Vitruvius*; and having, as Himself professeth, in the 56 *page* of the same Book, with no little pains, and charge, measured the whole work, and diligently searched the Foundations of it: seems to promise us a more full account in all particulars.

"This Antiquity (saith He) because the *Architraves* are set upon the heads of the upright stones, and hang as it were in the air, is generally known by the name of *Stone-heng*. The whole work, in general, being of a Circular form, is 110. foot diameter; double winged about, without a roof; anciently environed with a deep trench, still appearing about thirty foot broad. So that betwixt it, and the work itself, a large and void space of ground being left; it had from the Plain three open Entrances, the most conspicuous whereof lies North-east. At each of which was raised, on the outside of the Trench aforesaid, two huge stones, Gate-wise; parallel whereunto, on the inside, two others of less proportions. The Inner part of the work, consisting of an Exagonal figure, was raised, by due symmetry, upon the bases of four Equilateral Triangles, which formed the whole Structure. This inner part likewise was double, having within it also another Exagon raised; and all that part within the Trench, sited upon a commanding ground, eminent, and higher by much than any of the Plain lying without, and in the middest thereof upon a foundation of hard Chalk, the work it self was placed. Insomuch, that from what part soever they came unto it, they rose by an ascending hill.

"In the inmost part is a Stone appearing not much above the surface of the Earth,

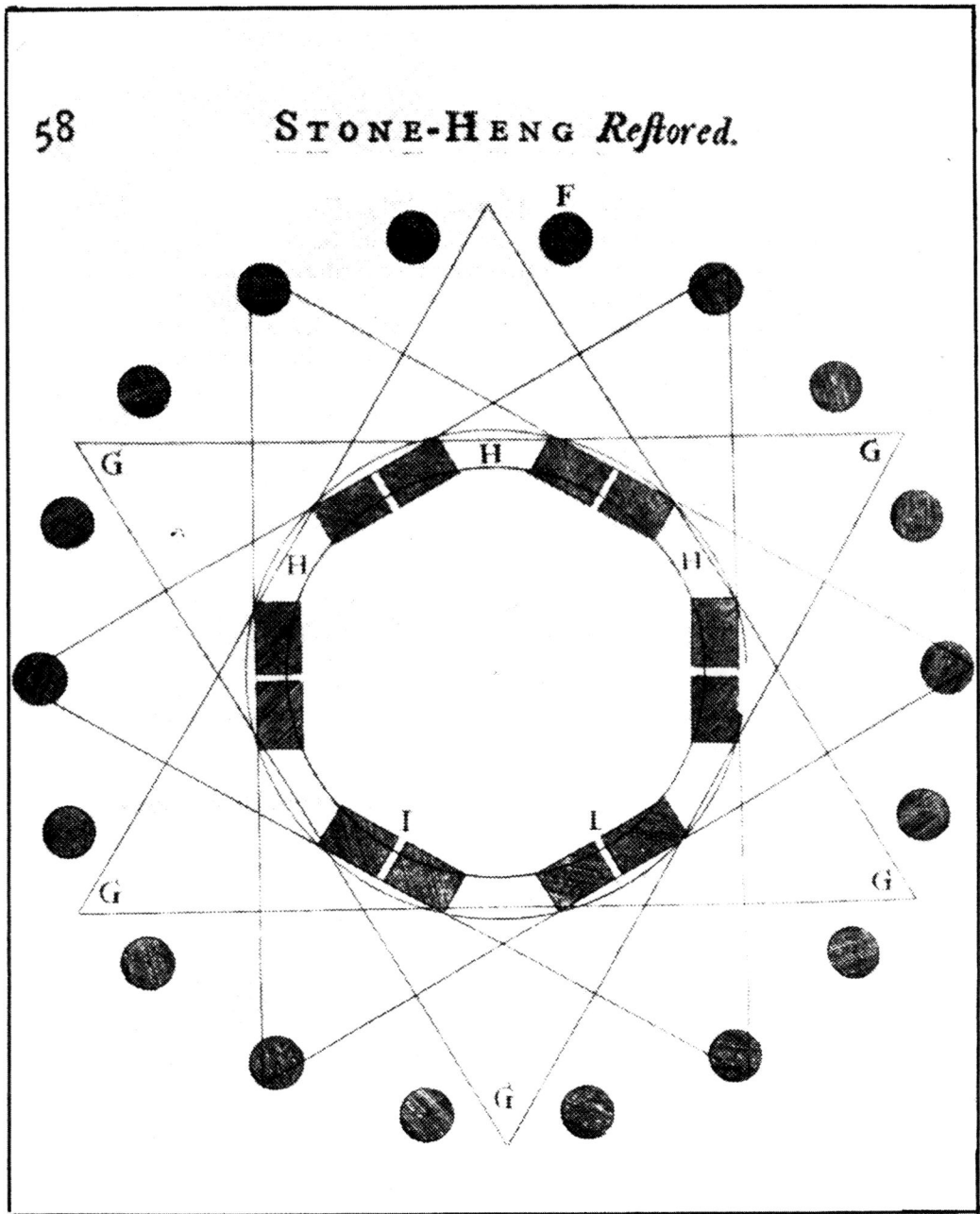

Fig. 83. *Imaginary ground plan of Stonehenge by Inigo Jones.*

and lying towards the East, four foot broad, and sixteen in length. Which, whether an Altar, or no, I leave to the judgment of others.

"The Great Stones, which made the Entrances from the outside of the Trench, are seven foot broad, three thick, and twenty high.

"Their Parallels, on the inside of the Trench, are four foot broad, and three thick; but so broken, their proportions in hight cannot be exactly measured.

"The stones, which make the Outward Circle, carry in breadth seven foot, in thickness 3 and ½, and in hight 15 and ½: each stone having two Tenons mortaised into the Architrave continuing upon them, throughout the whole circumference. For, these Architraves being joynted directly in the middle of each of the Perpendicular stones, that their weight might have an equal bearing; and up on each side of the joynt a Tenon wrought (as remains yet to be seen): it may positively be concluded thereby, the Architrave continued round about this Outward Circle.

"The smaller stones of the Inner Circle are two foot and ½ in breadth, 1. thick, and 6. high. These had no Architrave upon them, but were raised perpendicular, of a Pyramidal form.

"The Stones of the Greater Hexagon, 7. foot and ½ in breadth, three foot nine inches in thickness, and twenty foot in hight; each having one Tenon in the middle.

"The stones of the Inner Hexagon, 2. foot 6. inches broad, 1. foot and ½ thick, and eight foot high; in form Pyramidal, like those of the Inner Circle.

"The Architrave lying round about upon the Perpendicular stones of the Outward Circle, is three foot and ½ broad, two foot and ½ high or thick.

"The Architrave on the top of the great stones of the Outward Hexagon, 16. foot long, 3. foot 9. inches broad, 3. foot 4 inches high. This Architrave continuing onely from stone to stone, left betwixt every two and two, a void space, free to the air, uncovered.

"After this Survey (and some other Designs, that he fancied correspondent thereunto) He obligeth his Readers with the whole work in Prospective, as it now lies in its ruines, representing itself to the eye thus."

[Here Charleton refers to a Jones drawing he expects his readers to be familiar with. It is like my fig. 4 but with letters tagging certain features. Charleton addresses letter P and Q.]

> In which P. represents the manner of the Tenons, of a round form, mortaised into the Architrave of the Outward Circle: and
> Q. the Tenons of the like form, in the middle of the stones of the Greater Hexagon.

Reflecting upon these two Descriptions, and comparing them together with due care: You'l find them at open variance, and differing in so many, and so considerable particulars, that 'twill be a hard task for you to keep them from mutually discrediting each other. For

(1.) *Mr. Camden* expresly affirm's, He observed the Ranks, or Courses, in which all the Stones were erected, to be only *Three*, one within another; and *Mr. Jones* as confidently avouches, He found them to be *Four*.

(2.) The *Former* saith all those three Courses are *Circular*: the *Later* saith, of his four, two only are Circular, the other two *Hexagonal*.

(3.) *This* gives you a punctual account of *Three open Entrances*, marked with two huge stones perpendicularly raised on the outside of the Trench, and other two of lesser dimensions in like manner fited on the inside, in position parallel: *That* is utterly silent concerning any such matter; yea implicitly denies it, in that hee delivered, that all the stones observed the circumferences of their proper Circles.

(4.) In like manner, the *One* stumbles upon an *Altar-stone* (for such He conceived, and such He would have us believe it to be, notwithstanding his seeming to leave men to the liberty of their own judgment in that point:) over which the *Other* leaped cleerly, without so much as ever touching it.

(5.) *Mr. Camden* assignes to the Perpendicular stones of the largest size, twenty four foot of Altitude: but *Mr. Jones* will not allow them to exceed twenty foot.

Behold, here, a notable Example of the *discrepancy of Mens judgements, even in things easily determinable by the sense! and how hard it is to discern truth with others eyes!* What, then, shall we conclude on in the case? Upon whose relation may we, with greateset security to our belief, depend? If we compare the *Reputations* of these two Authors; we find them equally high and venerable: the One being worthily esteemed one of the principal *Antiquaries*, and most Learned men of his time; the Other as worthily reckoned among the most excellent *Architects* this Nation ever bred, and a general Scholar. If we ballance their several *Abilities* respective to the matter in hand; no great advantage of weight appears on either side: for if *Mr. Jones* were more conversant in *Vitruvius*, and more exact in the Rules of *Geometry*; Mr. Camden was not ignorant of the Art of Designing taught by the one, nor unacquainted with the use of the *Other*, as is evident from many passages in his immortal Writings. However, he was certainly skilfull enough in the common wayes of measuring and surveying, not to be mistaken in the dimensions and platform of Stoneheng. If we compute the *Times*, in which they severally took their draughts of this Wonder; the difference will be so small, as not to solve the variousness of them: for, they were Contemporaries, and not above forty years, at most, seem to have intervened betwixt the Writing of one and the other, concerning this Argument. A small space of time to wear off four foot of hardest stone from the heads of the Perpendiculars or Columns; especially considering not so much as an inch is diminished from their sides. And much too short a time, for so many new stones to grow up in, as *Mr. Jones* discovered more than the other perceived. Lastly, as for their *Veracity*; that's a thing sacred, admitting of neither dispute, nor comparison; and 'twere breach of Charity not to be confident of this; that both of them had so great devotion and reverence toward the majesty of Truth, as neither would dare to offend her, by willingly deluding the present and future ages, with counterfeit Certificates, or by adding or diminishing, where they pretend to exactness and fidelity. And yet notwithstanding, such is their misfortune, and our trouble, we cannot give credit to both at once: that one hath mistaken, is manifest; that both were mistaken, and about the same particulars, is improbable; to determine on which side the Error lies, is difficult, but by a new survey; and to reconcile them in all points, seems impossible. Wherefore, though the clue of my slender Observations upon the place, be not strong enough to conduct you out of this Labyrinth: yet, I hope, my zeal to truth may excuse my plainness and freedome, if I adventure to assure you, that having more than once or twice delighted my self with viewing this admirable Antiquity, and with all possible attentiveness of mind contemplated the form, order, and parts of it; I alwaies observed *Mr. Camdens* Draught to come much neerer in resemblance both to the work it self, and to the idea thereof formed in my Imagination out of its ruines, than that bequeathed to the world by *Mr. Jones*, though much more elaborate and artificial. Neverthelesse, the Model I have conceived of the whole Fabrique in General, being not cast in the mould of Architectonical Principles, nor adjusted by the maxims of Geometry; but rude and simple, such as my Eyes delivered in to my brain: I think it not worth the labour of Copying; but leave every man to the liberty of fancying as he pleaseth, when he hath sufficiently gazed upon the Original. In the mean time, let us proceed to our Capital Enquiry, *Who were the Authors of this stupendious Building,* that doth so amaze and amuse its beholders.

Excerpt 3. Today Stonehenge is the province of university archaeologists who argue from a rich store of excavated prehistory, and from sophisticated cross-cultural comparisons. Charleton's model for reasoning through the problem is no less sophisticated, although the resources he argued from were far more limited. These reduce to Camden's encyclopedic entry, his own field survey, classical references, and his correspondence with the equally learned Dr. Wormius.

In this excerpt Charleton critiques the claim for Roman architecture made by Jones, and then moves on to undermine Jones's conclusion that the monument was a temple erected to the heathen god Coelus. He brings to bear a thorough knowledge of classical letters, and cites them in his in-text references the way it still is done. Of unusual interest is his telling of the discovering at Stonehenge in the time of Henry VIII of a metal plate with writing inscribed on it, and how he consulted the best linguists of the day to translate it; they could not. Today, as I report in chapter 1, the riddle of this now lost tablet is at last resolved.

The reader may find this excerpt lengthy but it is too significant to ignore. Charleton wrote at the very start of Stonehenge studies, and developed a model that still applies even to a vastly different data base.

Mr. Jones *his Opinion, then, of the Founders, Antiquity and Design of Stone-heng, is*

That it was a work of the ROMANS, built by them, when they florished here in greatest peace and prosperity, and happily betwixt the times of Agricola's *government, and the reign of* Constantine *the Great, about 1560 years agoe; not as a Sepulchral Monument, but as a Temple, and particularly consecrated to the imaginary Deity of* Coelus, *or* Coelum, *from whence their superstitious belief derived the original of all things.*

The *Grounds* whereon He advanced, and *Reasons* with which He endeavoured to support this so new and strange surmise; being brought into order, and few words, are these that follow.

First, that the *Romans* were, and no other Nation could be Founders of *Stone-heng*, He argueth from (1.) the *Magnificence*; (2.) the *Order*; (3.) the *Architectonical Scheme*; (4.) the double *Portico* in the greater *Circle* of Stones, and another *Portico* in the *Cell*, or *Hexagon*; (5.) the *Manner* and *Position* of the Columns of the Building; and (6.) from the Roman *Reliques* frequently found neer the place.

Secondly, that it was a *Temple*, He would infer from (1.) the *Interval*, or spacious Court round about; (2.) the *Cell*, and its *Porticoes*; (3.) the *Altar*, and its position Eastward; (4.) the *Mixt*, or Compound *Order*; (5.) the *Aspect* of the whole Fabrique; and (6.) from the *Skuls of Beasts* digged up in the circumjacent ground.

Thirdly, that this so plausibly imagined Temple was consecrated in particular to the God, *Coelus*; He concludeth from (1.) the *Situation*; (2.) the *Aspect Hypæthros*; (3.) the *Manner*, or *Form*; (4.) the *Order*; (5.) the *Decorum* of the structure; (6.) the *Pyramidal* Figure of the stones; and (7.) from the *Kinds* of Beasts customarily offered in sacrifice to that Deity. And this is the Summary of all those particulars, from whose concurrent hints He seems to have deduced his Invention.

An Invention exceedingly fine and subtle, I confess; favouring of a pregnant Wit, and no small Learning, especially in the mysteries of ancient Architecture in use among the *Romans*; and therefore much applauded by some of more than vulgar judgment; yet not so firmly founded, as to be impregnable; nor so closely compacted in all its parts, as to keep out all weather of Contradiction. Wherefore though it be far from my design to batter and demolish it (for, in truth, it deserves to stand; though meerly for the pleasantness:) yet my devotion to truth, and the interest of my present disquisition concur to excuse my boldness, if having brought you to it, I adventure to shew you the several Flaws, chinks, and defects discoverable therein; leaving it at last to your own judgment, whether it be strong enough to secure any mans belief, that shall set up his rest in it.

Let us, therefore, begin at the First Partition, *viz. That Stone-heng was a piece of Roman Architecture*; and carefully view the strength of those Reasons alleged to prove it so to be.

(First,) As for the *Magnificence* thereof; what *Aristotle* (4. *Eth. cap.* 2.) terms μεγαλοπρέπειχ, the Latines *Magnificentia & Majestas*, doth not consist alone in the Magnitude or Massiness of either the Materials of a Building, or the whole Pile (for, then those huge stones lying one upon another, call'd *Wringchees*, in *Cornwall*, would be a magnificent structure): but in an artificial Decorum, or agreeable pulchritude conjoyned with greatness of bulk. Which two Qualities meeting together in any Fabrique, cause it to present it self to the eye with a certain twofold gracefulness or majesty, that instantly raiseth a kind of Respect, and where it is rare and excellent, a kind of delightfull Wonder also in the beholders. So that we use not to call Great things, Majestical, in respect of their large dimensions alone: nor Little things, Magnificent, notwithstanding their Elegancy. And this I conceive to be the adæquate notion of *Magnificence* among all Architects. Now, according to this notion, though the stones of *Stone-heng* be, indeed, extraordinarily big and ponderous; yet forasmuch as they are rude, rough, craggy, and difform among themselves, and destitute of any great Art or Elegancy in their general disposition and construction; I perceive my self under no constraint or necessity of apprehending it as a Magnificent building, at least in so high a degree, as *Mr. Jones* would have us believe, when He affirms, *that betwixt* Rome *and our island, there is no Monument, in which the Roman Magnificence is more conspicuous, then in this*. If by Magnificence He meant *Magnum apparatum*, the difficulty of the Means, strength of Engines, multitude of hands, length of time, &c. necessarily made use of in bringing together, and raising so many and so large stones; then doth his Inference fall to the ground: there being many antique Monuments yet remaining, some in *England*, others in *Scotland*, others again in *Denmark* and *Norway*; which consisting of the like materials, and those perhaps further fetcht too, could not but require like strength, labour, and art to their erection, and yet the *Romans* had no hand in setting up either of them; as shall be made appear, when the thread of my discourse hath brought me to mention them more opportunely. Furthermore, what judicious Eye, that hath once beheld the remains of *Diocletian's* Baths, *Nero's* Palace, *Marcellus* his Theatre, *Vespasians* Temple of Peace, the great *Cirque*, or other the monstrous buildings of the *Romans* in *Italy*; can afterward fancy any such thing as Roman Magnificence in this formless Uniform Heap of massy stones at *Stone-heng*? there being as little of proportion or resemblance betwixt this and those, as betwixt *St. Pancrace* Church, and *St. Pauls*; or as betwixt a Welsh montaineers cottage, and the Royal Palace of *Hampton Court*. Nor am I alone of this judgment; for the *Author* of the life of *Nero Cæsar*, formerly cited, apprehended so little of Magnificence in the thing, that from the very *Rudeness* thereof He concludes it (though erroneously) to have been a work of the *Britains*.

(Secondly,) As for the *Order*, which *Mr. Jones* affirms to be the *Tuscan*; that you may the more cleerly discern, whether any such thing was observed by the Builders of *Stone-heng*, in that work, or not, it is needfull for me to put you in mind at least, What that Tuscan Order is, what Conditions it hath that are Common to the other orders also, and what distinct Proprieties. The Ancient Roman Architects generally divided their structures *in parietes continuos, & intermissos*, into *Intire* or *Continned* walls, and *Intermissions* made by Columns or Pillars. Of these *Columns* they had, partly from the *Grecians*, partly of their own invention, Five different Kinds, or sorts; which reckoned according to their respective dignity and prefection, are the *Tuscan, Doric, Ionic, Corinthian*, and *Compound*, or (as it is commonly named) *Italic*. The *Tuscan* (which alone relates to our present business) *est plana, massiva, seu rustica columna, similis robusto alicui & benè artuato ruricolæ, viliter amicto*, is a plain, massive, or rustical Column, carrying some resemblance to a strong and well-limbed Country-man, meanly clad; as *Vitruvius* (*lib.* 4. *cap.* 1) not unfitly describes it. The *Conditions* common to this Pillar with the rest, are principally *Three*, according to *Sr. H.*

Wottons enumeration of them, *in prima parte Elementorum Architecturæ*, for the Excellency thereof translated into Latin by *John de Laet*. *First*, the Pillars of all the Orders are *Rotundæ figuræ*, of a Round figure. For, though some conceive the Column *Atticurges*, of which *Vitruvius* speaks (*lib.* 3. *cap.* 3.) was Square; yet was it lookt upon as irregular, and never admitted into the orders, but among other extravagant inventions, condemned by Him. *Secondly, Omnes diminuuntur & contrahuntur insensibiliter, plus aut minus, secundùm proportionem suæ altitudinis, ab tertia parte scapi sui sursum*, All are Contracted or lessened insensibly, more or less, according to the proportion of their altitude, from the third part of their Scape, or lower part, upward. Which *Guilielm. Philander*, (one of the best Interpreters of *Vitruvius*,) from the exact dimensions of sundry antique Remains survey'd by himself, prescribes *tanquam venustissimam diminutionem*, as the most comely and gracefull diminution; and most resembling the Taper growth of Pinetrees, from whose pattern the Figure of all Columns was first taken. *Thirdly, Omnes suos habent Stylobatas, altitudine tertiæ partis totius Columnæ, comprehensa, basi & capitulo*; All have their *Pedestals*, of the hight of the third part of the whole Column, from the base to the head. The *Proprieties* of the *Tuscan* order (to omit others of lesse importance) consist principally in two things, *viz.* the Proportion of the Longitude of the Pillar it self, and the *Intercolumnium*, or distance betwixt Pillar and Pillar. The *Hight*, or Length of the Pillar ought to be *Sex diametrorum crassissimæ partis inferioris ipsius scapi*, six Diameters of its thickness in the biggest part a little above the bottome. For *Vitruvius* (*lib.* 3. *cap.* 1) accounts the length of a Mans foot to be the sixt part of his whole body, in ordinary dimension: and Man, according to *Protagoras*, is τὸ τῶν αϖάντων χρημάτων μέτρον; *of all exact Symmetry the Prototype, or first Exemplar*. And the *Intercolumnium*, or Intervall betwixt the Pillars, is required to be *circiter quatuor illius diametrorum*, of about four Diameters. Now, these Qualifications of the *Tuscan* order being thus set down, on one side of the parallel: let us turn our Eyes upon *Stone-heng* and see what Analogy is to be found therein, to make up the other. (1.) At *Stone-heng*, very few, or none at all of the Upright stones, or Columns are *Round*, no nor in any degree related to that figure; but broad and flat, and mostly resembling Parallelipipeds, rather than Cylinders; as the eye witnesseth. So that here is a manifest inconformity to the Figure required indifferently in all the five orders. (2.) Their *Contraction*, or Lessening upward is not Uniform, but rudely various, in some greater, in others less, in none insensible, in all irregular: so as therein likewise they want the due proportion of Diminution common to all genuinely figured Columns. (3.) They have no *Pedestals* at all, being set in the ground; which is a third incongruity. (4.) The Perpendiculars of the Greater Circle are, according to *Mr. Jones* his measure, in altitude 15. foot and ½, in depth 3. foot, and in breadth seven foot. Where then is to be found the proportion of Longitude to six Diameters or the thickest part of the Column? (5.) Their *Intervalls*, or middle spaces seem to be about nine foot. For, *Mr. Jones* himself computes the length of each *Epistylium*, or *Architrave*, continued in round from Column to Column, to be precisely 16. foot; and there must be half the breadth of the Column, at each end, allowed for the meeting of the two Architraves in the middle, if not for the more firm bearing of their weight: so that measuring the distance of the supporters, by the remaining part of the Architrave, it will be nine foot. Which agrees not with the *Intercolumnium* of *Tuscan* Pillars. To conclude this paragraph, therefore; either the Conditions of the *Tuscan* Order here recited, are not according to the rules of Architecture taught by *Vitruvius*, and his excellent Interpreter, *Sr. H. Wotton*: or *Mr. Jones* was mistaken, when He conceived the Order of *Stone-heng* to be *Tuscan*.

(Thirdly,) As for the *Architectonical Scheme, in use among the* Romans, *consisting of four Equilateral Triangles inscribed within a Circle, by which He thought the whole work of* Stoneheng *designed and formed*; it is much easier imagined, than demonstrated to be really therein. For (1.) that Rule of *Vitruvius* (*lib.* 5. *cap.* 6) to which He referrs us for certification; if you take it intire, and not the later half only, as He cunningly did, runs thus. *Ipsius autem Theatri conformatio sic est facienda, ut quàm magna futura est perimetros imi, centro medio collocato circumagatur linea rotundationis; in eaque quatuor scribantur trigona paribus lateribus & intervallis, quæ extremam lineam circinationis tangant, quibus Astrologi, ex musica convenientia astrorum, ratiocinantur.* By the very first words whereof it is most manifest, the Rule it self concerns the designation, not of a round Temple, but of a *Theatre*; and the Context of the whole Chapter following declares it to have been invented for a threefold use, namely the most advantageous disposition of the *Proscenium, Scena,* and *Orchestra*; the equal diffusion of the voyces of the Singers and Actors; and the convenient ordering of Seats for the Spectators. But, what's this to *Mr. Jones* his conceipt of a *Temple*; and such a one too, as must bear the Aspect *Hypæthros, sive sub divo, i.e.* open at top? However, conceiving this Text might serve his turn, and the great name of *Vitruvius* give some authority to his Phancy, that otherwise would hardly pass among judicious men; he industriously usurped the quotation of it, by perverting the genuine sense to a wrong purpose; and to the end his Readers might be the longer in finding out the fraud, artificially omitting the citation of the particular Chapter, he leaves them to a tedious research through the whole Book, a labour so great, the patience of most, though Learned, would not extend to the enduring of it, upon so slender an occasion. (2.) The Question is, not whether this kind of Architectonical Scheme were anciently used by the *Romans*, in some of the publick Ædifices; but *whether* Stone-heng *was formed according to such a Scheme, or not? Mr. Jones*, indeed, hath expresly affirmed it: but, how hath he made it appear? That he hath drawn four Equilateral and Equidistant Triangles within the circumference of the Greater Circle of stones, so as all the Angles are terminated in the circular line, is not sufficient to prove it: forasmuch as every Novice in Geometry understands how to inscribe not onely 4. but 400. and many more such Triangles, in the *area* of a Circle much less in diameter, than that he describes. Nor is it sufficient, that he tell's us, *the intersection of the several Triangles fully demonstrateth after what manner the Greater Hexagon, made open at* Stone-heng, *was raised from the solid wall environing the* Cell *of the* Peripheros: because our sense assures us, there are no foot-steps or remains of any such solid wall of a circular form, raised where the intersections of the Triangles are supposed to be made; and because we have no evidence, but his single word, that there is any *Hexagon* at all in the work; whereas, neither *Mr. Camden*, nor the *Author* of Nero Cæsar, nor any other (for ought I could ever learn, and yet I have enquired of many Gentlemen who had carefully survey'd the Antiquity, and were well able to discern a Hexagon from a Circle) could ever perceive any such matter. Again, though he speaks of *Three Entrances leading into the Temple of* Stone-heng *from the Plain, and those likewise comparated by an Equilateral Triangle*: yet is it manifest even from his own Draughts of the work, and its Platform, that all the Perpendiculars or Columns of the Outward Circle are equidistant each from other; and if so, where are those Three Entrances? or how should we distinguish them from the other intercolumniary, or void spaces? All which considered, there remains (as I think) no tye upon any mans belief, that *Stone-heng* was a Roman Structure, in respect of the Scheme, by which it was designed and composed.

(Fourthly,) As for the *Double Portico reported to be in the outward Circle, and another within the Greater Hexagon, formed after the Roman fashion in structures of great Magnificence*: that you may be the better able to judge, whether He were in the right, yea or no; give me leave to acquaint You, what a *Portico* properly is, what the *Roman* Architects called a *Double Portico*, and what *Mr. Jones* termeth *Porticoes* in this place. *Vitruvius* (*lib.* 5. *cap.* 9) setting down precepts for the construction of *Porticoes* belonging to a Theatre, begins his discourse thus. *Post scenam Porticus sunt constituendæ, uti cum imbres repente ludos interpellaverint, habeat populus, quo se recipiat ex theatro*: "Behind the Scene are to be made Proticoes, to the end the people may have whither to withdraw themselves out of the Theatre, when suddain showrs disturb their sports. And *Philander* commenting upon these words, saith thus; *Porticus additæ sunt sacris ædibus, illustrium virorum domibus, & publicis ædificiis, necessitatis, aut ornamenti, animive caussa; sub eis repentinas pluvias vitabant, umbras ac frigora captabant, variis sermonibus diem consumebant, a meridie solem hyeme, a septentrione æstivas umbras excipientes*: "To sacred buildings, to the houses of great personages, and to publique ædifices are added Porches, for necessity, or ornament, or delight; under them they sheltred themselves from suddain rains, they retired for shade and coolness, and talked away the day; receiving Sunshine from the south in winter, and in summer shadow from the north. From whence it is most cleer, most certain, that all Porticoes are additional structures, wherein men may be protected from rain and sun; such as the memorable Porticoes of *Apollo Palatinus*, of *Augustus in campo Martio*, of the *Pantheon*, of *Antoninus Pius*, of the *Capitol* on the side of the *Capitoline* hill, in *Rome*. Of these Porticoes *some* are made with *parietibus continuis*, solid walls on one side, and Pillars on the other; as in all *Peristylia*, or paved walks enclosed with Columns, such as the costly Palace of *Urbin* at *Rome* is adorned with, such as the *Cloysters* in Monasteries, such as the walks under the *Old Exchange*, and those commonly called the *Piazzaes* of *Covent-Garden*. Others consist of solid walls on both sides, with rowes of Pillars set at distance from the walls; of which sort we have a glorious example in the *Portico* at the west end of *St. Pauls* Church, in designing and raising of which *Mr. Jones* himself was principal Architect. But *all* are *Tectæ*, Roofed or covered at top; otherwise how should they satisfie the use or end for which they were intended, namely to shelter men from excessive heat in summer, and from wet weather in all seasons of the year? As for *Double Porticoes*, they are no wayes different from single ones, except in this only, that they have a double order of range of Columns. For, *Philander* interpreting these words of *Vitruvius (loco citato) circa theatra sunt Porticus & ambulationes, quæ videntur ita oportere collocari, uti duplices sint, habeantque exteriores columnas Doricas, cum Epistyliis & ornamentis, ex ratione modulationis Doricæ perfectas*; expresly saith, *Porticus Duplices appellatæ sunt a duplici columnarum ordine*, Porches are termed Double, from the double order of Pillars, of which they are composed. And these, doubtless, are the adæquate notions of Porticoes, both simple, and double: and what every man understands, when he hears them spoken of. But what *Mr. Jones* intendeth by Porticoes in *Stone-heng*; is difficult to be conceived from his own discourse; and more difficult to be found in the work it self: so that we are confined to the liberty of conjecturing. By the double Portico, therefore, in the outward Circle or wing of stones; He means either the double row of Pillars set in round, of which the inner consisteth of smaller stones, such as he compares to *Pillasters*: or the space between each two Columns, with an *Architrave* over head. If the *first*; then it may be demanded, why the inner order of Columns are not equal in altitude to the outward, as they ought to have been by *Vitruvius* directions, and as they always were in Roman double Porticoes? and why is one order covered with Architraves, the other not? If the *other*; it may be objected, the Portico then can be but single, contrary to what it is supposed to be. The same may be said likewise of the other Portico imagined in the Greater Hexagon. But, whatever part of the Fabrique He fancied to be a Portico; thus much is evident, that it will not afford defence against the injuries of immoderate heat or rain; and therefore deserves not that title, in strictness of speech. And it seems, He that took the liberty so to call it, was put to a hard shift to blanch over the singularity of his conceipt: For, striving to assert it, to be customary among the old *Roman* Architects, to form the like Porticoes in their Temples, and more particularly in such Temples, as properly belonged to the Aspect *Hypæthros*, or were Roofless; rather than want the Patronage of *Vitruvius* in the case, he was forced to deprave the Text he alleged toward his defence. The words were lying in this order, (*lib*. 3. *cap*. 1. *sub finem*) *Reliqua omnia eadem habent quæ Dypteros, sed interiore parte columnas in altitudine duplices, remotas a parietibus ad circuitionem (ut porticus) Peristyliorum*: not as He (*pag*. 70) unfaithfully recites them, thus (observe I pray) *Hypæthros in interiore parte habet columnas remotas a parietibus, ad circuitionem (ut porticus) Peristyliorum;* adding and omitting what he thought fit. A course highly disingenious, and in the end as highly scandalous. For, whoso usurps the licence of falsifying the Text of any Author, much more of one so grave and oraculous, as *Vitrivius*, whatever advantage he imagines may arise from thence to his private opinion, in case the imposture be not detected: certainly it cannot countervail that shame and discredit that inevitably follows, when the judicious and examining Reader shall come, by having recourse to the Original, to find how grosly he might have been deluded, had he trusted to the Quotation. And *he that makes no scruple to impose an error, by corrupting another's Doctrine, forfeits the credit he expects to his own, and is always to be suspected of partiality to his Tenents, especially where he broacheth Novelties, and venteth them upon no other Reputation, but that of his single testimony.* It is but justice, therefore, if meeting with nothing in our Antiquity, that answers to any form of Porticoes, which, as Appendages to their Temples, were anciently erected by the *Romans*, and described by *Vitruvius*; nor having any other obligation to grant the being of any Portico there, besides *Mr. Jones* his bare conjecture, and that upon grounds obscure and fallible: I say, it is but justice if we suspect, that He onely imagin'd them to be such.

(5) As for the *Artifice, or Manner of Workmanship* shewn in *Stone-heng*, by which you are to understand onely the placing of the Upright Stones, answerable to Columns; most true it is, indeed, the old *Romans* used to set the Columns of publique Fabriques, at so much the less distance one from another, by how much greater the Columns were in Diameter, naming that particular kind of range, *Pycnostylos*, i.e. *Crebris Columnis*, the *close* order, from the close or thick standing of the Pillars. Nor is it less true, that in our Monument, the Perpendiculars, though extraordinary great in compass, have their intercolumnary spaces little in comparison; because of the weight of the incumbent Architrave, which might otherwise break of it self. And yet nevertheless I think it scarce warrantable thence to conclude, those Perpendiculars were erected by a *Roman* Artist. For, if you consult *Vitruvius* (*lib. 3. cap.* 2) about the true proportions of the Close order; you may soon be informed by him in these few words: *Pycnostylos est, cujus intercolumnio unius & dimidiatæ columnæ crassitudo interponi potest;* 'The *Pycnostyles* is that, where the Intercolumnium, or Intervall, is equal to the thickness, and half the thickness of the Column it self. To whom *Bernaldinus Baldus* fully assents, in his explanation of the word *Pycnostylos*, (*Lexic. Vitruvian. pag. 96.*) where he saith; *Inde species ista nomen adepta est, quod intercolumnium sit moduli unius tantum cum dimidio.* Then if you estimate the intervall from Perpendicular to Perpendicular, in the great Round of *Stone-heng*, by the length of the Architrave betwixt its two Supporters, according to my manner of computation formerly given, you will find it to be about 9 foot, and so inconform to the Rule of the Close order. After, perchance, you may give ear to my conjecture, That the Builder had respect chiefly to the length of the overthwart Stones, placing the Supporters accordingly, without any other consideration or precept of Art, rather of Necessity, than Choice: and that if he could have been furnished with Stones fit for Architraves, of larger dimensions in length and depth, (otherwise they could not have born their own gravity) in all likelihood he had proportionably enlarged the spaces of the Columns; it being evident, he made use of the greatest Stones he could get, of both sorts. But this is not material; it being sufficient, that the Rule of the *Pycnostylos* was not exactly followed in the position of the Columns at *Stone-heng*; and consequently, that the Manner is not *Roman*, as *Mr. Jones* would perswade.

(6) As for the manner of *fixing the Architraves upon the head of the Perpendiculars by Tenons and Mortises*; that likewise seems but an uncertain sign of *Roman* Masonry. For, those Architraves being to be placed *in Æquilibrio*, so as the point of Rest at each end ought to be there, where the weight was found equal on each side: all the Workman had to do toward their continuance in that posture, was, to contrive so to fasten them, as that no force of wind or tempest, nor any other (unless extreme) violence, by diminishing the

gravity on one side, might incline or sway them to sink down on the other; which could not otherwise be effected, but by corroborating the *Æquilibrium* by Tenons made in the Supporters, and let into holes or Mortesses in the Architrave, no kind of Morter or Cement being strong enough for that purpose. And thus much common reason might teach the Masons, without any great skill in Geometry, or having recourse to either the Rules or Patterns of *Roman* Architecture. Which, perhaps, was the cause why *Vitruvius* spake so little of this way of confirming great stones in buildings, as taking it for granted, the contrivement was so plain and obvious to men, even of but common understanding, as that it was needless for him to insist upon any Precepts concerning it: For, all I can meet with in his whole Volume, relating thereunto, is onely a slight, transitory, and obscure touch, (*lib.* 2. *cap.* 8.) which is this, *Quod si quis noluerit in id vitium incidere, medio cavo servato secundùm Orthostratas intrinsecus, ex rubro saxo quadrato, aut ex testa, aut silicibus ordinariis, struat bipedales parietes, & cum ansis ferreis, & plumbo frontes vinctæ sint: ita enim non acervatim, sed ordine structum opus poterit esse sine vitio sempiternum, quod cubilia & coagmenta eorum inter se sedentia, & juncturis alligata non protrudent opus, neque Orthostratas inter se religatos labi patientur*. From whence nevertheless little can be collected, that is capable of application to the manner of banding stones together in our Antiquity: all that is, we must be beholding to the industry of *Philander* for, who, after his interpretation of the word *Orthostratæ*, which signifies *upright Props*, such as the *Italians* term *Speroni, Philastri contraforti*, addeth, *Inciduntur in his canales, in quos, veluti in fœminas, aliud quidpiam, ceu masculum, ineat committaturque: cujusmodi sunt, quas nostri Mortesias, quasi Mordesias, à mordendo, vocant; comissuræscilicet genus, cum perpetuo canali induntur, inseruntur tabulæ, aut quippiam simile*. Besides, though Mr *Jones* alleged the authority of *Leo Baptista Albertus*, the *Florentine*, to prove, that in mighty Structures, where the stones were of extraordinary greatness, the *Romans* used to lay them without any unctuous incorporating Matter between: yet he neither hath, nor could bring under the hand of any Author a Certificate, that no other Nation did the like before, or until after the *Romans* had, by Conquest, or Commerce, civiliz'd them. And, therefore, it was somewhat boldly done of him, to infer that *Stone-heng* was a *Roman* structure, because the Architraves were compacted to their Supporters by Tenons and Morteses: when the Examples of the like way of Holdfasts for huge stones, among other Nations, (some of which were at that time barbarous) are infinite, and stand in the road-way of every man's observation.

(7 And lastly) As for the *frequency of Roman Relicks in Wiltshire*, such as Camps, Fortresses, Trenches, and the like, some of which are even to this day discernable, at least by their prints or footsteps, in places not far from *Stone-heng*; I shall willingly allow thus much, that conjoyned with History, they may be good testimonies of the lodging of *Roman* Armies in those places, and of their military traverses, during their War with the *Britans*; yet, seeing they carry no face of similitude, nor shew of relation to our Antiquity, the Laws of Logick will justifie my wariness and unbelief, if I doubt them to be so much as probable Arguments of the *Romans* being Authors also of that Work.

Having thus thread after thread, unravell'd Mr *Jones* his long Web of Reasons, which he thought so closely and artificially woven, as to be strong enough to bind his Readers to a belief of his Opinion, that *Stone-heng* was a *Roman* Structure: give me leave to add an Argument or two of mine own, of so much weight, as would have alone been sufficient to break asunder his whole contexture, had I not weakened it at all.

Mr. *Camden* in the close of his Discourse concerning *Stone-heng*, makes report of a certain Table, or plate of Metall, as it had been Tin and Lead commixt, found in or by the Monument, in the time of King *Henry* the viii. whereon were engraven many Letters, but in so strange a Character, that neither Sir *Thomas Eliot*, nor Mr. *Lilly* Schoolmaster of St. *Pauls*, could tell what to make of it; and so took no care to preserve it. Now certain it is, this Inscription was not left by the *Romans*, who generally wrote all their Memorials in their own Language, whose Character hath long out-lasted their Empire, continuing the same in all Ages; as appears even by their Coins of greatest Antiquity, and all their Monumental Epigraphs, of which *Camden* hath collected a great number, such as have been found in *England*, and *Gruterus* a large volume of others, dispers'd not onely through *Italy*, but all parts of the Earth, where ever the *Roman* Eagle pearch'd. Nor doth it appear to have been either *Greek*, or *Hebrew*, or *British*, or *Saxon*; because all these Languages and their several Characters, were well known to Sir *Thomas Eliot* and Mr. *Lilly*, who were excellent Linguists, and good Antiquaries, as the yet living Fame of one, and Writings of the other testifie. It remains, therefore, that these were *Barbarous* Characters: and if so, what hinders, but that we may guess them to be *Litteræ Runicæ, sive Gothicæ*, the *Runic* or *Gothic* Characters, such as were constantly used by the *Danes* in all their antique monumental Inscriptions, or Engravements? Especially since *John Speed*, in his Description of *Devonshire*, writes, That *near Exmore are certain remains of an antient work, namely, mighty Stones, set some in form of a Triangle, other inround, orderly disposed; and that upon one of them was an Engravement in* Danish *Letters, which could not be read by men most learned*. And that grave and universally learned man, *Olaus Wormius*, (Physician to the present King of *Denmark*, and not above four years past deceased, and who hath vouchsafed sometimes to honour me with his Epistles) in his first Book, *cap. 9. de Monumentis Danicis*, taketh special notice of this Inscription, and deploreth the unfortunate loss of it, with *Utinam bono publico communicatum fuisset; sorsan de rebus præclaris à nostratibus ibidem gestis testaretur*. That the *Danes* of old, affecting (as all other Nations of the world, however rude and illiterate) to perpetuate the remembrance of their notable actions and successes, delighted to raise Monuments of their Battels, Victories, and other Atchievments, as also of their Kings, principal Commanders, and great Persons; and leave short Records of the particular occasions of those Monuments, ingraven in *Runic* Letters; besides this, that they had none but the *Gothic* Language in use among them, is manifest from the testimony of *Saxo Grammaticus*, who *(in Præfation. Histor. Danic.)* recommends the observation thereof to his Readers, as a thing necessarily conducing to their understanding many, otherwise obscure passages in his History. *Nec ignotum volo*, saith He, *Danorum antiquiores, conspicuis fortitudinis operibus editis, gloriæ emulatione suffusos, Romani styli imitatione, non solum rerum à se magnificè gestarum titulos exquisito contextus genere, veluti Poëtico quodam opere perstrinxisse; verum etiam majorum acta patrii sermonis carminibus vulgata, linguæ suæ literis saxis ac rupibus insculpenda curasse*. And as for Precedents or *Examples* of that kind, they are so numerous, that *Olaus Wormius* his two Volumes, *De Monum. Danic. & de Literis Runicis*, mostly consist of such: otherwise perhaps I should have exercised your patience in reading some of those more conspicuous ones commemorated by *Saxo Grammaticus*, his Commentator, *Stephanus Stephanius, John Crantzius*, and other Writers of *Danish* Antiquities; that so I might have assisted the probability of my conjecture, that the Characters on the Plate found by *Stone-heng*, were *Runic* or *Gothic*. However, you have seen upon what fair grounds you may entertain a perswasion, that they were not *Latine*, and therefore not left by the *Romans*.

Again, This our Monument consisteth wholly of Stones *unwrought, rough,* and *rude*, as they lay in their beds of earth, (their *Tenons* and *Morteses* onely excepted) and of such variouis shapes, that the most curious eye can scarcely find a perfect similitude in any two of them: and Mr. *Jones* ought to have evinced, either by Testimonies authentick, or by Examples, that the *Romans* have ever raised any publick Structure of the like Materials; which being above his power (as I conceive at least) he warily omitted to attempt it, as he did the proof of many other particulars equally important toward the verification of his grand Position. Whereas *Olaus Wormius* hath been so liberal in his Contributions toward the maintenance of my Supposition, as to furnish me with not onely verbal Descriptions, but lively Draughts or Pictures also of sundry Antique *Danish* Monuments, as well in the Bullk and Rudeness of the Stones, as in the Order and Manner of their position and situation, much resembling our *Stone-heng*; and (as may be not obscurely collected from a Conference of Times, Actions, Histories, Ruines, &c.) not much different as to Antiquity. And this I think an Argument not unworthy your serious consideration; if not weighty enough to counterpoise all the reasons urged by Mr. *Jones*, to enforce his Dream, that the *Romans* were Authors of *Stone-heng*.

Having thus long entertained you, with examining the solidity of the *First Story* of our Architect's phantastical Building; Time and Order joyntly command me to usher you up to the *Second*: wherein I shall no longer detain you, than while I try the soundness of those Beams, upon which He imposed his so lofty conceipt, that *Stone-heng* was a TEMPLE. Which he presumes

(1) From the spacious *Court* lying round about it, agreeing with those of *Roman* Idolatrous Temples, wherein Beasts brought for Victims were slain, and into which none but Priests might enter. To which it may be objected, first, That the void space betwixt the utmost Circumvallation or Trench, in *Stone-heng*, and the Building it self, doth not exactly correspond with the *Atria* of *Roman* Structures; and therefore cannot, without corrupting the severe Dialect of Architects, be termed a *Court*. For, whoso attentively peruseth *Vitruvius* his Discourse *De Atriis*, *(lib. 6. cap. 4.)* will soon perceive, that He by the word *Atrium*, constantly means *primum ædificium, quod anteriori janua intrantibus occurrit*, the first Building that offers it self to the sight of those who enter by the fore-gate: And *Bernaldinus Baldus*, in his Note upon the first line of that Chapter, saith, *Arbitramur nos vetera Atria, nostrarum ædium parti illi respondere, quam vulgo* Anditum *dicimus,* Andatam, Caminatamve; *quæ quidem prima post ingressum ostii introgredientibus occurrit; eaque non quidem subdivalis, sed tecta & concamerata.* To which may be annex'd the agreeable judgment of *Claudius Salmasius (in Solinum, pag.* 1218.*) apparet Atrium, primò non fuisse vestibulum; neque aream Hypæthram; sed partem ædis sub tecto, at adeo penetrale, & fortasse concameratam porticum.* Seeing therefore, that the *Roman Atrium* always was covered at the top, and most frequently arched also; and that there is no such thing betwixt the outward Circle of Stones, and the great Trench environing it: Where is the Analogy or Resemblance supposed? Again, Indulging Him the liberty of our vulgar phrase, according to which the *Area*, or plot of ground, betwixt a Building and its Boundaries, may rightly enough be call'd a Court: yet, where is the necessity, yea, where the probability, that that Court was originally design'd and marck'd out for a place for the slaughter of Victims? Must all Structures environed with such *Areæ* be Temples? or all *Roman* Temples be accommodated with the like out-lets? If so, what will become of our Authors fancy, that those vast Stones standing in a Circle near *Long-Compton* in *Oxfordshire*, called *Roll-stones*, were antiently a Temple, and a *Roman* one too? for, these are destitute of all outward circumvallation or entrenchment. But the force of this Argument depends, perhaps, upon its conspiracy with its fellows; and therefore, if from them all put together, it shall appear, that our Monument was intended for a Temple; I shall no longer doubt, whether the void space of ground within the Trench be the Court belonging to it.

(2) From a large Stone, 16 feet long and 4 broad, appearing not much above the surface of the earth, in the Eastern part of the lesser Hexagon, which He takes for an *Altar*. Whereunto I cannot assent, for two considerations. First, the Humility of the Altar destroys the supposed Dedication of the Temple. For, the Rule of *Vitruvius*, how Altars ought to be placed in Temples, so as to carry a due Decorum, and visible Analogie to the nature and proprieties of that particular Deity therein to be worshipped, is this, *(lib. 4. cap. 8.) Altitudines Ararum sic sunt explicandæ, ut Jovi, omnibusque Cœlestibus quàm excelsissimæ constituantur; Vestæ, Terræ, Marique humiles collocentur.* Altars consecrated to *Jupiter*, and all *Celestial* Powers are to be made exceedingly tall or high; and those to *Vesta, Tellus*, and *Neptune*, humble or low; as in some sort representing the dwelling and domin-

ion of the respective Deity. So that, this Stone was either no Altar at all, or not ordained for Oblations to the god *Cœlus*. If it be objected, that the Stone perhaps was set *upright*; I answer, Then it was as much too *narrow* on the top, for the use assign'd, as now too *low* for the God to whom it is ascribed. Secondly, Mr *Jones*, in his Description of the Monument (as you may remember) speaks of three open *Entrances* leading from the Plain into the work it self, the most conspicuous of which lay *North-East*: which is openly inconsistent with the custome of the *Romans*, who always made the grand Entrance into the Temple, whatever it were, *è regione Altaris & Signi*, in that part, which was directly opposite to the place where the Altar and Statue stood erected; and the reason was, *Ut adoratum venientes Divinitatem suspicerent*, That the people coming up to make their adoration, might at their entrance have both Altar and Image in front, so as to behold them at first elevation of their eyes. Would you have Authority for this? Hear *Vitruvius* himself, *Ædes autem sacræ Deorum immortalium, ad regiones quas spectare debent, sic erunt constituendæ, uti, si nulla ratio impedierit, liberaque fuerit potestas ædis, Signum quod erit in Cella collocatum, spectet ad vespertinam cœli regionem: uti qui adierint ad aram immolantes, aut sacrificia facientes, spectent ad partem cœli orientis, & simulachrum quod erit in æde; & ita vota suscipientes contueantur ædem, & orientem cœli, ipsaque simulachra videantur exorientia contueri supplicantes & sacrificantes; quodque Aras omnes Deorem necesse esse videatur ad orientem spectare, (lib. 4 cap. 5)* Whence we may safely conclude, that if the position of the Altar were right, yet that of the principal Entrance leading up to it was wrong. But should we grant this to have been originally an Altar-stone; yet doth it not follow, that therefore the rest of the Building was a Temple: because in Stories, as well Sacred, as not, we read of many Altars standing alone, without Temples; and because it was one of the barbarous customes of the *Danes*, even in the stony Sepulchres of their mighty men, to erect Altars, and thereon to sacrifize to their Manes; witness *Olaus Wormius, (Monum. Danicor. lib. 1. cap. 6) Diversi ab his cernuntur Tumuli, saxis grandioribus undique cincti, ita ut utramque extremitatem mole vastiora reliquis claudant. In medio ut plurimum Ara extat. In hisce vulgus Gigantes sepultos credit, quorum ossa etiam haud raro 'e* [sic] *talibus effodiuntur. Sed ego ejusmodi integris etiam familiis destinatos puto, unde & in his Aræ, quæ communia sacrificia pro totius gentis incolumitate immolata excipiant*. With which if you compare *Stone-heng*, together with our vulgar tradition of Giants there interr'd, and the skuls of Oxen or Buls plowed up in the adjacent fields: You will find as much reason to believe it a Sepulchral Monument set up by that warlike and ambitious Nation, in the time of their tyranny here, with an Altar in the middle, for their Pagan and impious Sacrifizes, as, with Mr *Jones*, to conceive it a *Roman* Temple.

(Thirdly,) From the *use of the ancient* Romans *to erect the like Round Temples, that lay open without Walls, surrounded only with Pillars, and uncovered also on the top, or Roofless.* Which being his part to prove, and he finding it impossible; he betook himself to multiplication of Fictions, confusion of things cleerly distinct, and other disingenious shifts; such as have indeed amuzed and imposed upon vulgar heads, but can never convince the Learned and judicious, who are not ignorant, how strictly constant the *Roman* Architects were to their set Forms and Orders of Building, upon no occasion commixing or confounding them in publique structures, especially sacred ones, where the passenger was to be instructed at first sight, what Deity was adored within, by the peculiar forme of the Temple apparent without; that so he might prepare and address his devotion accordingly, without being mistaken either in the Object, or ceremonies of it. But, let us now judge Him unheard. He allegeth, out of *Vitruvius (lib. 4. cap. 7.)* that the *Romans* had round Temples of two divers Forms: whereof the one, named *Monopteros*, had neither continued walls about, nor Cell within, but was encompassed only with a round of Columns; the other, termed *peripteros*, had a Cell enclosed with a continued wall, and Columns set at convenient distance, so as to make a Portico round about on the outside. And this I allow to be true: but what though? our *Stone-heng* resembles neither of these Forms: not the *Monopteros*, because it hath a *Cell*, as Himself supposeth; not the *Peripteros*, because it wants a continued *wall* to incompass that Cell, as our eyes witness. Where then is the Similitude and Conformity? Why, rather than fail, our Author shall adventure to make that like to both, which really is like to neither. For stealing the outward Circle from the *Monopteros*, and the Cell from the *Peropteros*, and then again surrounding that same Cell (not with a Circle, as he ought, but) with a *Hexagon* of Pillars: of both Forms He makes a *Third*, not being able to withhold from confessing (so much had the joy of his 'Ευρηκα, ἑυρηηα, transported him) in the end, that it was a *New Invention*, which yet he needed not to have told us. So here you find him guilty of a double fault; confounding of two perfectly and irreconcileably distinct Forms of sacred Edifices; and converting a Circle, the essential and proper figure of all such Cells, as belonged to the *Peripteros*, into a *Hexagon*. Is this fair and candid dealing, think you, in a man of Letters? Doth it become one of the most famous Architects of our age, thus to build Castles in the air, and flye to a sanctuary made up of Fictions? But this is not all. From a strange and unheard of confusion of several Forms, He proceeds to blend together also several *Orders* of consecrated Buildings. For, He will have the Order, of which his Temple of *Stone-heng* must consist, to be partly *Tuscan*, partly *Corinthian*: affirming, that *as the plainness and solidness of the* Tuscan *order, appears eminently through the whole work, so the narrowness of the spaces betwixt the Stones, visibly discovers the delicacy and softness of the* Corinthian. Where (not to take notice of the manifest contradiction in the very terms) He incurrs a grand Error, in commixing, in one Temple, two so different Orders; when, by his own confession, (*pag*. 90.) *the* Romans *had for each of their Deities a certain particular Order of Temples, and observed that distinction of Orders so strictly, that they seldome or never varied them.* According to that of Vitruvius, (lib. 4. cap. 7.) *Non omnibus Diis iisdem rationibus ædes sunt faciendæ, quòd alius alia varietate sacrarum Religionum habet effectus.* And had they not done so, How could the *Roman* Architects of old, have been able, at first sight, to judge to what Divinity this or that Fane was peculiarly devoted? or, How could the Modern Architects of *Italy*, at this Day, by seeing onely the ruines of them, give such probable conjectures, concerning their antiquity and proper Dedication, as are very hardly to be contradicted? But, why am I thus prodigal of my time and pains, in shaking an opinion, that hath no foundation of either Precept, or Precedent from antient Architecture? especially when the Founder Himself was forced to excuse the fragility and weakness thereof, with this Plea; *The learned in Antiquities very well know, those things, which oblivion hath so long removed out of mind, are hardly to be discovered.* (*Pag*. 77.)

(4 And lastly) *From the Heads of Bulls, or Oxen, or Harts, and other such Beasts, digged up in or near this Antiquity*; as if no man could imagine other, but those were the Heads of such Beasts, as were antiently made Holocausts in that place. Why, is it not equally probable, they might be the skulls of Cattel slain for the sustenance of some one or other of those many Armies, that encamped on the adjacent Plain, where the Lines of their Entrenchments and Fortresses are yet visible? Was it not a common thing for Armies to carry along with them whole Herds of Beasts for their Provision, and to bury the bones of such as they killed, in places somewhat remote from their Camps? And, as for harts; it is well known, both by tradition among the Inhabitants of the neighbouring Villages, and by other testimonies yet remaining, that all the Plain from *Stone-heng* to *Ambresbury*, was, till within these 200 yeares, a Forest full of great Trees: and therefore not improbable, but the Heads of Deer might lie there, without any relation at all to *Stone-heng*. But grant them to be the Offall or Reliques of Sacrifices; yet what reason, they should be *Roman* Sacrifices, when the *Danes* also used the like, as may appear from what I lately delivered out of *Olaus Wormius*, of the custome of that Nation to offer Beasts in Sacrifice to the Ghosts of their deceased Commanders, upon their Sepulchral Monuments? This Argument, therefore, being as invalid as the rest, and altogether very unsatisfactory: it plainly

appears, that Mr *Jones* his Imagination had too powerful an Influence over his Reason, when He judged, upon such slender Evidences, that our Antiquity was antiently a *Roman* Temple.

We should, in the next place, consider His Reasons for the entitling this Structure to the God *Cælus*: but seeing it doth not appear to have been a Temple; 'twere in vain to be sollicitous about the *Dedication* of it. Omitting, therefore, to take notice of sundry Defects and Incongruities, as well Architectonical, as Historical, observable in that Later part of our Authors conceipt; as Errors that stand naked to every enquiring eye, and cannot hide themselves from even the Emblem of Justice: I here take my final leave of his so vulgarly admired *Book*; having, in memory that I perused it, first subscribed this short Animadversion, at the end of it. *Nunquam mihi placuit audaculorum quorundam ratio, quibus nihil est tam obscurum, tamque abstrusum, & procul ab hominum memoria positum, quod suarum conjecturarum sagacitate non fiat clarum, apertum, & cognitum. Nimium credulis ingeniis, & discendi cupidioribus rogati ultrove præstigiis & officiis imponunt, mentiuntur effossa marmora, atque adeo inscriptas urnas, quæ nusquam fuerint, imo quæ nec per somnum quidem viderint.* Which, though spoken by the grave *Philander*, in reproof of certain over-weening and audacious Wits, that thinking themselves quick-sighted enough to see through the darkness of oblivion, and make discoveries where Time had long since interposed its sable curtain; had pretended to find a Temple of the Sun, in the confused ruines of a Tower that stood upon the *Mons Quirinalis* in *Rome*, to that purpose counterfeiting Marble Pillars, and Urns, with formal Inscriptions: may yet be well accommodated to *Others*, who, ambitious to be thought *Argoses* in the ruines of Antiquity, spare not to point at things invisible, to descry in Monuments more than the Founders themselves ever designed, to form to themselves Examples that never were, and in favour of their own extravagant imaginations, to corrupt the testimonies of Authors most venerable, and falsifie the Records of antient Customs.

What the *Romans* claim was, You have heard, at large: hear now, in short, also [excerpt 4].

Excerpt 4. Having demolished the Jones thesis, Charleton now advances his own. Drawing on his correspondence with Dr. Wormius, and on the latter's six-volume work (in Latin) on Danish antiquities, Dr. Charleton selects the one type of monument that seems best to fit the Stonehenge case. Thanks to the Newberry Library in Chicago, I was able to consult the same original edition of *Danicorum Monumentorum* (1643) that Charleton looked into. His report on its contents is correct, a scholarly digest. No doubt he was impressed by Dr. Wormius's precise drawings of Danish field monuments, as well drafted as his own of Stonehenge (fig. 3).

In this excerpt, Dr. Charleton goes on to treat a number of like English antiquities, rings of standing stones, well known even in his day through accounts and crude drawings of them in Camden's popular encyclopedia. They are in fact prehistoric monuments (Burl 1979), although Camden ascribes them to historic times. In one case, the Roll-right Stones in Oxfordshire, he says formed the election court of Rollo the Dane. This suggestion naturally drew Charleton's attention as he reviewed other sites for possible Danish connections. Of course Charleton is today ridiculed for such speculation. Yet he organized into reasoned argument what data he had to hand from wide-ranging sources. All the same he stumbled upon the very insight I support in this book.

The Title of the DANES to Stone-heng;

Which is grounded chiefly upon Custom, and Presidents. For that they, more than any other Nation whatsoever, were in old time, and even a good while after the refinement of their barbarous Manners, and conversion to Christianity, accustomed to erect Monuments of huge Stones, upon several memorable occasions; and such Monuments, that compar'd to our (or their) *Stone-heng,* seem to agree therewith in most, if not all points of resemblance; whereof many are at this day extant in *Denmark* and *Norwey*: is not hard to prove, from the undoubtable testimonies of their best Historians and Antiquaries.

Olaus Wormius (lib.2mo *Monum. Danic.*) being to reduce into order that great multitude of Stony Monuments in his Country, of which, as the most worthy to be commemorated, He had proposed to himself to treat; first makes a general division of them into *Two Classes*: namely, *Literata, quæ ex saxis constabant literatura prisca, vulgo Runica, exteris Gothica, exaratis,* Letter'd Monuments, such as consisted of large stones, with Inscriptions of *Runic,* or *Gothic* Characters, speaking their occasions and intentions; and *Illiterata, quæ ex rudibus quibusdam illiteratis, certo tamen ordine & serie dispositis,* Unletter'd, which were composed of rude stones, without engravements, but so disposed after a certain manner, as that the Beholder might from the order of their position collect, upon what Accidents, and for what Ends or Uses they had been set up. So that *These,* though destitute of the Elements of Language, were not absolutely Dumb, but spake their particular purposes in a more obscure Dialect of Figures, and were read in the Alphabet of their proper Platforms. Then he subdivides this later sort into *Five* distinct *Ranks*; namely, into *Sepulchra,* Tombs containing the bones of eminent persons defunct: *Fora,* places of Judicature, where Right and Justice were administred, according to the Laws and Customs of the Country: *Duellorum Strata,* Cirques or places of Duells, or Camp-sights: *Trophea,* Trophies, where Battells had been fought, and the Enemy defeated: and *Comitialia loca,* places wherein Kings and Supreme Commanders were elected by the General Suffrages of the People, and Inaugurated with great Pomp and publick Solemnity, such as the rudeness of that Nation, and the simplicity of those times afforded. This Scheme being drawn, as the rule of his Method; He thence-forward proceeds to Examples of each kind. And we are obliged therein to follow Him step by step; that so we may the sooner, and without deviation, arrive at a competent degree of satisfaction, whether any, and which of all those different sorts of Antique Monuments hath so near a resemblance of *Stone-heng,* as that we may, from the apparent *similitude* of their *forms,* infer a probable *affinity* in their *Origines* and *Designations*; which is the period of our travail.

As for the *Literata,* which carry their Age and Titles engraven on their fronts; they lie not in our way, our Antiquity having no Inscription on any of its Stones: and though that Plate of Metall with barbarous Characters, of which we have formerly taken notice, might probably appertain unto it; yet is not that sufficient to appropriate it to the order of Monuments, whose dignity and value consist chiefly in their *Epigraphs.* Ranging it, therefore, among the *Illiterata*; let us a while insist upon a particular survey of those: beginning at the Antique *Danish.*

Sepulchres.

Whereof I meet with some, in *Olaus Wormius,* that are in more than one point of analogy correspondent to *Stone-heng.*

One stands in *Seland,* on a plain, near the high-way leading to a certain small Town, called *Birck*; formed according to this description of our Author. *Ex saxis rudioribus mediocribus, quadrata in longitudinem tendens, ducta est area; huic tres colles seu Tumuli inclusi, undique circa radicem, ejusdem fermè magnitudinis saxis cincti. Major meditullium occupans, in apice aram habet ex saxis quatuor stupendæ magnitudinis exstructum, ita ut tria quartum maximum & planum sustineant.* "A plot of ground, of a square running out in length, is empalled with rude stones, not of the largest scantlings: in which are included three Mounts of Earth, circumscribed at their bases with stones of the like bigness. The greatest Mount, standing in the middle, hath on its top an Altar made up of four stones of stupendious magnitude, so as three standing in Triangle, support the fourth upon their heads, which is the greatest of all, and plain or flat.

A *Second*, situate not far from the same place, and somewhat more eminent, consisteth of a *Tumulus*, or mount of earth cast up, under which, the common people have a Tradition, that a Giant, whose name was *Langbeen Kiser*, was antiently buried; and encompassed with fifty six stones of prodigious bulks. *Moles hæc saxo percussa, reboat, ut concameratum opus subesse colligere facile quis possit*, saith our Author; this massive Structure being knock'd hard with a stone, yields a great sound like the Ecchoes of Vaults, so that it is easily to be collected, that there is an arched or vaulted hollowness underneath.

Here let us make a stand for a minute or two, and reflect upon a few particulars that offer themselves to our observation. *First*, these two Sepulchral Monuments are situate in *Campis patentibus*, in open and spatious fields; a cleer evidence, the *Danes* (as many other Nations) anciently used to bury in large and wide plains. *Secondly*, they threw up mounts of Earth over their dead: and those of two sorts, according to the qualities of the persons inhumed. For, of these *Tumuli*, such as were simple and naked, served to denote the interrment of Common Souldiers, together with their inferior officers, slain in battel upon the place: but those compassed about with great stones, set in single, double, or treble order, were designed to conserve the memory of great Captains or Generals. For *Wormius* touching upon these *Tumuli*, left this remark concerning their Distinction. *Qui rudiores sunt, ex sola terra in rotunditatem & conum congesta constant; ex iis, qui una vel multiplici Saxorum serie circa basin cinguntur, exercituum Imperatoribus, aliisque Magnatibus dicati creduntur; ut Simplices nullis ornati lapidibus, militibus strenuis, & athletis de patria benè meritis.* Howsoever, in those Martial times, when no vertue could render any man noble or great, but Fortitude, and Honour lay in the strength rather of the Arm, than of the Head; the Armies of this Nation constantly preferred monuments of mighty stones, much above those *Tumuli*, or (as we call them) *Burrows*; nor ever entrusted the fame of their Worthies to such simple and homely conservatories, but only in places where Rocks and Quarries were scarce. This we learn from a very remarkable text in the Commentaries of *Petrus Lindebergius. Sciendum autem, quòd Dani, cum propter defectum saxorum Pyramides ac Obeliscos extruere minime potuerint, olim in memoriam Regum & Heroum suorum ex terra coacervata ingentem molem montis instar eminentem statuerint.* From whence it is very plain, that the old *Danes* used not to inhume their Chieftains and highest Commanders under Tombs of Earth, but in case of necessity, where neither the place of the battel, in which they were slain (if they dyed in war) nor the Country neer it, afforded them stones of dimensions fit for Pyramids and Obelisques. Otherwise they made use of stones of the largest size they could possibly get: sparing no pains nor cost to raise them up into the most magnificent Fabriques, their little skill in Architecture could amount to. Hereupon *Wormius; Ætatis progressu plus operæ in Magnatum tumulis positum videtur. Nam, non solum iis grandes cippos patriis literis notatos imposuerunt, defuncti titulos exhibentes: sed etiam tumulos ipsos tam in æpice, quam circa basin visendæ magnitudinis cinxere saxis, aream insuper quadratam adjicientes, quæ totam molem grandioribus includeret, &c.* To which we may opportunely subjoyn a parallel record of *Christianus Cilicius (lib. 1. Belli Dithmarsici.) Erant*, saith He, *Magnatum Danicorum sepulturæ in sylvis & agris, tumulosque aggestis lapidibus vestientes muniebant; quod genus complures passim adhuc visuntur, qui Gigantum Strata vocantur.* Mark here the near affinity of the very Name; *Stone-heng* being by all our Authors, who have mentioned it, called *Chorea Gigantum,* the Giants Dance, and the most magnificent Stony Monuments of the *Danish* Princes, *Strata Gigantum,* the Giants pavements or paths. The *last* observable is, that in many of their Sepulchral piles they placed an Altar; *eo fine,* saith *Wormius, ut ibidem in memoriam defuncti quot annis sacra peraguntur;* that they might yearly offer sacrifices to the defunct, at least in memory of them, upon the place of their inhumation. Of this we have a sufficient confirmation from a note of *Ubbo Emmius,* (lib. 1. Histor. Fris. pag. 21.) *Commemoratione dignum videtur, quod in Regione hac ingentis molis saxa complura, quæ nulla vectatione, nulla vi hominum illac deportari potuisse, ob magnitudinem credas, congesta inveniantur, quorum ea dispositio est, ut Aras referre videantur. Nam jacentibus nonnullis, alia iis imposita sunt plana, relictumque foramen, per quod reptare homo possit*: "it deserves commemoration, that in this Country are found multitudes of Stones congested of so vast masses, that you would believe them impossible to be removed by any Engines, by any the greatest strength of Men; and so disposed, as to represent Altars. For upon the heads of some, others are imposed, of a plain figure, and a hole or empty space left underneath, through which a man may creep. Nor ought it to seem so singular and strange a piece of Superstition, for a phlegmatique and dull headed Northern Nation, to set up Altars in the midst of such ample and massive Tombs: when Temples themselves first grew up out of meaner Sepulchres, even among the Grecians. This perhaps, you'l smile at, as a paradox; and therefore it behooves me to produce some credible Authority to assert it. *Clemens Alexandrinus* (*in Protreptico*) is the man, who both expresly avoucheth it, and brings several Instances to prove it, thus. *Superstitio templa condere persuasit. Quæ enim prius hominum sepulchra fuerunt, magnificentiùs condita, Templorum appellatione vocata sunt. Nam apud Lariscam civitatem in arce, in templo Palladis, Acrisii sepulchrum fuit, quod nunc sacrarii loco celebratur: in arce quoque Atheniensi, ut est ab Antiocho in nono Historiarum scriptum, Cereris sepulchrum fuit: in templo vero Palladis, quem Poliada Græci appellant, jacet Erichtonius,* &c. But we have made too long a Hault in this place, and it more imports us, to proceed to

"A *Third* notable Example of Stony Sepulchres in *Denmark.* Which composed of a *Tumulus* or Burrow cast up in the middle, and three orders of huge stones set in manner of Columns, at equal distance, the outmost making a large quadrangle of fifty paces length in each side, the other two perfect Circles one within another; presents it self to the admiration of passengers, on a plain, about a mile from *Roeschild,* and neer the high way that leads from thence to *Frederisksburgh.* Of this *Ol. Wormius* hath given a perfect Draught, (*Monument Danicor. pag. 35.*)"

For a *Fourth,* I have, among many others, chosen the notable Monument of King *Harald Hyldetand* (whose courage, continency, and wisedome, together with his happy successes in warr, are highly celebrated by *Saxo Grammaticus*) which yet remains neer *Lethra,* or *Leire,* in *Seland,* anciently the seat of Kings, now a decaid obscure village: *saxis grandioribus stipatum, in meditullio immensa mole quadra, minoribus aliis innixa exornatum;* compassed about with stones of extraordinary greatness, and in the middle ennobled with one Square stone, or rock, of an immense bulk, resting upon the heads of others of inferior magnitude; whose picture, though in too small a module, is taken also by our Author.

Now, from the various structure of these four grand Sepulchres, neither of which doth fully quadrate with other; it is manifest, the Founders were not strict in observing any such set form of placing their stones, that might at first view distinguish them from other Monuments; unless in this onely, that the Exterior Muniment or pale of great stones was commonly either exactly square, or neerly approaching that regular figure. And yet sometimes they varied from that also, as *Wormius* himself confesseth. For, albeit in his general description of the fashion of this sort of Sepulchres, he tells us, they had *aream quadratam, quæ totam molem grandioribus saxis includeret:* yet afterward, in the same Chapter, he mentions some, that had not been formed according to that rule. His words are, *Diversi ab his quidam cernuntur tumuli, figura oblongiori, congerie depressiori, saxis grandioribus undique cincti, ita ut utramque extremitatem mole vastiora reliquis claudant, &c.* But of this first King of Unlettered Danique Monuments, we have taken a sufficient survey. Let us pass, therefore, to the *Second*, viz. *Fora*, or

Places of Judicature.

Where judgment was publickly given concerning Right, and litigious sutes determined betwixt subject and subject, according to the Known laws and constitutions of the country; and that either immediately by the King himself, where the parties concerned were Noble, or the matter in controversie important; or otherwise by his deputed Judges, in cases of less moment. These Courts were, like Justice her self, naked, and open; standing, not in Cities, nor Towns, but in fields and spacious campanias; nor covered with roofs, but with a kind of rude magnificence made only of a certain plot of ground, of a Quadrangular, or Oval figure, set apart by an enclosure of the vastest stones, that could possibly be had, placed like Columns, at equal distance; with one great stone, for a judgment seat, in or neer the middle; as appears from the remains of Two (anciently very eminent) yet visible in *Denmark*.

The *One* in *Seland*, neer the city 𝔇𝔯𝔢𝔱𝔥𝔦𝔫𝔤; whose manner of structure, and capacity *Ol. Wormius* having with great diligence survey'd, he thus describes it. *Vidi illud quadraginta sex saxis stupendæ magnitudinis cinctum fuisse, eminente in ejus meditullio grandiusculo quodam; omnia vero in ovalem disposita erant figuram, itaquidem, ut utrinque ad latera, circa medium porta quasi, vel aditus pateret meridiem & septentrionem versus. Longitudo nonaginta passus æquabat, latitudo viginti.* This *Forum*, or 𝔗𝔦𝔫𝔤 (in the *Danique* language) was begirt about with forty six stones of wonderfull magnitude, and had one great stone standing in the middle: all the stones of the Enclosure were disposed into an Oval figure, so that about the middle, on each side, was left as it were a gate, or Entrance, one toward the South, the other toward the North. The length of the oval was ninety paces, the breadth twenty.

The *Other* neer 𝔄𝔞𝔩𝔪𝔲𝔫𝔱𝔬𝔯𝔭, *undique cautibus septum,* hemm'd in on all sides with stones equal to *Rocks*: which gave name to the place where it stands, that being called 𝔗𝔦𝔫𝔤𝔢𝔱, to this day. Many other of the same kind are to be seen in other Provinces of *Denmark*; saith our *Author*.

As these Courts of Justice were rude in their Fabrique, so for many Ages together, were the ways of *Trial* practised in them. For, from *Frotho Magnus*, who swayed the *Danish* Sceptre, about the most happy time of our *Saviour's* Nativity, down along until the Reign of *Suenotto*, in the year of our Lord 986, all weighty and difficult controversies were decided *per Monomachiam*, by Duel; the Defendant being obliged to combat the Plaintiff openly within the lists of the Court, and prove the goodness of his cause by the sharpness of his weapons, without other Advocate but his own courage. A very savage and unequal manner of trial this! where always the Sword of Justice was put into the hand of the Criminal, where many times Right had no Vindication but from Fortune, and the most Innocent, if overcome, was either to die upon the place of his purgation, or, what's more grievous, to become Slave to his unjust Accuser. Yet men were hereto bound by a severe Law, made by the said *Frotho*, and recited by *Saxo Grammaticus*, (*Hist.Danic.lib. 5.*). After, the Beams of the Christian Faith shining on those northern Nations, and in some degree overcoming the gloominess of their barbarous Manners and Customes; that Law was abrogated, and in the place of Duels, the somewhat less cruel, but not much less uncertain way of Trial *per Ordelium*, by *Fire-Ordeal*, succeeded; and was continued in the same Courts, till about the year of Christ 1350. It was condemned by a decree of the *Lateran* Council, and an Edict of King *Woldemarus* II, an Extract of which you may find in

Wormius, (Monum. Danic. lib. I cap. II) Then began all causes to be determined by the judgment of twelve *Jurors*, as here with us in *England*; not but this way was much more ancient, (for it is ascribed to *Regnerus* sirnamed 𝔏𝔬𝔡𝔟𝔯𝔬𝔤, who ruled in *Denmark* about the year of Christ 820; and as some *Danish* Writers boast, was derived from him to our *Etheldred*) but it seems not to have been either by universal custome established, or by strict and penal Laws enforced, so as totally to exclude the *Ordeal* in all cases, until the said *Woldemarus* his days. And *Harald* the vij[th], after the abolition of Duels, introduced a new, but pernicious manner of determining contentions, by which the Party accused might purge himself of whatever Crime charged upon him, *Solo juramenti sacramento*, by onely his own single Oath, *idque contra omnem testium fidem*, and that against the clearest testimony of Witnesses: as *Saxo Grammat.* hath left upon record, *(lib. II.)* But the unreasonableness hereof was so great, and the evil conferences so many, that it could not continue long. Notwithstanding the ways of Trial were thus various; yet the places were still the same, namely, these open and rude Courts here described. From which we pass to the Third sort of *Danique* unletter'd Monuments, *viz.*

Places of Combats, or Fights.

These were, indeed, always designed by Great stones, but not constant to any one Figure, so as to be thereby alone distinguishable, without the help of Tradition. For, though *Saxo Grammat. (lib. I. cap. 29.)* willing to give some directions, how, from the several Ordinations of the Stones, Posterity might guess aright at the several Occasions, upon which they were set up; delivers this as a general Rule: *Recto & longo ordine pugilum certamina; quadrato turmas bellantium, & sphærico familiarum designantia sepulturas; ac cuneato equestrium acies ibidem, vel prope, fortunatius triumphasse:* yet *Wormius* professeth, he much doubted whether this order were everywhere strictly observed, or not; afterward alleging Examples of different Figures.

One he mentions out of the Author of *Histor. Bremensis, (lib. 2. cap. 9.)* that consisting of one mighty Stone, was erected in memory of a Duel fought near a place named 𝔄𝔤𝔯𝔦𝔪𝔢𝔰𝔴𝔢𝔡𝔢𝔩, in which a famous Combatant, 𝔅𝔦𝔲𝔯𝔤𝔲𝔦𝔡𝔬, overcame and slew a Champion of the *Slavi*, and acquired immortal honor.

Others he speaks of that were marked with many huge stones set equally distant each from other, in a *streight* line; some that were truly *Cirques*, and some *Quadrangular*: all which, together with the Laws and Manner of such Camp-fights betwixt the Champions of several Kings, You may see fully decribed by him, *(Monum. Danic. lib. I. cap. 9.)* In the mean time I hasten to the *Danish*.

Trophies,

Or Monuments of great *Battels* fought, and *Victories* obtain'd. Which, though agreeing among themselves, in their durable and massie Materials, are nevertheless irreconcilably discrepant in their Forms. So that in these, as well as in the other sorts hitherto survey'd, the Founders seem to have entrusted the remembrance of their glorious Successes, as much to the voice of Fame, and popular Tradition, as to the obscure signification of any one Figure or Scheme observed in the Monuments themselves: or else varying the Platforms of their Triumphal Piles, according to the various circumstances of their Encounters, and fortunate Achievements, and the commodities of the place; they left Posterity, who could not arrive at certain knowledge of those Circumstances, to grope after their particular Stories, in the darkness of uncertain conjectures. This our Author, *Ol. Wormius*, was too ingenuous to excuse, or conceal; and therefore though, in compliance with the former perswasion of his Country, he tells us, *Integri exercitus stragem lapidum quadrata in plano dispositione indicasse*, "That the antient *Danes* by stones disposed into a Quadrangle, shewed the overthrow of a whole Army of their Enemies, upon or near that place: yet he immediately subjoyns, *Verum non ubique ab omnibus præcise observatnm* [sic] *fuisse hunc ordinem ac dispositionem saxorum, planè mihi persuadeo*; "But I perswade my self fully, that this order or disposition of the stones, was not precisely observed by all, in all places. However, it imports us not to pretermit an *Example*, or two, of these huge Triumphal Antiquities.

In the Diocess of *Bergen*, on a wide mountainous place, near a Village, called 𝔗𝔶𝔩𝔫𝔢𝔰, you may, with a delightful wonder, behold six stones of an incredible magnitude, resembling Pyramids, erected at equal distances, in two semi-circles, one within another; each environed with two entire circles of lesser stones of Oval figure; and in the middle of the intercolumnary spaces in each semi-circle, a great multitude of the like stones heaped one upon another, till they amount toward a Cone: and all in a most elegant order, set up in memory of a bloody Battel fought upon the place; as the people of the Country report by hear-say from their fore-fathers, though their relations differ in many circumstantial particulars. After this description, our Author addeth, *Plura ejusdem generis & alibi in eadem Diœcesi videre & observare licèt, figura quidem diversa, sed eundem in usum fabrefacta*.

But, what need we travel into *Denmark*, for Patterns of this kind of Monuments, when we have two most notable ones here at *home*, one in *Cornwal*, another in *Oxford-shire*? which, if you have not beheld with your own eyes, and dare give credit to Mr *Camdens*, you may have them represented to you in these his Descriptions.

"Near St *Neoths* in *Cornwal* (saith he) upon a plain adjacent to a wondrous pile of Rocks heaped up together upon one stone of lesser size, fashioned naturally in form of a Cheese, so as it seemeth to be pressed like a Cheese, whereupon it is named, *Wring-Cheese*; are to be seen many great stones, on some sort four-square, of which seven or eight are pitched upright, of equal distance asunder. The neighbour Inhabitants term them *Hurlers*; as being by a devout and godly error perswaded, they had been Men sometimes transformed into Stones, for profaning the Lord's Day with hurling the Ball. Others would have it to be a Trophy or Monument, in memorial of some Battel. And so doubtless this was, and not improbably left by the *Danes*.

"Not far from *Burford*, upon the very border of *Oxford-shire*, is an antient Monument, to wit, certain huge stones placed in a circle. The common people call them *Roll-rich stones*, and dream they were sometimes Men, by a miraculous Metamorphosis turned into hard stones. The Draught of them, such as it is, pourtraied long since, here I represent unto your view. For, without all form, and shape they be, unequal, and by long continuance of time much impaired. The highest of them all, which without the Circle looketh into the earth, they call the King; because he should have been King of *England* (forsooth) if he had once seen *Long Compton*, a little Town lying beneath, and which one may see, if he go some few paces forward: other five, standing at the other side, touching as it were one another, they imagine to have been Knights mounted on Horseback; and the rest the Army. These would I verily think to have been the Monument of some Victory, and haply erected by *Rollo* the *Dane*, who afterward conquered *Normandy*. For, what time He with his *Danes* troubled *England* with depredations, we read, that the *Danes* joyned Battel with the *English* thereby, at *Hoch Norton*; a place for no one thing more famous in old time, than for the woful slaughter of the *English* in that foughten field, under the Reign of King *Edward the Elder*."

To these may be annexed another eminent Trophy, known by the name of *Stipperstones*, standing upon *Huckstowe* Forrest in *Shropshire*, consisting of great piles of stones, and others like Rocks perpendicularly erected thickly together, and set up to perpetuate the renown of a fatal defeat given to the *Britans* by *Harald*. Concerning which *Giraldus Cambrensis* hath this clear testimony. Harald *in person being himself the last footman, with foot-men, and, light arms, and victuals answerable for such an Expedition in* Wales, *valiantly went round about through all* Wales, *so as that he left few or none alive. And for a perpetual memory of this Victory, you may find very many great stones in that country erected after the antique manner upon hillocks, in those places wherein He had been Conqueror, with these words engraven,* Hic fuit Victor Haraldus: *Here was Harald Conqueror.* Now these being sufficient instances of *Danique* Triumphal Monuments, it remains onely that we search after some of their *Loca Comitialia,* or

Places designed for the Election and Inauguration of their Kings.

In which, not onely their Noble-men and Grandees, but also the Commons being upon summons assembled from all parts of the Nation; used to consult and vote about matters of State of greatest importance, more especially upon the death of the Prince; and in that case, to give their Suffrages for the next in blood, or power, to succeed him. This business, as being of most concernment to the Publick, was performed with pomp and solemnity answerable; the manner and Ceremonies whereof are concisely set down by *Saxo Grammaticus;* thus. *Lecturi Regem veteres affixis humo saxis insistere, suffragiaque promere consueverunt, subjectorum lapidum firmitate facti constantiam ominaturi:* "Our Fore-fathers being to elect their King, used to stand upon stones pitch'd upright in the ground, and to give their suffrages; by the firmness of the stones upon which they stood, tacitly declaring the firmness of their act, and as by a good Omen foreshewing the durability of his government." And *Ol. Wormius* more fully describing the manner, both of the open Senate-House, and of the Election it self, saith, *Reperiuntur in his oris loca quædam, in quibus Reges olim solemni creabantur pompa, quæ cincta adhuc grandibus saxis, utplurimum duodecim, conspiciuntur, in medio grandiore quodam prominente, cui omnium suffragiis electum Regem imponebant, magnoque applausu excipiebant. Hic & comitia celebrabant, & de regni negotiis consultabant. Regem vero designaturi, Electores saxis insistebant forum cingentibus, decreti firmitudinem pronunciantes:* "in this Country are beheld certain Courts or Parliament, in which heretofore Kings were elected with solemn state; which are surrounded with mighty stones, for the most part twelve in number, and one other stone exceeding the rest in eminency, set in the middle, upon which (as upon a Regal Throne) they seated the newly elected King, by the general suffrage of the assembly, and inaugurated him with great applause and loud acclamations. Here they held their great Councils, and consulted about affairs of the Kingdome. But when they met together to nominate their King, the Electors stood upright upon the stones environing the Court, and giving their voyces, thereby confirmed their choice."

This rudely-magnificent Custome of Electing the supreme Magistrate, in such open circles of huge stones, and after such a manner; as it was of highest Antiquity, so was it likewise of greatest Duration among the *Danes.* For, *Bernhardus Malincrot (in libr. de Archi-cancellariis, p.* 158.) through a long series or descent of their Kings, brings it down to the time of the Emperor *Charls the fourth,* who publishing that so renowned golden Bull *de Electione Imperatorum,* gave occasion to the abrogation of it.

Yea, so sacred were these Courts, in such high esteem and veneration were they held, for many hundreds of years together; that even in time of publick peace and tranquillity, the Candidate King was *de jure* obliged there to receive his solemn Inauguration, and assume the Ensigns of Royalty: as if the Place and Ceremonies were essential parts of his right to soveraignty, and the votes of his Electors much more valid and authentique, for being pronounced in that *Forum.* And if it hapned that the King fell in some forein expedition, by the hand of the Enemy, or by a less glorious death; there ensued an *Inter-regnum,* till such time as his surviving Army had in some convenient plain brought together a multitude of the largest stones they could possibly find, and set them both for the interrment of his Corps, and the election of his Successor: and this as well because they reputed an Election in such a place, a good addition of title; as because many great and irreparable incommodities might redound to the Republique during that pause or respite of Government, in case the new election were deferred, until they had returned to their own Country, and assembled the best part of the Nation in some one of their ancient Kings-benches, as they may be properly enough termed, considering their dignity and use. To authorise this, which otherwise might be thought somewhat romantique, I am provided of a text out of a very grave and faithfull writer of that Nationa, *Suaningius*; which is well worthy my recital, and your special consideration; being that which gave me the first hint for my conjecture touching the End or purpose, for which *Stone-heng* was built. The text is this; *Locum publicæ Regiæ electionis postquam incolis convenientem, ad quem, nulla obstante itineris difficultate, omnes qui erant vocati, venire possent, elegissent; saxa grandia singulari opera atque studio conquiri, atque in eundum locum, quem electioni Regiæ destinarant, comportari curarunt. Neque enim tum, quemadmodum hodie, destinata electioni Regum certa erant loca, sed pro arbitrio sententiaque eorum, qui autoritate & potentia alios antecellebant, eligebantur. Huc comportate saxa conscendentes hi, quibus eligendi jus commendatum erat, circumstante populo, suffragia ex iis ferebant*: and may be thus Englished. "When for the publick election of the King, they had made choice of a place convenient, to which all that were summoned might, with the least difficulty of travail, repair; they took care, that stones of extraordinary greatness should be, with singular labour and diligence, sought forth, and brought together in the same place, which they had appointed for the Royal Election. For, they were not then, as now a dayes, certain appointed places for that affair; but such were chosen, at the pleasure and judgment of those, who excelled others in authority and power. Upon the stones brought hither, those to whom the right of electing was delegated, mounting up, delivered their suffrages, the people standing round about below." The same in every particular is confirmed by the learned *Stephanus Stephanius*, in his Commentaries upon the first Book of *Saxo Grammaticus* his History of *Denmark*; whither I remit the unsatisfied.

As for *Examples* of this noblest and most magnificent sort of Monuments; *Olaus Wormius* hath furnished us with Three very conspicuous ones; one in *Seland*, neer 𝔏𝔢𝔦𝔯𝔢, called 𝔎𝔬𝔫𝔤𝔰𝔱𝔬𝔩𝔬𝔫, or Kings throne; another in *Schoneland*, not far from *Lundie*, in which homage was annually paid to King *Olaus*, and *Christianus* the first was with royal solemnity inaugurated and invested with regal ornaments; a third neer *Viburg*, in the *Cimbric* territory, in which common tradition will have *Dane* the first to have been likewise elected, and inthroned, as the name 𝔇𝔞𝔫𝔢𝔯𝔩𝔦𝔲𝔫𝔤, which to this day it bears, seems to witness. And the reason he gives, why there is one in each of these three Provinces, is, that anciently they were distinct Principalities, and under the dominion of as many petty Kings, though now reduced under the soveraignty of a Monarch, the present King of *Denmark*.

Nor are we destitute of the like in *England*. For, in *Cornwall*, on a large plain, called *Biscaw Woun*, near a village named *St. Buriens*, stand erected, in a circle, nineteen huge stones, distant each from the other about twelve foot; with one stone far higher and greater than the rest in the Centre. Which though *Camden* supposeth to be some Trophy left by the *Romans*, under the later Emperors; or else by *Athelstane* the *Saxon*, when he had subdued the *Cornish* men: yet considering, on one side, that the *Romans* used not to eternize their victories here, or elsewhere, by any such Trophies; and, on the other, that there was a time, when the *Danes* also had not only *Cornwall*, but all *England* beside, under their barbarous subjection; and that this Monument doth in all particulars correspond with the Courts of Elections Royal in *Denmark*, of which I am now speaking; considering this, I say, no reason appears to the contrary, but I may assent to the opinion of *Wormius*, that it was, after a great defeat of the English *Saxons*, by his Country-men, erected for the Election of their own King, and the investiture of him with the soveraignty of his newly acquired Principality.

Excerpt 5. Now Charleton musters all the foregoing to arrive at his conclusion: a systematic eight-point comparison of Stonehenge and Worm's Danish *comitalia loca*. This is his brilliant insight, partly right for the right reasons, and partly for the wrong ones.

The rest of his book goes on to question his own hypothesis. A true scientist present at the creation of the Royal Society, his "devotion to truth" is the only constant. He says new evidence is bound to come to light and new ideas come about: exactly what has happened with the advent of modern archaeology. In my view this but confirms his tentatively-offered theory: Stonehenge as a royal election court.

Here, perhaps, You'l be a little surpriz'd, if I adventure to make our *Stone-heng* it self bring up the rear of this last and most Gigantique division of *Danique* Antiquities. But, it is my Conjecture; the ultimate scope of my so laborious Enquiry; the point in which all the lines of this long discourse concentre. Wherefore, having now at length brought you to a place, where You may at once behold the strength of all those several Reasons, that conspired to suggest that opinion to me: it is fit I should draw them together in as small a compass, as I can, and so present them to your consideration, while what hath been delivered both of all the *Danish* Unletter'd Monuments in general, and in particular of their *Courts for Election of Kings*, is yet fresh in your memory. And this, I conceive, may be most concisely, and most advantagiously effected, by way of Parallel, or Comparison, in this plain and easie Method.

The Ancient Courts of Parliament in Denmark *alwayes*	STONE-HENG likewise
I.	I.
WEre situated in large and open Plains and not far from some Town, of competent reception, at least for people of the best Quality: and	STands in a spacious Plain, about two miles distant from Ambresbury, anciently a Town of great note: and
II.	II.
In, or neer to the middle of the Kingdom; that such as were summoned to convene, upon the Election of a King, or other affair of publick importance, might repair thither with equal conveniency: and	In a mediterranean or mid-land Country; for so Camden calls Wiltshire: and
III.	III.
Upon a greatly rising ground, for the advantage of prospect, and that the Common people assembled to confirm the suffrages of the Electors, by their universal applause and congratulatory acclamations; might see and witness the solemn manner of the election.	Uppon a plot of ground somewhat more eminent, than the circumjacent Plain, which enlargeth the prospect of the Pile, and which cannot be approached but by an easie ascent, on all sides.
IV.	IV.
Were open on the Top, and sides; that so the King elect standing in the middle, might be beheld from all quarters of the neighbouring Plain; and the Votes of the Electors the better heard by the multitude,	Is uncovered above, or roofless, and environed not with continued walls, but stones pitcht upright; so that such as stand on any side without, may perceive what's done within.

standing round about, at a becoming distance.

V.

Made onely of huge stones, the largest that could possibly be found any where in the Country; rude, unhewn, of no certain figure.

VI.

And these set upright, at equal distance each from other, in a Circle; that so the Electors standing upon them might make a round:

VII.

With one stone taller and bigger than the rest, erected in the Centre, for the King to stand upon, and shew himself to the people, at the time of his Inauguration, and receive their joyfull Acclamations, wishes of felicity, and other testimonies of submission and fealty.

VIII.

Without any Inscription, or Letters ingraven upon any one of the Stones: because the Fabrique was sufficiently Known by its proper Form; and the Use in a peculiar manner customary to the *Danes*.

V.

Made of stones of vast magnitude; and unhewn, as they came from the Quarry, of no regular figure: and

VI.

These set in round, equally distant among themselves, and perpendicular;

VII.

With one Stone, in the inmost circle (now lying along and broken, but at first set upright, and then probably placed at the very centre of the whole work) whose remaining fragments put together make, according to Mr. Jones *his accompt, sixteen feet in length; Which is as likely to have been a* Kongstolon *(as the* Danes *call theirs) or Kings throne, as an altar.*

VIII.

Having no Epigraph, cut, or trencht in any of the Stones; as carrying a sufficient evidence of its Designment and use, in the figure of its platform, and perfection in all essential parts; and speaking its Founders, in the (in those dayes) well-understood language of its vastness, and the similitude it bore to others erected by the same Nation in their own Country.

Thus far, You see, the *Parallel* holds in all particulars, even to a high degree of Resemblance; there being no one thing in the *Antique Courts of Parliament* yet remaining in *Denmark*, which is not be to found also in our *Stone-heng*. Some things, I must acknowledge, are observed in *This*, more than in *those*: and lest I might be thought over-favourable and partial to my own Conceipt; if I should omit to note them; I shall particularly observe what they are.

The key to the present work is Charleton's eight-point comparative analysis above, especially item VII. On that basis I have ventured, in plate V:2, to picture the king of Stonehenge being elected as he stands high on his election stone, his electors on lower ones, while a popular assembly looks on. The scene, however, is projected back into the Bronze Age: my refinement of Charleton's Iron Age scenario.

Appendix *III*

A Novelization of Charleton's Theory by Leon Stover

In the last section of chapter 3, I mention a novel about Stonehenge (Stover 1972). This was done with the science fiction writer Harry Harrison, a friend I admired for his artful skill in working realistic technicalities into fiction. In this case we brought in methods for the construction of Stonehenge, as well as the ancient techniques of tin smelting, bronze making, and the sailing of sea-going vessels for long-distance trade.

The novel took off in direct response to Professor Atkinson's discovery of the Mycenaean dagger carving on stone 53. We back-plotted our story to show, at the end, how that carving got there. Fig. 84 pictures it once again, this time with an ax-head carving at bottom left (at top right is part of the one already shown). Such carvings are everywhere, the Stonehenge kings' stock in trade. The novel dramatizes these transactions, with Teutons on the continent in particular.

This novel in turn prompted another thesis novel, *Stonehenge 2000 B.C.*, by Bernard Cornwell (2000), who wrote me to say as much. Cornwell's record as an historical novelist, given to dutiful homework on various periods, is outstanding, so when he says his Stonehenge novel offers a "different interpretation," I give it serious attention. Although he has temples aplenty and astronomical alignments at Stonehenge itself, his religious thesis is a worthy rebuttal to my political one. I welcome his creative offering, knowing that none of us can ever do more than approximate a coherent theory.

Woven into my plot is Dr. Charleton's political theory of Stonehenge, which seems appropriate since he himself was a writer of novels on top of everything else.

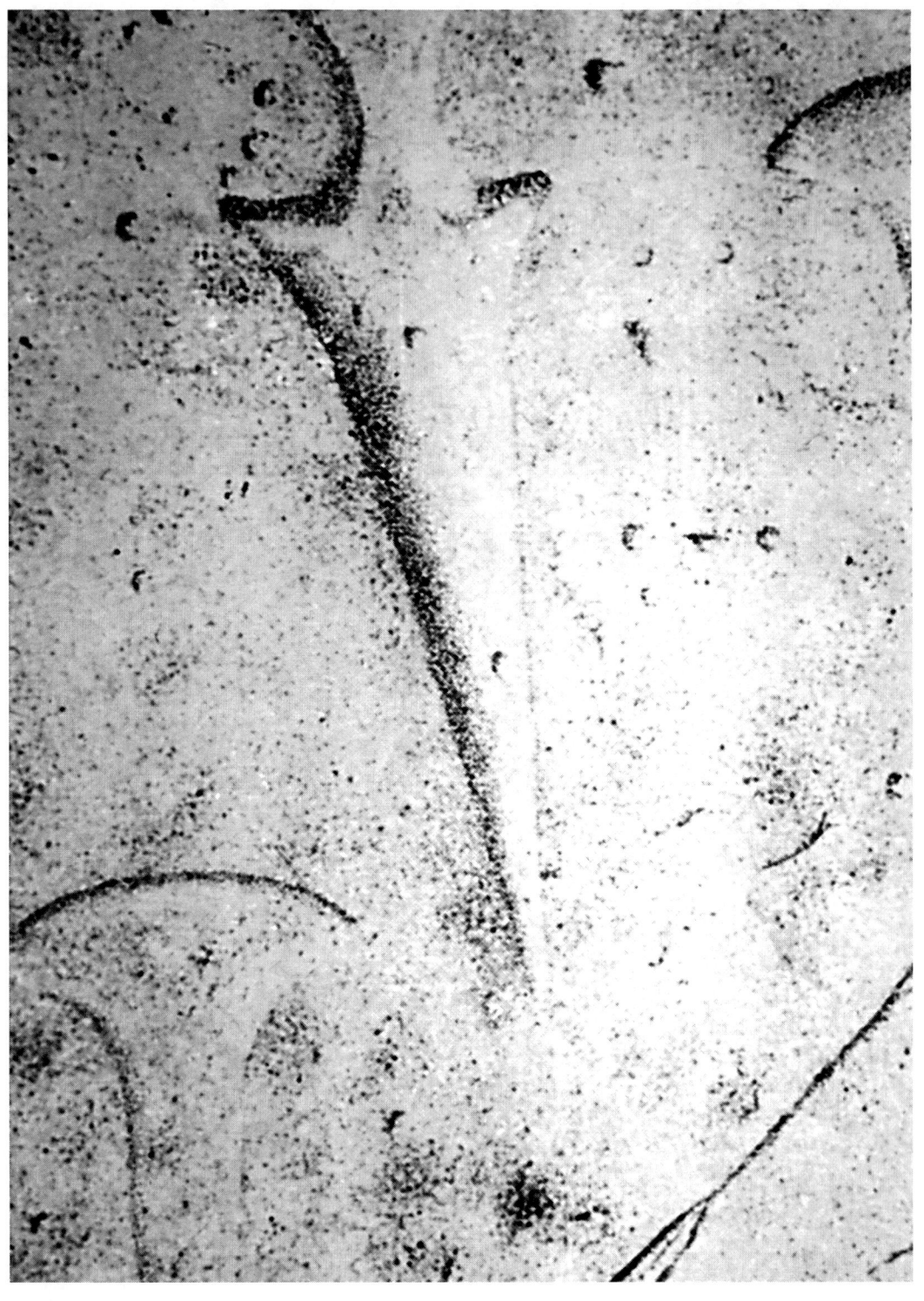

Fig. 84. *Dagger carving on stone 53, with bronze ax-head carving at bottom left and part of another at top right. The ax-heads are always depicted haft down, blade up.*

Indeed, it served to deepen my interest in his line of thinking and I went on to further explicate it in *Stonehenge: The Indo-European Heritage* (Stover 1978). By that time, however, a radiocarbon date for Stonehenge III had been arrived at, which made it 500 years too early for Mycenaean involvement, fictional or otherwise.

Nevertheless, Mr. Harrison and I brought out a second edition, the unabridged version, because our original publisher found the text too long. So many interesting details were left out we determined to get the full story on record. Not that a change in dating was ignored. I added a lengthy Afterword, plus bibliography, explaining all the ins and outs of this issue, at the same time justifying the use of Celtic mythology from Iron Age Ireland in recreating a Bronze Age culture in southern England. That still stands.

The title of the unabridged edition is *Stonehenge: Where Atlantis Died* (Stover 1983). This proved to be irresistible in every translation, including Russian, Polish, and Finnish. Many readers, I suspect, were disappointed when they learned that the real grabber, Atlantis, was no unsolved mystery, to be fantastically imagined any which way, but archaeological fact established ever since 1909. Plato's Atlantis (one small round island and one larger rectangular island) is none other than Thera (also called Santorini) and Crete. These were the main islands of the Minoan thallassocracy, a Bronze Age maritime empire rival to the Mycenaean empire centered on the Peloponnesus (Galanopolis and Bacon 1969; Hood 1971; Luce 1969).

The actual struggle between these two empires is the novel's premise, based on Plato's own words in the *Critias*.

> The Greek cities were in command of the one side and fought through the whole of the war, and in command of the other side was the king of Atlantis, which was an island once upon a time, but now lies sunk by earthquakes.

The following bold and dramatic promise of what is to come prefaces the novel.

> This was the world.
> The blue waters of the Mediterranean were at the heart of it. The world was the islands in this sea and the lands that ringed its shores. Journey was by water, across the sea, and up the rivers of fresh water that fed it.
> This was the world where bold warriors battled with bronze swords. Without bronze there could be no warriors — just as without tin there could be no bronze. Copper alone was too soft to make a warrior's weapon. Therefore no journey was too difficult, no effort too great, to obtain the tin that transformed the abundant and malleable copper into noble bronze.
> Only the boldest warriors dared to voyage to the ends of the world, to venture up the rivers to find this tin. Only the bravest dared to go beyond the land-rimmed sea, out through the narrow straits into the storm-filled Atlantic beyond. To sail north in the cold fog, to the icy island in the ocean where, with heroic effort, the tin could be found.
> This was the world one thousand and five hundred years before the birth of Christ.

The first of two maps (fig. 85) illustrates the geography of Plato's account of this epic struggle. Cartographic features are for the most part named to suggest the ancients' world-view. Down at bottom right are the home islands of the Atlanteans (Minoans), to the left Mycenae. Top left is the Island of the Yerni (Britain), the vital source of tin for Mycenae, only to be contested by Atlantis. Its tin mine in midreaches of the Danube River have already been attacked by agents of Mycenaean intrigue, and so the war moves on to Britain where Atlantis is defeated by default: Thera blows up.

The second map (fig. 86) details the Island of the Yerni. At bottom left is the Mycenaean tin mine, vital to the war with Atlantis. At center are the five strongholds (duns) of the Yerni (proto–Celts) in constant conflict with each other. These duns are located in the five regions mapped in fig. 86, where in this book four under-kings ruled beneath the Stonehenge overking. In the novel the term dun is borrowed from the Irish and Scottish Gaelic for fortress, fortified place, royal residence, castle, etc. The novel, however, never mentions Yerni kings but only bull-chiefs, a term taken from the *Rig-Veda*, where "cow chiefs" so name the leaders of the Aryan invasion of India. The term calls attention to the importance of wealth in cattle to the political leadership of the chiefdoms or kingdoms of early Indo-European society everywhere. So Yerni bull-chiefs it is.

Now for the novelistic story line. King Perimedes, like Agamemnon in Homer, is ruler of the Argolid, now at war with King Atlas of Atlantis, founded by the legendary King Minos, who ruled the Minoan sea-empire contesting the Mycenaean land-empire: the two sides in Plato's account of a great war extending beyond Mediterranean waters. Perimedes receives word from a survivor of a raid on his tin

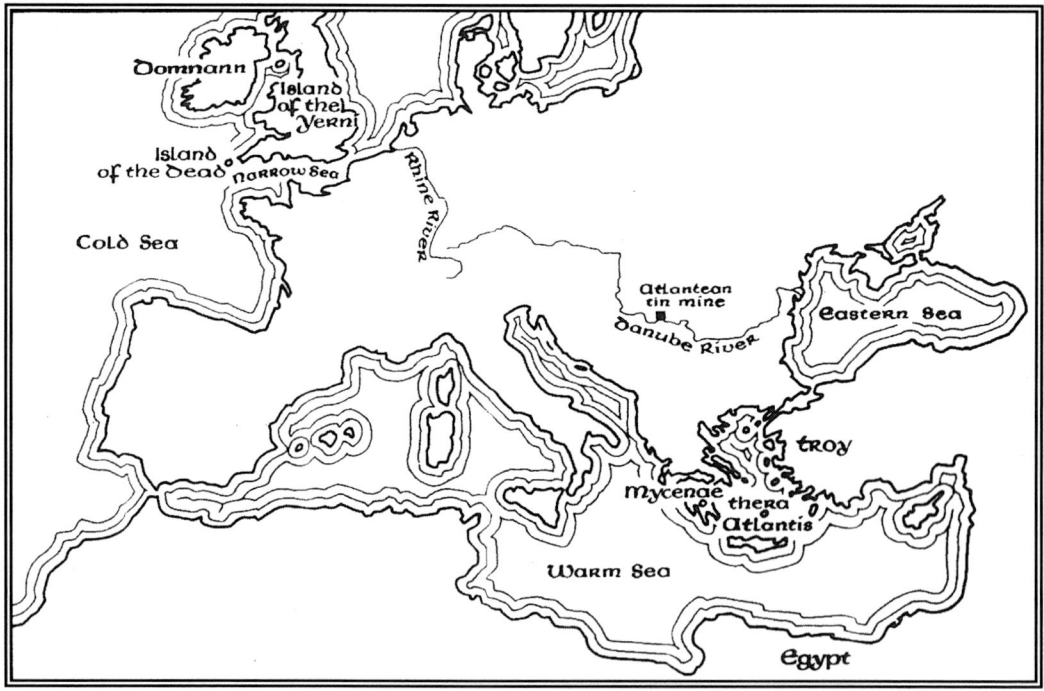

Fig. 85. *World-map of the war between Mycenae and Atlantis; from Stover 1983.*

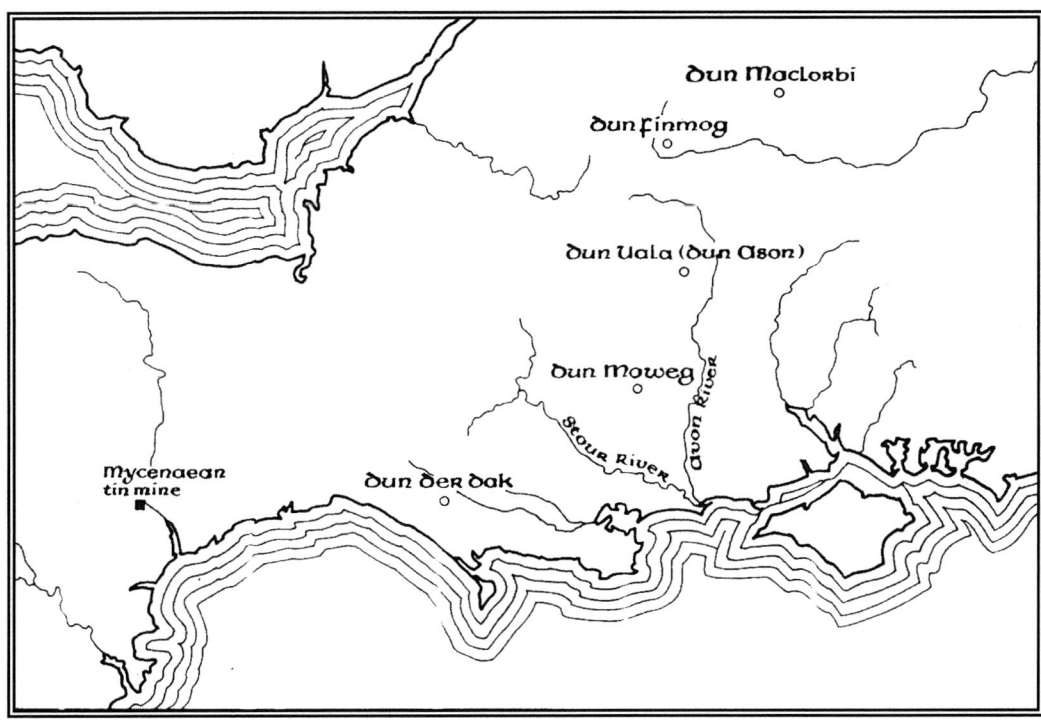

Fig. 86. *Map featuring details of the Island of the Yerni; from Stover 1983.*

mine far to the north, carried out by Yerni warriors. In the event they were led to do so by a sinister Atlantean agent from Troy. His trick was to get the warring Yerni chiefdoms unified in attacking the Mycenaean tin mine: greater heroic glory in that than in fighting each other.

Perimedes decides to send his son prince Ason to the trouble spot and find some way to settle the Yerni problem. Ason takes on this difficult mission, but asks that he bring along his homoerotic friend Inteb, the Egyptian architect who, through trade relations with pharaoh Thuthmosis IV, had just completed building the cyclopian walls and Lion Gate of Mycenae's hilltop citadel. The two arrived at a monumental solution, the building of Stonehenge with Ason, a skilled warrior, installed as bull-chief of all five regions. The Atlanteans counter in force and capture Ason, who is taken back to the palace of Knossos on Crete to face King Atlas. At that moment Thera explodes, a tsunami swamps the palace, and Ason in triumph yells, "Die, Atlantis, die!" Inteb leaves a memorial at Stonehenge, that carving of the royal dagger of Mycenae on stone 53.

Two excerpts from the novel follow. The first is my favorite, a digest of heroic poetry exampled in the Irish hero tales: praise-poetry recited by Druidic bards (see Chadwick 1912; Chadwick and Chadwick 1932). In this case the proto-Druid Nemed sings extravagant praise of Ason just after he defeated, in single combat, the boastful leader of a Yerni dun opposed to Ason's unification project.

Nemed chants with rising enthusiasm before his Yerni audience.

Much of the material was familiar, old lines repeated and used in different ways. This only increased the warriors' appreciation, rather than lessening it. They nodded at the parts they knew well.

> Sound of thunder and rushing wind,
> A crashing, a breaking,
> Rock tearing, ground ripping,
> Such sounds to deafen the ears.
>
> The sounds that I heard were men at war,
> Shield shock of shield against shield.
> Axes striking and breaking,
> Skulls crushed.
>
> What fighting was done then,
> Deep voices of heroes
> And battling warriors, raging with anger,
> Grim wild men, great bull-chiefs.
>
> There was Ason,
> In the midst of gore, seeking blood,
> Man of the long knife, bellowing bull.
>
> Then they met,
> then Ason struck.
> Cleft Uala's head,
> Drove the blow to his navel —
> Then a second cross-wise stroke
> Brought him down in three pieces.

Nemed drew a deep wavering breath, loud in the silence, and shouted the remainder without stopping or even pausing.

> Drenched with blood and gray with brains,
> He cut away
> > jaw from head,
> > head from trunk,
> > arms from trunk,
> > bend from arms,
> > wrists from bend.
> > fists from wrists,
> > thumbs from fists,
> > nails from thumbs,
> > legs from trunk,
> > knees from legs,
> > calves from knees,
> > feet from calves,
> > toes from feet,
> > nails from toes,

And he sent these limbs and parts
Flying front and back like bees
Buzzing about in the sunlight.

Loud shouts of appreciation followed this, and buzzing sounds that would not stop until Nemed had regained his breath and repeated the part about the bees again.

Next is a passage describing how Inteb, under Ason's unquestioned authority, got the Yerni to line up for the splitting of a great sarsen slab into usable sizes. The point here, looking back from the Celtic example, is that Yerni warriors were unaccustomed to coordinated action. Caesar recalls his Gaulish foes fighting as individuals (like the hero of *Beowulf,* "most eager for renown") who fall to his legions disciplined to fight by the numbers: heroic ethic versus military ethic.

The warriors are instructed to come armed with heavy stone mauls, twenty selected.

"There is room for no more. The honor is for these warriors, who will do what no one has ever done before."

They swaggered about, then climbed onto the great slab with him, calling out boasts to the scowling warriors left behind. They brought the mauls with them. With the aid of the Mycenaeans, Inteb pushed the warriors into a line against the far edge of the stone. Shoulder to shoulder, they stretched the length of the slab, listening with pained attention as Inteb explained what they had to do. It was not complex, but they were not used to working together, had never done anything in unison before in their lives. It was a concept they found difficult to understand. He made them repeat the motions, over and over, many times before they got it right. Small stones, no bigger than a man's fist were passed up and they used these as they practiced. Inteb had drawn two charcoal lines the length of the slab, a pace apart, and he kept redrawing the lines as their shuffling feet obliterated them. There were mutterings of complaint over the stupid hot thing they were doing — but no one smiled. Inteb repeated the instructions with a voice rapidly growing hoarse.

"That's it, all in a line, your feet on that marked line. Not standing in front of it or behind it, but *on* it. Good. Raise your mauls, as high as your head, hold them there ... *hold* them until I give the word, and all together, just for once, *drop them!*"

The small rocks clattered down, most of them on the marked line in an irregular fall, rolling about and some dropping over the edge to the ground. The watching crowd had been cleared back by the Mycenaeans, but small boys ran forward to retrieve the fallen stones and pass them back up. They were enjoying themselves, if no one else was.

"No, leave them there," Inteb ordered. "And throw the rest of the stones away. We'll do it now with the mauls."

There were excited shouts at this announcement, and the warriors called to one another as they kicked the small stones away and bent to pick up the waiting mauls. It was an impressive sight, the tall, sweat-drenched warriors, shoulder to shoulder the length of the great slab, with Inteb standing behind them. The crowd was silent.

"Lift!" Inteb called out and they bent and a ripple moved down the line as they straightened and the green mauls rose in the air.

"Hold, hold!" he shouted, since some of the warriors were slower than the others and one, cursing, dropped the stone on his foot. Then they were all up, high, higher...

"*Drop them!*"

The great weight of hard stone fell with a rolling thunder, and the warriors jumped back.

Nothing happened. Inteb shouted hoarse orders above the growing murmur from the crowd.

"Not good enough, nor at the same time, not on the line. Do it right or it can't be done at all, you great hulking dim-brained animals. Lift together, hold together, drop together, hold together, drop together ... *drop!*"

Again, nothing — but a rising growl of anger from the warriors as well as the crowd. The Mycenaeans raised their weapons and shields, and Ason jumped up next to Inteb and paced behind the warriors' backs.

"Killers of dogs!" he shouted. "This is harder than killing. This is something you must do right — or I will slay you all. This you will do."

By force of will he kept them there, shouting aloud now in protest, raising and dropping the mauls again — with no result. With the flat of his sword Ason drove back the men who tried to turn away, cursing them in three tongues, so that they once again grabbed up the mauls.

"Over your heads, you eaters of turds!" he called out. "High, higher, hold them there, all of you, do what I tell you, do it right, because this time they fall together and they fall on the line the correct way, bring them down ... *now!*"

Shouting angrily, the Yerni warriors hurled the stones down with a crashing roar, and the solid rock beneath their feet shivered.

With a growing, crackling, rushing roar it sheared in half, fell away, a great broken slab that dropped and cracked, spraying fragments out at the screaming, running crowd.

Dumbfounded, the warriors looked down at what they had done.

The immense slab of stone had broken along its entire length, along the line Inteb had drawn upon its surface.

How-to-do-it passages like this are woven into a tale of high adventure set in ancient times: a Bronze Age thriller. Along the way, however, its entertainment value is not without instructive content, the business of a serious thesis novel.

Appendix *IV*

Excerpt from *Stonehenge* by William Stukeley (1740)

William Stukeley, M.D. (1683–1765), began his career as a young country doctor in Lincolnshire. Avidly disposed to antiquarian interests, by age 30 he took Stonehenge as a special passion, strongly admixed with a religious mission. The reverse of Dr. Charleton, he feared the scientific world view would destroy the true foundations of Christianity, already shaken by seventeenth-century Deism in Charleton's time. Strangely enough, Stukeley's lasting contribution was to make Druidism central to the national folklore.

The full title of Stukeley's book is *Stonehenge, a Temple Restor'd to the British Druids*, by which he means restored to "Patriarchal Christianity," the founding faith. He says

> My intent is (besides preserving the memory of these extraordinary monuments, now in great danger of ruin), to promote, as much as I am able, the knowledge and practice of ancient and true Religion, to revive in the minds of the learned the spirit of Christianity ... to warm our hearts into that true sense of Religion, which keeps the medium between ignorant superstition and learned free-thinking, between enthusiasm and the rational worship of God, which is no where upon earth done, in my judgement, better than in the Church of England.

Stukeley had entered Holy Orders in 1729, but his antiquarian pursuits continued unabated, even as he entered upon the heated theological question of the day: how to reason out a basis for religious faith acceptable to all sectarian parties among the reformed churches and free-thinkers. His answer, in the Stonehenge book of 1740, was to be found in the "Natural religion" of the native Druids. Having come from ancient Phoenicia, descended from the land of the Canaanites in the time of Abraham, they brought with them the original "patriarchal religion."

Druids, of course, were familiar to the British public ever since Aylett Sammes first translated Caesar's account of his Gallic wars in *Britannia Antiqua Illustrata* (1676). The one illustration that most impressed was that of a learned Druid, impossible book in hand (see fig. 12). This image Stukeley adapted to his own purpose, to portray ancient wise men of a sort who would never indulge the barbaric acts of human sacrifice described by Caesar (see fig. 68). These remade Druids are now the standard model for those mock-druids who attend the midsummer sunrise at Stonehenge every year, drawing huge tourist crowds and getting national television coverage. They are rather benign and altogether high minded.

Two of Stukeley's exemplary Druids are pictured in fig. 87. One of them stands at the temple's front door, looking very like the memorable Aylett Sammes image of 1676, except that he has no book in hand, although Stukeley credits his British Druids with literacy in the Phoenician alphabet. The other one stands within, facing the entrance with arms upraised. His object of worship, however, is the altar stone directly behind him. Title of the drawing is "A Peep into the Sanctum Sanctorum."

The temple itself is restored to the finish of well-dressed stones no less elegant than those drafted by Inigo Jones for his Roman Temple. Stukeley, at least, gets the overall design correct. He was, in fact, a scrupulous draftsman of prehistoric ruins of every sort. His field drawing of Stonehenge in fig. 88 is accurate in every detail, including the leaning of that great trilithon pillar (stone 56), not pushed upright until 1901 by the Ministry of Works. The seated man rests on a broken half of stone 80, Stukeley's Altar Stone (his coinage).

Professional archaeologists regard Stukeley as the least reliable of the antiquarian amateurs, way out there on the lunatic fringe for his fanciful Druids. Yet they rely on his field drawings for lost features of the prehistoric landscape, and they still denominate Stonehenge a "temple" almost by default: what else *could* it be if not a religious edifice? Dr. Charleton had a political solution but this, however sane the learned argument, is dismissed out of hand because of the impossible Viking connection. In this book I have dared to justify Charleton's concept by removing his royal election court to the Bronze Age, and to make over Stukeley's ridiculous Druids as the proto–Druidic designers of Stonehenge. Reflection upon the history of ideas about Stonehenge finds that some are more useful than others to the interpretation of indisputable archaeological findings, empirical facts that do not and cannot explain themselves.

Inigo Jones offers a perfect example of how culture-bound a theory can be. His Roman temple mirrors exactly the classical revival he led under the reign of James I. Charleton clearly reflects the cultural ambience of the Restoration after Charles II regained the English throne. Nevertheless he broke through to a suggestive theory applicable to a Bronze Age kingdom. Stukeley's baggage was the current religious controversy he engaged, with his Druids earning him lasting scorn. In his defense, however, allow me to point out the significance of his original title,

Fig. 87. *Stukeley's drawing, derived from fig. 12, of a British Druid standing at the doorway into the Stonehenge sanctuary, another within.*

Appendix IV

Fig. 88. *Stukeley's field drawing of the ruins of Stonehenge, the Altar Stone under the seated figure.*

The History of the Temples of the Ancient Celts.* The term "Celt" was just then coming into use by British antiquaries as a substitute for "Briton," in recognition of the fact, brought out by French antiquaries, that the Celtae or Gauls were the same people as the Ancient Britains (see Piggott 1968:152*f*). Stukeley, therefore, is a precocious contributor to Celtic studies, which today so much enrich our retrospective understanding of the proto–Celtic builders of Stonehenge.

In the excerpt below, Chapter 1, Stukeley reviews the works of Inigo Jones and Walter Charleton and faults them for restoring Stonehenge to the wrong people, Romans and Danes respectively. The right people are the British Druids of Phoenician origin. To validate this notion he refers to excruciating measurements he took at Stonehenge and other monuments. He concludes that their builders used the Hebrew cubit as the basic unit of cadastral mensuration. This is no less fanciful than the so-called megalithic yard (= 2.72 feet) deduced by the astronomical theorists (see Thom 1967).

**The same intent lies behind his later book of 1743 on Avebury,* Abury, a Temple of the British Druids, with Some Others. *His field drawings of this complex monument show missing stones valuable for historians to know about, as do those lost at nearby West Kennet Long Barrow.*

Excerpt from Stonehenge *(Stukeley)*

STONEHENGE
A WORK of the
𝔅𝔯𝔦𝔱𝔦𝔰𝔥 𝔇𝔯𝔲𝔦𝔡𝔰
Describ'd.

Chap. I

Of the Situation of Stonehenge *in general. That it was a temple of the Druids, of the patriarchal mode, who were a most ancient oriental colony. In later times, the* Belgæ *from the continent, conquer'd this country from them. Whence these stones were brought? Of their nature, magnitude, weight. Of the measure of the Druids, the ancient* Hebrew *cubit, and its proportion to the* English *foot.*

THE *Wiltshire* downs, or *Salisbury* plain, (as commonly call'd) for extent and beauty, is, without controversy, one of the most delightful parts of *Britain*. But of late years great encroachments have been made upon it by the plough, which threatens the ruin of this fine champain, and of all the monuments of antiquity thereabouts. Monuments, we can scarce say, whether more wonderful in themselves, more observ'd, or less understood! among them, *Stonehenge* has been eminent from the remotest ages, tho' 'tis not the greatest, most considerable, or most ancient. But 'tis my intent to begin my discourse from it, because the latest, and from thence proceed upwards in our inquiries, about the times and authors of these stupendous works, the temples of the Druids in our Island: for I cannot doubt that *Stonehenge* was such. The idea we conceive of the distance of time, when these kind of works were made, cannot be ill-form'd, if we consider, that the utmost accounts of 'em we have in writing, are from the *Britons*, the remains of the people who lived here, at the time of the *Roman* invasion. This is mention'd in some manuscripts of *Ninnius* before the *Saxons* and *Danes* came over. And the oldest *Britons* speak of this only by tradition, far above all memorial. They wonder'd at *Stonehenge* then, and were as far to seek about the founders and intent of it, as we now. They have recourse to magic, as is usual, when they would account for any thing seemingly so much above human power, to accomplish. They tell us, these stones of immense bulk were brought from a plain, in the middle of *Ireland*, and the like. Which reports give us only no obscure hint of their true authors, the Druids, who were fam'd for magic, and were driven last into *Ireland*, in the time of the *Romans*. There they built such like works again, or their brethren had built before; till Christianity, to which the greatest and purest part of their own doctrine was akin, soon put an end to their polity, which the *Roman* arms could not do. And they embrac'd that religion, to which their own opinions and rites had so direct a tendency. This is the sentiment of *Origen* on *Ezekiel* iv. And 'tis sufficiently evident, if we consider, that the first planters of Christianity in *Ireland*, immediately converted the whole island, without so much as the blood of one martyr. Nay, the Druids themselves, at that time the only national priests, embraced it readily, and some of them were very zealous preachers of it, and effectual converts of others. For instance, the great *Columbanus* himself was a Druid: the apostle of *Ireland, Cornwall, &c.* We need not be surpriz'd at this, when we assert, that there is very much reason to believe, these famous philosophic priests came hither, as a *Phœnician* colony, in the very earliest times, even as soon as *Tyre* was founded: during the life of the patriarch *Abraham*, or very soon after. Therefore they brought along with them the patriarchal religion, which was so extremely like Christianity, that in effect it differ'd from it only in this; they believed in a Messiah who was to come into the world, as we believe in him that is come. Further, they came from that very country where *Abraham* liv'd, his sons and grandsons; a family God almighty had separated from the gross of mankind, to stifle the seeds of idolatry; a mighty prince, and preacher of righteousness. And tho' the memoirs of our Druids are extremely short, yet we can very evidently discover from them, that the Druids were of *Abraham*'s religion intirely, at least in the earliest times, and worshipp'd the supreme Being in the same manner as he did, and probably according to his example, or the example of his and their common ancestors.

All this I shall prove, in the pursuit of this work. But before we come to speculation, intend to give an exact description of their several temples, and the like works; for such will be a good foundation for us to build upon. That we may proceed from things evident and more known, to those less known, and which we design to make evident, as well as we are able, and the nature of it will permit. A matter so immers'd in the dark mist of time, where very few scatter'd traces remain, must needs bespeak the reader's candor. The dignity of the subject will excuse my boldness in attempting one so difficult. And however I succeed in accounting for these wonderful works; at least, I shall be instrumental in preserving their memory, in giving just drawings of them.

Stonehenge, by the extravagant grandeur of the work, has attracted the eyes and admiration of all ages. And the reformation, upon the revival of learning among us, the curious began to consider it more intimately, I cannot say successfully. Mr. *Camden* rose as the sun of antiquity, that put out former lights, and, like Cæsar, affrights all that value a reputation, from attempting any thing in his way. His great skill in *Roman* learning, and our *English* history, only enabled him to be, as it were, silent on *Stonehenge*. He saw with excellent judgment, that neither *Roman* nor *English* had place there, or could serve to illustrate it. He writes modestly, as his manner was; "Of these things I am not able so much to give an accurate account, as mightily to grieve, that the founders of this noble monument cannot be trac'd out." He could not persuade himself that either *Romans*, *Saxons* or *Danes* had any hand in it. And as for his representation of it in picture, I verily believe, it was drawn only from fancy or memory, or by some engraver from his oral description. A.D. 1620, king *James* I. being at the earl of *Pembroke*'s seat at *Wilton*, and agreeably surpriz'd with the sight of *Stonehenge*, consulted the famous architect *Inigo Jones*, upon it; thinking it a matter in his way. This great man, who deservedly may be stiled the *English Vitruvius*, gave his opinion of it, as a *Roman* work; and left, I suppose, some few indigested notes in writing thereupon. From which his son-in-law *John Webb* compos'd an intire treatise, endeavouring to prove it. But they that are acquainted with *Roman* architecture, or have consider'd *Stonehenge*, must needs be of a different opinion. And as my Lord Bishop of *London* well observes, in his notes on *Camden*, "it cannot be safe to close with Mr. *Jones*, tho' his book otherwise be a learned and ingenious piece." *Inigo Jones* lived 30 years after this, and yet Mr. *Webb* makes an apology for his work, "that if he had surviv'd to have done it, with his own hand, it would have been better." But 'tis very reasonably believ'd, that tho' *Inigo Jones* was an extraordinary genius in architecture, yet he wanted many qualifications for an author, especially in such a work as *Stonehenge*. 'Tis my opinion, that had his architectonic skill been united to Mr. *Camden*'s learning, he could never have demonstrated *Stonehenge* to be a *Roman* work. Afterwards, Dr. *Charleton* publish'd a piece against *Webb*'s performance, and certainly has said enough to overthrow it, tho' he could not with equal success establish his own opinion, that it was the work of the *Danes*. Whereas *Olaus Wormius* finds no such monuments among the *Gothic* nations: which, as Mr. *Toland* observes, is answer sufficient to his allegation. *Webb* answer'd the Doctor's book, and by turns effectually demolish'd his opinion, but could not still vindicate his own. Yet from all their disputations, no spark was struck, towards a discovery of the real truth. What is the worst part in both performances of Mr. *Webb*, his representation of the real monument in his drawings, is fictitious. And, as Mr. *Aubry* rightly observes, "in endeavouring to retrieve a piece of architecture in

Vitruvius, he abuses the reader with a false representation of the whole." It requires no great pains to prove this, nor need we take much time to be satisfy'd in it: the work is still extant. As soon as a judicious eye comes upon the spot, we discern that *Webb*'s equilateral triangles forming the cell are fancies: his three entrances across the ditch are so too; and that he has turn'd the cell a sixth part from its true situation, to favour his imaginary hypothesis. But 'tis against my inclination to find fault with the labours of others, nor do I thereby seek to bribe the reader in my own favour. I had a great pleasure for several years together, in viewing and examining these noble remains of our ancestors. What I wrote about them, was for my private amusement, and that of friends. And I publish them only for the honour of my country, and in hopes that such a publication will not be unserviceable to religion; which is my ultimate view.

Tho' *Stonehenge* be the proudest singularity of this sort, in the world, as far as we know: yet there are so many others, manifestly form'd upon the same, or kindred design, by the same measure, and for the same purpose, all over the *Britanic* isles; that we can have no room to doubt of their being made by the same people, and that by direction of the *British* Druids. There are innumerable, from the land's end in *Cornwall*, to the utmost northern promontory in *Scotland*, where the *Roman* power never reach'd. They are to be found in all the islands between *Scotland* and *Ireland*, isle of *Man*, all the *Orkney* islands, *&c.* and numerous in *Ireland* itself. And there is no pretence, as far as I can see, for any other persons or nations being the founders of them. They are circles of stones, generally rude, of different diameters, upon elevated ground, barren, open heaths and downs; chiefly made of stones taken from the surface of the ground. There are no remembrances of the founders, any other than an uninterrupted tradition of their being sacred; that there is medicinal virtue in them; that they were made by the *Irish*; that they were brought from *Afric*; that they were high-places of worship; sanctuaries; bowing, adoring places; and what names they commonly have, intimate the same thing. And in many places the express remembrance and name of Druids remain, and the people bury their dead in or near them to this day, thinking them holy ground. Mr. *Toland* in his history of the Druids, p. 23. tells us, "In *Gealcossa*'s mount in *Inisoen* in the county of *Dunegal*, a Druidess of that name lived; it signifies white-legg'd, according to the ancient manner in *Homer*'s time. On that hill is her grave and her temple, being a sort of diminutive *Stonehenge*, which the old *Irish*, at this day, dare not any way profane." Many instances of this sort, of all these particulars, we have in our island: particularly the temple on *Temple-downs* by *Abury*. Whatever is dug up in or near these works are manifestly remains of the Druid times; urns, bones, ornaments of amber, glass beads, snake-stones, amulets, celts, flint-hatchets, arrow-heads, and such things as bespeak the rudest ages, the utmost antiquity, most early plantations of people that came into our island, soon after *Noah*'s flood. I have all the reason in the world to believe them an oriental colony of *Phœnicians*; at least that such a one came upon the first *Celtic* plantation of people here: which reasons will appear in the progress of this discourse. I suppose in matters of such extraordinary antiquity, it would be absurd to set about a formal demonstration; and those readers would be altogether unreasonable, that expect we prove every fact here, as they would do by living witnesses, before a court of judicature. When all is consider'd, that I have put together on this affair, a judicious person, I presume, will agree, I have made the matter sufficiently evident, and as much as the nature of things requires.

In the times just preceding the coming of the *Romans* into *Britain*, the *Belgæ*, a most powerful colony from the *Gallic* continent, had firmly seated themselves all over the country, where *Stonehenge* is situate, quite to the southern sea; taking in the fourth part of *Wiltshire*, and all *Dorsetshire*. *Wiltshire* has its name from the river *Willy*, which in *Welsh* is *wyli*, in *Latin*, *vagire*, from its noise. A river of like name in *Northamptonshire*. Upon the former river at *Wilton*, probaby liv'd the *Carvilius*, one of the four kings that fought *Julius*

Cæsar, the picture of whose *tumulus* we have given towards the end. The *Belgæ* came into *Britain* upon the south, as other *Celtic* nations before had fix'd themselves from the east, *Kent*, the *Thames*, &c. such as the *Cantii, Segontiaci, Atrebates*, &c. so that in *Cæsar*'s time, all the south and east parts of *Britain* were dispossess'd of their original inhabitants, and peopled from the continent: and this very work of *Stonehenge* was in the hands of the *Belgæ*, who built it not. In my *itinerarium curiosum*, p. 181. I observ'd no less than four successive boundary ditches here, from the southern shore; which with good reason, I suppos'd, were made by the *Belgæ*, as they conquer'd the country by degrees, from the aboriginal inhabitants. This shews, they must have been a long while about it, that the *Britons* disputed every inch of ground with them, and that for two reasons; as well because of the extraordinary beauty and goodness of the country, as fighting *pro aris & focis* for their great temple of *Stonehenge*: not to speak of that other great temple, a little more northward, at *Abury*. The *Segontiaci* had got *Hampshire*, to the east of them, before, as far as the *Colinburn* river, and the *Atrebates*, *Berkshire*. The first ditch runs between the river of *Blandford*, formerly *Alauna*, and the river of *Bere*, the piddle in *Dorsetshire*, two or three miles south of it. The second runs to the north of *Cranborn* chase, upon the edge of *Wiltshire*, by *Pentridg*: it divides the counties of *Dorset* and *Wilts*. The third is conspicuous upon *Salisbury* plain, as we pass from *Wilton* to *Stonehenge*, about the two-mile stone, north of *Wilton*: it is drawn between the river *Avon* and the *Willy*, from *Dornford* to *Newton*. The fourth is the more famous *Wansdike*, of great extent. *Gwahan* in old *British* signifies *separatio, distinctio* guahanu *seperare*, and *that* undoubtedly gave name to the ditch. The method of all these ditches, is, to take the northern edge of a ridge of hills, which is always steep; the bank is on the south side. And in my itinerary, p. 134. I show'd a most evident demonstration, that it was made before the time of the *Romans*, in the passage of the *Roman* road down *Runway* hill. *Wansdike* is the last advanc'd post of the *Belgæ* northwards, and that it was made after *Stonehenge* was built, is plain, because the stones that compose the work, were brought from *Marlborough* downs in north *Wiltshire*, beyond the dike; and as then in an enemy's country. And most probably it was built before the *Belgæ* set footing in *Britain*, because of the great number of barrows or sepulchral *tumuli* about it, which, no doubt, were made for the burial of kings and great men.

The stones of which *Stonehenge* is compos'd, beyond any controversy, came from those called the gray weathers, upon *Marlborough* downs near *Abury*; where is that other most wonderful work of this sort, which I shall describe in my next volume. This is 15 or 16 miles off. All the greater stones are of that sort, except the altar, which is of a still harder, as design'd to resist fire. The pyramidals likewise are of a different sort, and much harder than the rest, like those of that other Druid temple call'd *the Weddings*, at *Stantondrew* in *Somersetshire*. Dr. *Halley* was at *Stonehenge* in the year 1720, and brought a piece of it to the Royal Society. I examin'd it with a microscope. 'Tis a composition of crystals of red, green and white colours, cemented together by nature's art, with opake granules of flinty or stony matter. The Doctor observ'd from the general wear of the weather upon the stones, that the work must be of an extraordinary antiquity, and for ought he knew, 2 or 3000 years old. But had the Doctor been at *Abury*, which is made of the same stones, he might well from the like argumentation conclude, that the work as old again as *Stonehenge*, at least much older, and I verily believe it. Nevertheless the current of so many ages has been more merciful to *Stonehenge*, than the insolence of rapacious hands, (besides the general saccage brought upon the work of old) by the unaccountable folly of mankind, in breaking pieces off with great hammers. This detestable practice arose from the silly notion of the stones being factitious. But, alas! it would be a greater wonder to make them by art, than to carry them 16 miles by art and strength; and those people must be inexcusable, that deface the monument for so trifling a fancy. Another argument of vulgar incogitancy, is, that all the wonder of the work consists, in the difficulty of counting the stones; and with that, the infinite numbers of daily visitants busy themselves. This seems to be the remains of superstition, and the notion of magic, not yet got out of peoples heads, since Druid-times. But indeed a serious view of this magnificent wonder, is apt to put a thinking and judicious person into a kind of ecstacy, when he views the struggle between art and nature, the grandeur of that art that hides itself, and seems unartful. For tho' the contrivance that put this massy frame together, must have been exquisite, yet the founders endeavour'd to hide it, by the seeming rudeness of the work. The bulk of the constituent parts is so very great, that the mortaises and tenons must have been prepar'd to an extreme nicety, and, like the fabric of *Solomon*'s temple, every stone tally'd; and neither axes nor hammers were heard upon the whole structure. Nevertheless there is not a stone at *Stonehenge*, that felt not, more or less, both ax and hammer of the founders. Yet 'tis highly entertaining to consider the judicious carelessness therein, really the grand gusto, like a great master in drawing, secure of the effect: a true master-piece. Every thing proper, bold, astonishing. The lights and shades adapted with every inconceivable justness. Notwithstanding the monstrous size of the work, and every part of it; 'tis far from appearing heavy: 'tis compos'd of several species of work, and the proportions of the dissimilar parts recommend the whole, and it pleases like a magical spell. No one thinks any part of it too great or too little, too high or too low. And we that can only view it in its ruins, the less regret those ruins, that, if possible, add to its solemn majesty.

    The stones of the gray weathers are of a bastard sort of white marble, and lie upon the surface of the ground, in infinite numbers, and of all dimensions. They are loose, detach'd from any rock, and doubtless lay there ever since the creation, being solid parts thrown out to the surface of the fluid globe, when its rotation was first impress'd. All our Druid temples are built, where these sort of stones from the surface can be had at reasonable distances; for they are never taken from quarries. Here is a very good quarry at *Chilmark* in this country. *Salisbury* cathedral, and all the great buildings are thence; but 'tis a stone quite different to our work. It was a matter of much labour to draw them hither, 16 miles. My friend the reverend Dr. *Stephen Hales*, the excellent author of vegetable statics, and other works, computed them as follows. The stone at the upper end of the cell, which is fallen down and broke in half, is in length (says he) 25 feet, in breadth 7 feet, and in thickness at a medium $3\frac{1}{2}$, amounts to 612 cubic feet. Now a cubic foot of *Hedington* stone weighs near $154\frac{1}{4}$ pounds troy. If *Stonehenge* stone be of the same specific gravity, it will amount to 94,348 pounds, which is $31\frac{1}{2}$ tuns. But if this be of the same specific gravity as *Burford* stone, which weighs to $155\frac{1}{4}$ the cubic foot, then it will weigh 95,319 pounds troy, or 32 tuns. If it be equal to *Blaidon* stone, which is 187 pounds troy *per* cubic foot, then it weighs 114,444 pounds troy, or 38 tuns. But I am sure that the stone is of considerably larger dimensions, than what Dr. *Hales* has stated it at, and that the sort of stone is much heavier than that of the largest specific gravity he speaks of, and that it amounts to more than 40 tuns, and requires more than 140 oxen to draw it; yet this is not the heaviest stone at the place.

    The notion we ought to entertain of *Stonehenge* is not a little enhanc'd, by the discovery I made from frequent mensurations there. It gave me the opportunity of finding out the standard and original measure, which the people us'd, who made this and all other works of this kind. And this precludes any tedious disputation against the opinion of authors; for whoever makes any eminent building, most certainly forms it upon the common measure in use, among the people of that place. Therefore if the proportions of *Stonehenge* fall into fractions and uncouth numbers, when measur'd by the *English*, *French*, *Roman*, or *Grecian* foot, we may assuredly conclude, the architects were neither *English*, *French*, *Roman* or *Greeks*. Thus, for instance, when the accurate *Greaves* tells us, the door of the *Pantheon* (which is of one stone) is of *English* foot-measure 19 foot $^{602}/_{1000}$ within: should we not be apt to assert at first sight, that the architect in so costly a work, did not chuse his measures at random, but intended that this dimension should be 20 feet? When we consider this building is at *Rome*, and that it amounts to 20 *Roman* feet, must we not conclude, it was erected by the *Roman* standard? adding too, that all the rest of the dimensions of this stately structure fall aptly and judiciously into the same scale. So as long as any *vestigia* of St. *Paul*'s cathedral remain, the *English* foot, by which it was built, will easily be known. I must prepare the reader for a right understanding of our Druid edifices, by informing him, that *Stonehenge*, and all other works of this nature in our island, are erected by that most ancient measure call'd a cubit, which we read of in the holy scriptures, and in ancient profane authors. I mean the same individual measure, call'd the *Hebrew, Egyptian, Phœnician* cubit; most probably deriv'd from *Noah* and *Adam*. 'Tis the same that the pyramids of *Egypt* and other their works are projected upon; the same as that of *Moses*'s tabernacle, *Solomon*'s temple, &c. and we may reasonably pride ourselves in possessing these visible monuments of the old measure of the world. My predecessor Bishop *Cumberland* shows, enough to satisfy us, that the *Egyptian* and *Hebrew* measure was the same, tho' he has not hit upon that measure, to a nicety. My friend and colleague Dr. *Arbuthnot* has been more successful, in applying it to such parts of the greater pyramid, as evidently establish its proportion, to our *English* foot, from the measures *Greaves* has left us: and shows it to be 20 inches and ⅘ of *English* measure. Thus the Doctor observes the side of the greater pyramid at base, is 693 *English* feet; which amounts exactly to 400 *Egyptian* cubits, a full and suitable number for such a square work, and without question the originally design'd measure, the *stadium* of old. I have taken notice that *Inigo Jones* observ'd the like dimensions, in laying out the plot of *Lincoln's-Inn-fields*. The Doctor adds many more instances, deduc'd in the same way, to confirm it. I add, that *Greaves* says, the lowermost steps of the pyramid are near 4 feet in height, which amounts to 2 cubits and 2 palms. They are 3 foot in breadth, *i.e.* 1 cubit 4 palms. The length of the declining first entrance is 92 feet and an half, *i.e.* 55 cubits. The length of the next gallery is 110 feet, which amounts to 60 cubits. There is another gallery in the pyramid, of the same length. Mr. *Webb* says the diameter of *Stonehenge* is 110 feet. This would tempt one to suspect the same measure us'd in both. Thus the diameter of the like work at *Rowldrich* in *Oxfordshire*, describ'd by Dr. *Plot*, is 35 yards, *i.e.* 110 feet, grossly measur'd. Father *Brothais* in his observations on upper *Egypt*, in our *Phil. Trans.* found a door-case made of one stone, in a magnificent building, it was 26½ feet in height, this is 15 cubits. Dr. *Huntington*, in the same *Trans.* says, he found the sphynx standing by the northern pyramids to be 110 feet in circuit, *i.e.* 60 cubits. *Ptolomy* in his IVth book, and *Pliny* XXXVI.——speak of the obelisk rais'd by king *Rameses* at *Heliopolis*, which Mr. *Webb*, p. 34. gives the length of in *English* feet, 136. This is 80 cubits. That which *Augustus* set up in the *circus maximus* at *Rome* upon reduction of *Egypt*, *Webb* says, is 120 feet 9 inches, which amounts to 70 cubits. Another, *Augustus* set up in the *campus martius*, which he says is 9 foot higher, *i.e.* 5 cubits. He speaks again of that erected by *Fontana* before St. *Peter*'s, 81 feet, which was 50 cubits. I suppose the base being injur'd, it was cut a little shorter. This at the base, he says, is 9 foot square, *i.e.* 5 cubits. The *Vatican* obelisk is 170 foot high, which is 100 cubits. 12 foot broad at bottom, which is 7 cubits; at top a third part less.

Hence we gather, the measure of the shew-bread table of the *Jews*, a cubit and half in height, *Exod.* xxv. 23. It had a golden crown about it, meaning a moulding, or verge or cornish, as upon our tea-tables. דר *peripheria, corona*, because 12 loaves were to be pil'd upon it. It was 31 inches in height, that of our ordinary eating-tables. And we shall find by this same cubit divided into its 6 tophach's or palms, all our Druid works are perform'd. 'Tis not to be wonder'd at, that it should come into *Britain*, with an eastern colony under the conduct of the *Egyptian, Tyrian, Phœnician Hercules*, (who was the same person) about *Abraham*'s time, or soon after, as I have good reasons to believe, which will be shown in its proper place.

Bibliography

Adams, Frank Dawson
    1938 *The Birth and Development of the Geological Sciences*. London: Constable.

Ashbee, Paul
    1960 *The Bronze Age Round Barrow in Britain*. London: Phoenix House.
    1970 *The Earthen Long Barrow in Britain*. Toronto: University of Toronto Press.
    1978 *The Ancient British: A Social-Archaeological Narrative*. Geo Abstracts: University of East Anglia, Norwich, England.

Atkinson, R.J.C.
    1956 *Stonehenge*. London: Hamish Hamilton.
    1966 "Moonshine on Stonehenge." *Antiquity* 40: 212–16.
    1975 "Megalithic Astronomy—A Prehistorian's Comments." *Journal of the History of Astronomy* 6: 42–52.
    1980 *The Prehistoric Temples of Stonehenge and Avebury*. London: Pitkin Pictorials for HMSO.

Aubrey, John
    1665 "Monumenta Britannica or Miscellany of British Antiquities. Vol. 1, Section 1, Templa Druidum; Stoneheng." MS in the Bodleian Library, Oxford.

Aveni, Anthony F.
    1980 Review of Stover 1978. *Archaeology*, vol. 33, no. 4 (July-August): 64f.

Barclay, Edgar
    1895 *Stonehenge and Its Earthworks*. London: D. Nutt.
    [1902] *The Ruined Temple Stonehenge*. London: St. Catherine Press.

Branston, Brian
    1980 *Gods of the North*. London: Thames and Hudson.

Bray, Warwick, and David Trump
　1972　*The Penguin Dictionary of Archaeology*. London: Penguin Books.

Brøndstedt, Johannes
　1965　*The Vikings*. Tr. by Kalle Skov. London: Penguin Books.

Burl, Aubrey
　1979　*Rings of Stone: The Prehistoric Stone Circles of Britain and Ireland*. New York: Ticknor & Fields.

Caesar, Julius
　1980　*The Battle for Gaul [Commentarii de Bello Gallico]*. Tr. by Anne and Peter Wiseman. Boston: David R. Godine.

Cáhill, Thomas
　1995　*How the Irish Saved Civilization*. New York: Doubleday.

Chadwick, H.M.
　1912　*The Heroic Age*. Cambridge: Cambridge University Press.

Chadwick, H.M., and Chadwick, N.K.
　1932　*The Growth of Literature, Vol. 1: The Ancient Literatures of Europe*. Cambridge: Cambridge University Press.

Chancy, William A.
　1970　*The Cult of Kingship in Anglo-Saxon England: The Transition from Paganism to Christianity*. Manchester: Manchester University Press.

Childe, V. Gordon
　1926　*The Aryans: A Study of Indo-Europeans*. Reprinted 1970, Port Washington, N.Y.: Kennikat Press.
　1942　*What Happened in History*. Harmondsworth: Penguin Books.
　1957　*The Dawn of European Civilization*, 6th ed. London: Routledge and Kegan Paul.

Clarke, D.V., T.G. Cowie and Andrew Foxon, eds.
　1985　*Symbols of Power at the Time of Stonehenge*. Edinburgh, Natural Museum of Antiquities of Scotland: HMSO.

Coles, I.M., and A.F. Harding.
　1979　*The Bronze Age in Europe: An Introduction to the Prehistory of Europe c. 2000–700 B.C.* London: Methuen.

Cornwell, Bernard
　2000　*Stonehenge 2000 B.C.* A novel. New York: HarperCollins.

Crittall, Elizabeth, ed.
　1973　*A History of Wiltshire* I:2. Oxford: Oxford University Press.

Cunnington, M.E.
　1929　*Woodhenge*. Simpson: Devizes.

Daniel, Glyn
　1958　*The Megalith Builders of Western Europe*. London: Hutchinson.
　1972　*Megaliths in History*. London: Thames and Hudson.

Davidson, H.R. Ellis
　1964　*Gods and Myths of Northern Europe*. London: Penguin Books.

Demakopoulou, Katie, Christiane Eluère, Jorgen Jensen, Abrecht Jockenhövel, and Jean-Pierre Mohen, eds.
    1993 *Gods and Heroes of the European Bronze Age*. London: Thames and Hudson.

Dick, Oliver Lawson, ed.
    1949 *Aubrey's Brief Lives*. London: Martin Secker & Warburg. Edited from MSS in the Bodleien Library, Oxford.

Drews, Robert
    1993 *The End of the Bronze Age: Changes in Warfare and the Catastrophe ca. 1200 B.C.* Princeton: Princeton University Press.

Dumézil, Georges
    1958 *L'Idéologie tripartie des Indo-Europeens*. Brussels: Collection Latomus, volume 31.
    1973 *Gods of the Ancient Northmen*. Tr. by Einar Haugen. Berkeley: University of California Press.

Dunkling, Leslie, and Gordon Wright.
    1987 *Dictionary of Pub Names*. London: Routledge & Kegan Paul.

Ettlinger, Ellen
    1952 "The Association of Burials with Popular Assemblies, Fairs and Races in Ancient Ireland." *Études Celtiques*, vol. 6: 30–61.

Fletchner, Richard
    1997 *The Barbarian Conversion: From Paganism to Christianity*. New York: Henry Holt.

Fox, Aileen
    1964 *South West England*. London: Thames and Hudson.

Galanopolis, A.G., and Edward Bacon
    1969 *Atlantis: The Truth Behind the Legend*. Indianapolis: Bobbs-Merrill.

Gantz, Jeffrey, tr.
    1981 *Early Irish Myths and Sagas*. London: Penguin Books.

Gelling, Peter, and Hilda Ellis Davidson
    1969 *The Chariot of the Sun and Other Rites and Symbols of the Northern Bronze Age*. London: J.M. Dent.

Geoffrey of Monmouth. Tr. by Lewis Thorpe.
    1966 Geoffrey of Monmouth, *The History of the Kings of Britain*. London: Penguin Books.

Gimbutas, Maria
    1965 *Bronze Age Cultures in Central and Eastern Europe*. The Hague: Mouton.
    1973 "Old Europe c. 7000–3500 B.C.: The Earliest European Civilization Before the Infiltration of the Indo-European Peoples." *Journal of Indo-European Studies* 1: 1–20.
    1974 "An Archaeologist's View of PIE in 1973." *Journal of Indo-European Studies* 2: 289–308.

Green, Miranda J.
　1997　*The World of the Druids.* London: Thames and Hudson.

Green, Miranda J., ed.
　1992　*Dictionary of Celtic Myth and Legend.* London: Thames and Hudson.

Grinsell, L.V.
　1958　*The Archaeology of Wessex.* London: Methuen.
　1975　*Legendary History and Folklore of Stonehenge.* St. Peter Port, Guernsey, C.I., Britain, Toucan Press.
　[1978]　*The Stonehenge Barrow Groups.* Salisbury, England: Salisbury and South Wiltshire Museum.

Hamilton, J.R.C.
　1968　*Excavations at Clickhimin, Shetland.* Ministry of Public Buildings and Works, Archaeological Reports 6. Edinburgh: HMSO.

Hanning, R.W.
　1966　*The Vision of History in Early Britain: From Gildas to Geoffrey of Monmouth.* New York: Columbia University Press.

Harrison, Richard J.
　1980　*The Beaker Folk: Copper Age Archaeology in Western Europe.* London: Thames and Hudson.

Harrison, W. Jerome
　1901　*A Bibliography of Stonehenge and Avebury.* Devizes, England: C.H. Woodward.

Hawkins, G.S.
　1965　*Stonehenge Decoded.* New York: Doubleday.

Heller, Mikhail, and Aleksandr M. Nekrich
　1986　*Utopia in Power: The History of the Soviet Union from 1917 to the Present.* New York: Summit Books.

Hood, Sinclair
　1971　*The Minoans.* London: Thames and Hudson.

Ingram, J.
　1807　*An Inaugural Lecture on the Utility of Anglo-Saxon Literature, to Which Is Added the Geography of Europe by King Alfred.* Oxford: Oxford University Press.

Jones, Inigo
　1655　*The Most Notable Antiquity of Great Britain, Vulgarly Stone-Heng, on Salisbury Plain, Restored, by Inigo Jones, Esquire, Architect General to the Late King.* London: D. Browne.

Kellaway, G.A.
　1971　"Glaciation and the Stones of Stonehenge." *Nature* 233: 30–35.

Kendrick, T.D.
　1928　*The Druids: A Study in Keltic Prehistory.* London: Methuen.

Lincoln, Bruce
　1981　*Priests, Warriors, and Cattle.* Berkeley, University of California Press.

Lockyer, Norman
   1906   *Stonehenge and Other British Monuments Astronomically Considered*. London: Macmillan.

Long, W.
   1876   "Stonehenge and Its Barrows." *The Wiltshire Archaeological and Natural History Magazine* 16.

Lopez, Robert
   1966   *The Birth of Europe*. New York: M. Evans.

Luce, J.V.
   1969   *The End of Atlantis*. London: Thames and Hudson.

MacAlister, R.A.S.
   1931   *Tara, a Pagan Sanctuary of Ancient Ireland*. London: Scribner's.

MacKillop, James, ed.
   1998   *Dictionary of Celtic Mythology*. Oxford: Oxford University Press.

Mallory, J.P.
   1989   *In Search of the Indo-Europeans: Language, Archaeology and Myth*. London: Thames and Hudson.

Megaw, J.V.S.
   1970   *Art of the European Iron Age*. New York: Harper & Row.

Mongait, A.L.
   1961   *Archaeology in the U.S.S.R.* Tr. from the Russian of 1955 by M.W. Thompson. London: Pelican Books.

Mylonas, George E.
   1966   *Mycenae and the Mycenaean Age*. Princeton, N.J.: Princeton University Press.

Newall, R.S.
   1929   "Stonehenge." *Antiquity* 3: 75–88.

North, John
   1996   *Stonehenge: A New Interpretation of Prehistoric Man and the Cosmos*. New York: Free Press.

Pearson, John
   1973   *Arena: The Story of the Colosseum*. New York: McGraw-Hill.

Petrie, George
   1839   "On the History and Antiquities of Tara Hill." *Transactions of the Royal Irish Academy*, Vol. XVIII: 25–232.

Petrie, W.M.F.
   1880   *Stonehenge*. London: Edward Stamford.

Piggott, Stuart
   1962   *The West Kinnet Long Barrow: Excavations 1955-56*. Ministry of Works Archaeological Reports No. 4. London: HMSO.
   1967   *Celts, Saxons, and the Early Antiquarians*. Edinburgh: Edinburgh University Press.
   1968   *The Druids*. London: Thames and Hudson.

Raftery, Barry
    1994 *Pagan Celtic Ireland: The Enigma of the Irish Iron Age.* London: Thames and Hudson.

Renfrew, Colin
    1987 *Archaeology and Language: The Puzzle of Indo-European Origins.* London: Jonathan Cape.

Saunders, Eleanor
    1973 *The Prehistoric Monument of Durrington Walls.* Salisbury: Salisbury and South Wiltshire Museum.

Shipley, Joseph Twadell
    1984 *The Origin of English Words: A Discursive Dictionary of Indo-European Roots.* Baltimore: Johns Hopkins University Press

Stone, E.H.
    1924 *The Stones of Stonehenge.* London: Robert Scott.

Stover, Leon
    1978 *Stonehenge: The Indo-European Heritage.* Chicago: Nelson Hall. In Britain as *Stonehenge and the Origins of Western Culture.* London: Heinemann.

Stover, Leon, with Harry Harrison
    1972 *Stonehenge, a Novel.* London: Peter Davies; New York: Scribner's.
    1983 *Stonehenge: Where Atlantis Died.* New York: Tor Books. Unabridged edition of the above.

Stukeley, William
    1740 *Stonehenge, a Temple Restor'd to the British Druids.* London: W. Innys and R. Manby.

Tacitus
    1948 *Tacitus on Britain and Germany.* Tr. by H. Mattingly. With introduction, notes, glossary, and maps. London: Penguin Books.

Taylor, Isaac
    1876 Brief communication in *Notes and Queries,* series 9, vol. 3: 43f.

Taylor, J.J.
    1978 *Bronze Age Goldwork in the British Isles.* Cambridge: Cambridge University Press.

Thom, A.
    1967 *Megalithic Sites in Britain.* Oxford: Oxford University Press.

Thomson, George
    1949 *Studies in Ancient Greek Society: The Prehistoric Aegean.* Reprinted from the London edition by Citadel Press, New York.

Tierney, J.J.
    1960 "The Celtic Ethnography of Posidonius." *Proceedings of the Royal Irish Academy* 60, sec. C, no. 5: 189–275.

Vlahos, Olivia
    1968 *The Battle-ax People: Beginnings of Western Culture.* New York: Viking Press.

Wainwright, Geoffrey
    1989 *The Henge Monuments: Ceremony and Society in Prehistoric Britain.* London: Thames and Hudson.

Wainwright, George J., and I.H. Longworth
    1968 *Durrington Walls: Excavations 1966–1968.* London: Society of Antiquities.

Webb, John
    1665 *A Vindication of Stone-Heng Restored.* London: R. Davenport for Tho. Basset.

Wilson, David M., ed.
    1980 *The Northern World: The History and Heritage of Northern Europe.* London: Thames and Hudson.

Index

Agricola 127
Ambrosius 7
Aristotle 109 footnote
Athenaeus 17, 106
Atkinson, R.J.C. 29, 31, 36, 38, 39, 46, 54, 85, 99, 155; "Moonshine on Stonehenge" 28
Aubrey, John 14, 23, 59
Avebury 14

Bacon, Sir Francis 121
Baum, L. Frank: *The Wonderful Wizard of Oz* 76 footnote
Beowulf 105, 161

Caesar, Julius 64, 68, 69, 70, 78, 96, 97, 105, 117, 118, 161; *The Battle for Gaul* [Commentarii de Bello Gallico] 17, 58, 94, 164
Camden, William 143; *Britannia* 125f
Carter, Howard 67
Celts 58 *et passim*
Charles I 8, 9
Charles II 3, 8, 12, 121, 128, 164
Charles IV, Holy Roman Emperor 91, 113
Charleton, Walter 7–20; *Chorea Gigantum* 7
Childe, V. Gordon 74, 82; *The Aryans* 70
Clarke, D.V.: *Symbols of Power at the Time of Stonehenge* 63
Cornwell, Bernard: *Stonehenge 2000 B.C.* 155

Cromwell, Oliver 8, 9
Cunnington, M.E. 98

Daniel, Glyn: *Megaliths in History* 17
Däniken, Erich von: *Chariots of the Gods?* 31; *Erinnerungen an die Zuklunft* 31; *Gods from Outer Space* 31
Demakopoulou, Katie: *Gods and Heroes of the European Bronze Age* 63
Dindshenchas (Book of Place Names) 102, 106f, 112
Diodorus Siculus 17; *Bibliotheca Historica* 105
Dryden, John 9, 121

Evans, Sir Arthur 51, 54

Freud, Sigmund 76 footnote

Geoffrey of Monmouth 17, 125, 126; *Historia Regum Britanniae* 7
Gimbutas, Maria 74
Green, Miranda J.: *Dictionary of Celtic Myth and Legend* 70
Grinsell, L.V.: *Archaeology of Wessex* 93

Harrison, Harry 155, 157
Harrison, Richard J.: *The Beaker Folk* 79
Harvey, William 9
Hawkins, Gerald 62; *Stonehenge Decoded* 19, 28

Heller, Mikhail, and Aleksandr M. Nekrich: *Utopia in Power* 76 footnote
Henry VIII 11
Herodotus 74
Hittites 117
Homer 64, 72, 87, 105, 114, 158; *The Iliad* 3, 67, 102, 105
Howard, Sir Robert 121

James I 8, 9f, 164
Jones, Inigo 9f, 122, 127, 128, 132, 143, 164, 166; *The Most Notable Antiquity of Great Britain* 8
Jones, Sir William 72

Kellaway, G.A. 17
King Agamemnon 67, 72, 110, 114, 158
King Alfred 8, 11, 29; *The Geography of Europe* 114
King Arthur 7
King Vortigern 7

Lockyer, Sir Norman 72
Lyell, Sir George: *Principles of Geology* 16

"MacDatho's Pig" (Irish hero tale) 109
MacKillop, James: *Dictionary of Celtic Myth and Legend* 70
Merlin 7, 17, 125
Mongait, A.L.: *Archaeology in the U.S.S.R.* 82, 84
Morgan, Lewis H.: *Ancient Society* 78 footnote

Newall, R.S. 51, 53f, 56, 57
Newton, Sir Isaac 10
North, John: *Stonehenge* 20

Petrie, Sir Flinders 22
Piggott, Stuart 46
Plato 81: *Critias* 157, 158; *Republic* 71, 76 footnote

Pope Boniface IV 69
Posidonius 17, 58, 80, 95, 105, 106
Prokofiev, Sergei Sergeevich: *The Scythian Suite* 73
Prose Edda 72

Rig-Veda 69, 70, 74, 75, 78 footnote, 158
Robin Hood (film) 104
Rogers, William 126

St. Augustine 76 footnnote
St. Patrick 63, 64
St. Sebastian 96
Sammes, Aylett 95; *Britannia Antiqua Illustrata* 94, 164
the Scythians 73
Stone, E.H. 16, 35; *Stones of Stonehenge* 14, 36
Stover, Leon: *Stonehenge: The Indo-European Heritage* 157; *Stonehenge: Where Atlantis Died* 157
Strabo 17, 94, 96, 105; *Geograhica* 95
Stukeley, William 21, 23, 91, 94, 114, 115; *Stonehenge* 3, 17, 113, 163–166

Tacitus, Cornelius 117; *Germania* 97
Táin Bó Cúalnge (Irish epic) 102, 106
Thomsen, Christian 4, 10, 12
Thuthmosis IV 159
Tutankhamen 67

Verse Edda 72
Vikings 12, 30, 80, 91, 92, 106, 125, 164
The Vikings (film) 104
Vitruvius (Marcus Vitruvius Pollio): *De Architectura* 127
Vlad IV 96f

Webb, John 128; *A Vindication* 122
Wormius, Olaus (Old Worm) 9, 11f, 92, 93, 113, 131, 152; *Danicorum Monumentorum* 10, 143